3

College Reading

HOUGHTON MIFFLIN
ENGLISH FOR ACADEMIC SUCCESS

John Avery
Green River Community College

Linda Robinson Fellag
Community College of Philadelphia

SERIES EDITORS

Patricia Byrd

Joy M. Reid

Cynthia M. Schuemann

Houghton Mifflin Company
Boston   New York

Publisher: Patricia A. Coryell
Director of ESL Publishing: Susan Maguire
Senior Development Editor: Kathy Sands Boehmer
Editorial Assistant: Evangeline Bermas
Senior Project Editor: Kathryn Dinovo
Manufacturing Assistant: Karmen Chong
Senior Marketing Manager: Annamarie Rice
Marketing Assistant: Andrew Whitacre

Cover graphics: LMA Communications, Natick, Massachusetts

Printed in the U.S.A.

Library of Congress Control Number: 2004112229

ISBN: 0-618-23022-X

123456789-CRW-08 07 06 05 04

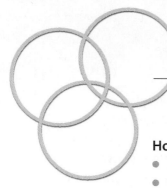

Contents

Houghton Mifflin English for Academic Success Series

Houghton Mifflin English for Academic Success Series

SERIES EDITORS

Patricia Byrd, Joy M. Reid, Cynthia M. Schuemann

○ What Is the Purpose of This Series?

The Houghton Mifflin English for Academic Success series is a comprehensive program of student and instructor materials. For students, there are four levels of student language proficiency textbooks in three skill areas (oral communication, reading, and writing), and a supplemental vocabulary textbook at each level. For both instructors and students, a useful website supports classroom teaching, learning, and assessment. In addition, for instructors, there are four Essentials of Teaching Academic Language books (*Essentials of Teaching Academic Oral Communication*, *Essentials of Teaching Academic Reading*, *Essentials of Teaching Academic Writing*, and *Essentials of Teaching Academic Vocabulary*). These books provide helpful information for instructors who are new to teaching and for experienced instructors who want to reinforce practices or brush up on current teaching strategies.

The fundamental purpose of the series is to prepare students who are not native speakers of English for academic success in U.S. college degree programs. By studying these materials, students in English for Academic Purposes (EAP) programs will gain the academic language skills they need to learn about the nature and expectations of U.S. college courses.

The series is based on considerable prior research as well as our own investigations of students' needs and interests, instructors' needs and desires, and institutional expectations and requirements. For example, our survey research revealed what problems instructors feel they face in their classrooms and what they actually teach; who the students are and what they know and do not know about the "culture" of U.S. colleges; and what types of exams are required for admission at various colleges.

Student Audience

The materials in this series are for college-bound ESL students at U.S. community colleges and undergraduate programs at other institutions. Some of these students are U.S. high school graduates. Some of them are long-term U.S. residents who graduated from a high school before coming to the United States. Others are newer U.S. residents. Still others are more typical international students. All of them need to develop academic language skills and knowledge of ways to be successful in U.S. college degree courses.

All of the books in this series have been created to implement the Houghton Mifflin English for Academic Success competencies. These competencies are based on those developed by ESL instructors and administrators in Florida, California, and Connecticut to be the underlying structure for EAP courses at colleges in those states. These widely respected competencies assure that the materials meet the real world needs of EAP students and instructors.

All of the books focus on . . .

- Starting where the students are, building on their strengths and prior knowledge (which is considerable, if not always academically relevant), and helping students self-identify needs and plans to strengthen academic language skills
- Academic English, including development of Academic Vocabulary and grammar required by students for academic speaking/listening, reading, and writing
- Master Student Skills, including learning style analysis, strategy training, and learning about the "culture" of U.S. colleges, which lead to their becoming successful students in degree courses and degree programs
- Topics and readings that represent a variety of academic disciplinary areas so that students learn about the language and content of the social sciences, the hard sciences, education, and business as well as the humanities

All of the books provide . . .

- Interesting and valuable content that helps the students develop their knowledge of academic content as well as their language skills and student skills
- A wide variety of practical classroom-tested activities that are easy to teach and engage the students
- Assessment tools at the end of each chapter so that instructors have easy-to-implement ways to assess student learning and students have opportunities to assess their own growth
- Websites for the students and for the instructors: the student sites provide additional opportunities to practice reading, writing, listening, vocabulary development, and grammar. The instructor sites provide instructors' manuals, teaching notes and answer keys, value-added materials like handouts and overheads that can be reproduced to use in class, and assessment tools such as additional tests to use beyond the assessment materials in each book.

◯ What Is the Purpose of the Reading Strand?

The four books in the Reading strand focus on the development of reading skills and general background knowledge necessary for college study. These books are dedicated to meeting the academic needs of ESL students by teaching them how to handle reading demands and expectations of freshman-level classes. The reading selections come from varied disciplines, reflecting courses with high enrollment patterns at U.S. colleges. The passages have been chosen from authentic academic text sources, and are complemented with practical exercises and activities that enhance the teaching-learning process. Students respond positively to being immersed in content from varied disciplines, and vocabulary and skills that are easily recognized as valuable and applicable.

Because of the importance of academic vocabulary in both written and spoken forms, the Reading strand features attention to high-frequency academic words found across disciplines. The books teach students techniques for learning and using new academic vocabulary, both to recognize and understand the words when they read them, and to use important words in their own spoken and written expressions.

In addition to language development, the books provide for content and academic skill development with the inclusion of appropriate academic tasks and by providing strategies to help students better understand and handle what is expected of them in college classes. Chapter objectives specified at the beginning of each chapter include some content area objectives as well as reading and academic skills objectives. For example, student work may include defining key concepts from a reading selection, analyzing the use of facts and examples to support a theory, or paraphrasing information from a reading as they report back on points they have learned. That is, students are not taught to work with the reading selections for some abstract reason, but learn to make a powerful connection between working with the exercises and activities and success with teacher-assigned tasks from general education disciplines. The chapter objectives are tied to the series competencies which were derived from a review of educator-generated course expectations in community college EAP programs and they reflect a commitment to sound pedagogy.

Each book has a broad "behind-the-scenes" theme to provide an element of sustained content. These themes were selected because of their high interest for students; they are also topics commonly explored in introductory college courses and so provide useful background for students. Materials were selected that are academically appropriate but that do not require expert knowledge by the teacher. The following themes are explored in the Reading strand — Book 1: Society, Book 2: Enduring Issues, Book 3: Diversity, and Book 4: Memory and Learning.

The series also includes a resource book for teachers called *Essentials of Teaching Academic Reading* by Sharon Seymour and Laura Walsh. This practical book provides strategies and activities for the use of instructors new to the teaching of reading and for experienced instructors who want to reinforce their practices or brush up on current teaching strategies.

The website for each book provides additional teaching activities for instructors and study and practice activities for students. These materials include substantial information on practical classroom-based assessment of academic reading to help teachers with the challenging task of analysis of student learning in this area. And, the teacher support on the series website includes printable handouts, quizzes and overhead transparency forms, as well as teaching tips from the authors.

◯ What Is the Organization of *College Reading 3*?

College Reading 3 prepares high-intermediate level students for the demands of college-level academic reading.

Themes

Six chapters of readings in sociology, psychology, marketing, health and nutrition, genetics, and history present concepts and language that many students will encounter in future courses. The academic disciplines have been chosen to match courses that ESL students most often take in U.S. colleges and universities.

Competencies

College Reading 3 develops the reading competencies listed on page xv and referred to as objectives at the start of each chapter. Additional content-specific objectives are also listed there. These competencies are developed and reinforced in logical sequence based on reading assignments and hierarchical task complexity.

Reading Development

- Chapters 1 and 2 present essential reading skills—previewing, finding main ideas and major points, noting organizational patterns, transferring insights gained across reading passages, and working with charts and graphs.
- Chapters 3 and 4 develop the above skills and introduce summarizing and paraphrasing, responding to short answer test items, making inferences, analyzing the use of statistics as support, and identifying audience and purpose in a reading.
- Chapters 5 and 6 expand on reading skills by having students refine paraphrasing skills, identify and understand academic citations, recognize metaphors in a scientific reading, distinguish between essential concepts and explanatory material, and reflect on key theories.

Academic Success

Special feature elements include reading strategy boxes, Master Student Tips to highlight important advice for students, and Power Grammar notes to draw attention to grammar shifts that influence meaning. Rather than "grammar in context," *College Reading 3* exploits "grammar from [the] context," of the readings.[1] For example, through reading, students learn to examine parts of speech, explanation or

---

1. Byrd, P. and Reid, J. (1998) *Grammar in the Composition Classroom*. Boston: Heinle.

definition markers, and language features that characterize different writing styles found in academic passages.

Content Knowledge

- Several readings per chapter theme facilitate sustained content reading.
- Content skill building is present in every chapter: from the scientific method to analysis of author's intent and purpose.

Vocabulary Development

Vocabulary development is a key feature of *College Reading 3*, so each reading selection was analyzed for its Flesch-Kincaid Grade Level, and other factors to ensure that readings were appropriate for this level.

The Web Vocabulary Profiler[2] was used to identify academic[3] and high-frequency[4] vocabulary items in each selection. These analyses aid teachers tremendously in determining which vocabulary items should be stressed in pre- and post-reading activities. *College Reading 3* features a range of vocabulary-building activities aimed at student retention of academic and high-frequency words.

Academic vocabulary words in the reading selections are unobtrusively marked with dotted underlines and a footnoted glossary provides extra help for students when needed.

Chapter Organization and Exercise Types

Each chapter is clearly divided into sections marked *Reading Assignment 1, 2,* etc. The reading assignment sections include common features which indicate pre-reading, reading, and post-reading activities. Following the reading assignment sections, each chapter has a final component called Assessing Your Learning at the End of a Chapter.

2. The Web Vocabulary Profiler, maintained by Tom Cobb, analyzes a reading to identify academic and high-frequency vocabulary words within the text. A link to his site can be found by visiting our site at www.hmco.com
3. *Academic words* refers to the Academic Word List compiled by Dr. Averil Coxhead of Victoria University of Wellington is a list of 570 word families commonly found in academic texts from all subjects. A link to her site with the complete list can be found by visiting our site at www.hmco.com
4. *High-frequency* vocabulary words refer to the 2,000 most frequently used words, the General Service List of English words, also known as the West List (1953).

Getting Ready to Read

Schema-building activities—photographs, group discussions, etc.—activate students' prior knowledge before reading. Students also study potentially unfamiliar vocabulary and key concepts and terms in the academic discipline before they read.

Reading for a Purpose

In this section, readers are guided to read for specific information through pre-reading tasks such as prediction of ideas, formation of pre-reading questions responding to short pre-test items, and other exercises. These activities focus readers' attention on a particular purpose for reading: finding key ideas.

Demonstrating Comprehension

Instead of monotonous comprehension exercises, *College Reading 3* features a variety of interest-peaking activities to monitor comprehension. After each reading, there is not just one or two, but multiple opportunities to assess comprehension. Main idea, major points, supporting ideas, text organization, and confirmation of pre-reading tests and other activities provide repeated checks of students' understanding of reading.

Questions for Discussion

Once students demonstrate a basic understanding of a reading selection, they delve more deeply into its content and language through group and pair discussions. Students write complete sentence answers to the questions after their discussions to exploit the language gained from reading in developing writing skills.

Reading Journal

The reading journal feature also facilitates the reading-writing link. Students express reactions to key ideas in reading or write extended answers to discussion questions. Journal writing also serves as another way to check reading comprehension.

Learning Vocabulary

Each chapter includes directed vocabulary learning exercises and strategy suggestions for students.

Focusing on (Subject Area)

Here students are exposed to more in-depth exercise types that focus on content learning expectations or assignments from the different discipline areas associated with each chapter.

Linking Concepts

In this section, readers synthesize information gained from two or more sources and transfer ideas from reading to their experiences. Students express these connections in discussion and writing.

Assessing Your Learning at the End of a Chapter

This final section of each chapter asks students to revisit the chapter objectives in a reflective manner, and review for a test. Then, a practice self-test tied to the objectives is provided. Students can test themselves on their understanding and retention of important content and language features in the readings. The items in the student practice tests are similar to items included on the sample tests provided for instructors to use. (Visit the series website at www.college.hmco/esl/instructors/.) Finally, academic vocabulary from the chapter is also revisited, and a For Further Study web link reminder is provided for students.

Acknowledgments

At Houghton Mifflin Company, ESL editor Susan Maguire made the project a reality, and developmental editor Kathy Sands Boehmer kept our team of educator-writers on track and supplied us with the essential reviews to make our initial efforts more effective. Series editors Patricia Byrd (Georgia State University), Joy Reid (University of Wyoming), and Cynthia Schuemann (Miami Dade College), as well as all the team members, lent an enormous store of theoretical and pedagogical knowledge to the series. To Reading strand editor Cynthia Schuemann, for her assiduousness, we extend our sincere thanks. Cynthia was not only a series editor and Reading strand editor, but as a Reading strand co-author, she and Cheryl Benz empowered and inspired us to match their level of professional dedication and quality.

To our families, we recognize your love, encouragement, and good humor which has sustained us, and for this we simply thank you for your part in making this project even possible.

Finally, students are the core reason that teachers endeavor to improve methods and materials. Our students at Green River Community College and Community College of Philadelphia are especially deserving. Work and family responsibilities, urban, cultural, and language challenges— all of these impact our students as they strive toward their academic goals. Above all, we dedicate these materials to them and wish them every success.

The following reviewers contributed practical comments:

Harriett Allison, Gainesville College

Michael Aymie, Bunker Hill Community College

A. Mara Beckett, Glendale Community College

Jennifer Britton, Valencia Community College

Lori Cawthorne, Bunker Hill Community College;

Amy Drabek, Queens College

Duff Galda: Pima Community College

Kathleen Kelly, Passaic Community College

Daryl Kinney, Los Angeles City College

Linda Linn, San Jacinto College

Erin Lofthouse, San Francisco City College

Carole Marquis, Santa Fe Community College

Brian McClung, Brookhaven College

Marilyn Mirman, Baltimore City Community College

Cynthia Solem, San Jose City College

Mary Swidey, Bristol Community College

Stephanie Vogel, Suffolk Community College

Regina Weaver, Portland State University

Colleen Weldele, Palomar College

Vivette Beuster, Green River Community College

Richard Alishio, Green River Community College

Susan Kay Donaldson, Tacoma Community College

Laura Walsh, City College of San Francisco

○ What Student Competencies Are Covered in *College Reading 3*?

Description of Overall Purposes

Students develop the ability to comprehend lengthier texts on diverse academic topics by applying appropriate reading strategies.

Materials in this textbook are designed with the following minimum exit objectives in mind:

Competency 1: (level/global focus) The student will read academic texts with general education content. (Text sources include materials from Houghton Mifflin secondary and some college "essentials" textbooks, approximate readability levels 9–13).

Competency 2: (flexibility) The student will adjust reading strategies according to text (e.g., applying personal schema to survey and predict, and varying reading speed).

Competency 3: (components) The student will analyze the use of facts and examples to support and explain generalizations, statements of theory, and implicit main ideas or assumptions. These distinctions will aid the student in prioritizing what to learn for test-taking purposes (e.g., distinguishing more relevant from less relevant or irrelevant pieces of information).

Competency 4: (organization) The student will use a wide range of textual clues to identify text style and structure (method of development) of a reading with particular attention to commonalities and differences found across disciplines.

Competency 5: (vocabulary) The student will develop vocabulary by applying effective strategies to clarify, analyze, and learn the meaning of new words in non-literary text, and the student will understand the figurative use of language in literary text.

Competency 6: (vocabulary) The student will discriminate, select, and learn important words pertinent to specific academic reading contexts.

Competency 7:
(critical thinking)

The student will demonstrate the ability to apply the following critical thinking skills when reading. The student will:

a. make plausible inferences or interpretations.
b. develop a perspective through exploration of beliefs, arguments, and theories.
c. ask significant questions.
d. transfer insights gained from readings to other contexts and identify significant similarities or differences in perspectives or application.
e. clarify and analyze the meaning of text (e.g., through outlining, paraphrasing, and summarizing).
f. synthesize information gathered from more than one source in order to give an informed opinion.
g. apply content knowledge to academic tasks.
h. identify an author's purpose, point of view, or tone when reading literary text.

Competency 8:
(culture)

The student will understand and discuss common cultural references.

Competency 9:
(study strategies)

The student will apply effective study skill strategies.

⭕ **What Are the Features of the Reading Books?**

The Houghton Mifflin English for Academic Success series is a comprehensive program of student and instructor materials. The fundamental purpose of the program is to prepare students who are not native speakers of English for academic success in U.S. college degree programs.

The Reading strand of the Houghton Mifflin English for Academic Success series focuses on the development of reading skills and general background knowledge. It is dedicated to meeting the academic needs of students by teaching them how to handle the reading demands and expectations of freshman-level college classes. The four books provide reading selections from authentic academic text sources and practical exercises and activities that enhance the teaching-learning process. Students respond positively to being immersed in vocabulary, content, and skills that are easily recognized as valuable and applicable.

Authentic Academic Reading Selections: The reading selections come from varied disciplines reflecting high-school academic preparation and college freshman-level courses with high enrollment patterns. The selections represent true reading demands college students face.

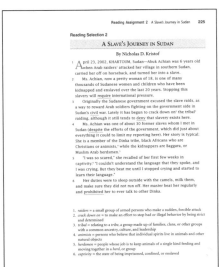

Content and Academic Skill Development: In addition to language development, the books provide for content and academic skill development with the inclusion of appropriate academic tasks and by providing strategies to help students better understand and handle what is expected of them in college classes.

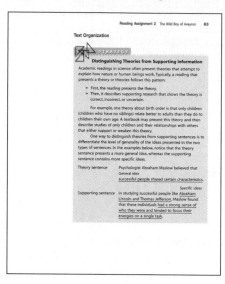

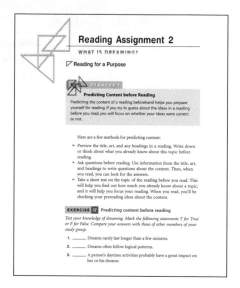

Academic Vocabulary: Academic vocabulary is important in both written and spoken forms, so the Reading strand features attention to high-frequency academic words found across disciplines. The books teach students techniques for learning and using new academic vocabulary and provide many practice exercises.

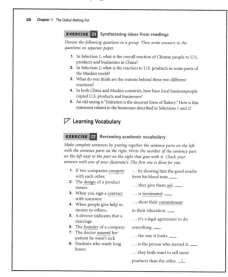

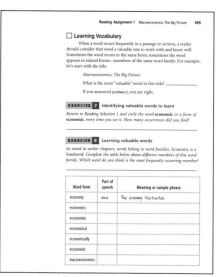

Integrated Review and Assessment: Each chapter closes with revisiting objectives and vocabulary and a practice test.

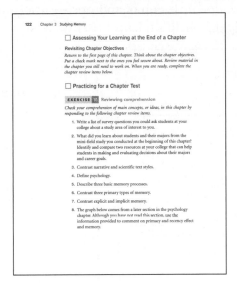

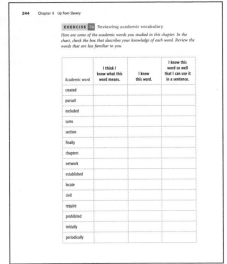

Master Student Tips: Master Student Tips throughout the textbooks provide students with short comments on a particular strategy, activity, or practical advice to follow in an academic setting.

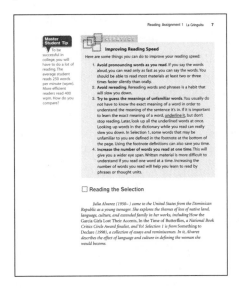

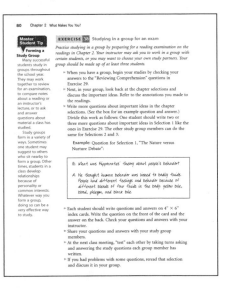

Power Grammar Boxes: Students can be very diverse in their grammar and rhetorical needs so each chapter contains Power Grammar boxes that introduce the grammar structures students need to be fluent and accurate in academic English.

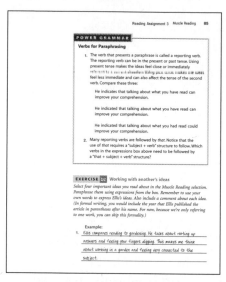
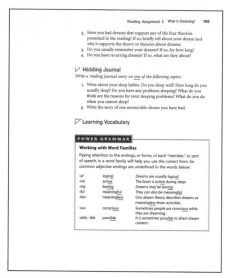

Ancillary Program: The following items are available to accompany the Houghton Mifflin English for Academic Success Series Reading strand:

- Instructor website: Additional teaching materials, activities, and robust student assessment.
- Student website: Additional exercises and activities.
- The Houghton Mifflin English for Academic Success series Vocabulary books: You can choose the appropriate level to shrinkwrap with your text.
- *The Essentials of Teaching Academic Reading* by Sharon Seymour and Laura Walsh is available for purchase. It gives you theoretical and practical information for teaching reading.

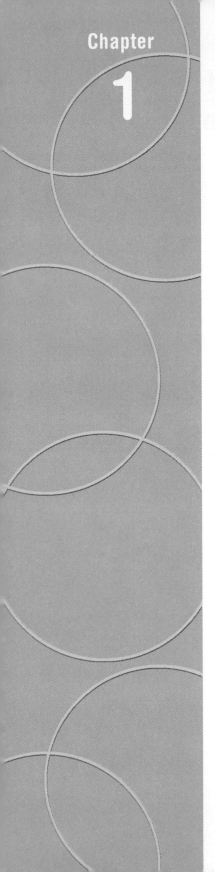

Race and Ethnicity

ACADEMIC FOCUS: SOCIOLOGY

Academic Reading Objectives

After completing this chapter,
you should be able to:

✓ Check here as you
master each objective.

1. Preview texts to aid comprehension ☐
2. Read and understand a section of a sociology textbook ☐
3. Create a guided outline of a reading selection ☐
4. Analyze the use of facts and examples used to support generalizations ☐
5. Identify a common organizational pattern for explanations ☐
6. Clarify and summarize the meaning of a text passage ☐
7. Transfer insights gained across reading passages ☐
8. Form a study group to review reading selections ☐

Sociology Objectives

1. Describe similarities and differences between race and ethnicity ☐
2. Name the characteristics of minority groups ☐
3. Identify patterns of repression a society may exhibit toward minority groups ☐
4. Evaluate how completely various minority groups have joined a dominant society ☐

Reading Assignment 1

○ Getting Ready to Read

One job of sociologists is to observe how individuals belong to various groups of people. Two of these groups of people are racial and ethnic minorities. In this chapter, the authors tell us race is based on "physical differences among people," while ethnicity is "based on cultural factors." Look at the pictures and think about how you would group these individuals.

Group A

How are the above men the same? How are they different?

Group B

How are the above men the same? How are they different?

Group C

How are the above women the same? How are they different?

EXERCISE 1 Participating in class discussion

Form a small group of three or four classmates and discuss the following questions related to the pictures on page 2. You might not agree on all the answers. It's okay to disagree.

1. When you looked at the pictures, what kinds of differences did you notice? What kinds of similarities did you find?
2. In the selection you will read about race and ethnicity, the authors state that race is based on "physical differences among people" while ethnicity is based on "cultural factors." How would you define the terms *race* and *ethnicity* in your own words? How are they different from one another?
3. Which groups of people shown in the pictures are of the same race, but from different ethnic groups?
4. Which groups of people shown in the pictures are from the same ethnic group, but from different races?
5. Which ethnic and racial groups are represented in your class?
6. Are all racial and ethnic groups treated equally in American society or in other societies? Explain any differences you see between groups or societies.

○ Learning Vocabulary

What Is the Academic Word List?

Researchers have found that certain words appear over and over again in academic readings. These same words appear across academic disciplines, from textbooks in sociology and world history to articles on business and computer science, so they are important words to learn and remember. Common academic words are marked in the reading selections in this textbook with dotted underlines. You may already know some of these words, but others may be new. Develop a system for recording new words and definitions so that you can study and remember them. Make learning the unfamiliar academic vocabulary words a priority, and you will not only expand your vocabulary *but also* perform better in academic courses. The identified words are found on the Academic Word List (AWL). To view the complete AWL, visit our website http://esl.college.hmco.com/students.

Vocabulary Strategies: Using the Academic Word List

A useful vocabulary learning strategy is to keep a reading and vocabulary journal. As you read, write down new words you want to learn with reminders about the meaning of the words. Reminders could include a definition, synonym, translation, or the word in a phrase. When the word reappears in a new text, you will be ready. Your reading comprehension will increase as will your reading speed. As you learn the words through reading, by doing these exercises, and with the help of a dictionary, put them in a reading journal. See the "Keeping a Reading Journal" box near the end of this chapter for a more detailed description of a reading journal. Words that you study and use are words that you will remember.

EXERCISE 2   Scanning for academic vocabulary

*Scan through the pages of Reading Selection 2, starting on page 15, to find and preview these AWL words. The words may appear more than once. Write down the paragraph number next to the word the **first** time it appears. The first two are done for you as examples.*

1.	minority	1	12.	ethnicity	___
2.	sociologists	1	13.	traits	___
3.	aspect	___	14.	traditionally	___
4.	military	___	15.	migration	___
5.	dominant	___	16.	accurately	___
6.	established	___	17.	data	___
7.	norms	___	18.	uniform	___
8.	structure	___	19.	categories	___
9.	majority	___	20.	available	___
10.	discrimination	___	21.	culture	___
11.	identified	___	22.	trends	___

23. comprise   ____   35. maintaining   ____

24. diverse   ____   36. targeted   ____

25. retain   ____   37. responded   ____

26. generation   ____   38. negative   ____

27. voluntary   ____   39. submission   ____

28. intense   ____   40. withdrawal   ____

29. factors   ____   41. status   ____

30. participate   ____   42. distinctive   ____

31. respond   ____   43. process   ____

32. ranging   ____   44. acknowledges   ____

33. transferred   ____   45. unique   ____

34. estate   ____

○ Reading for a Purpose

STRATEGY

Previewing

Good readers understand what they read and remember the information for quizzes, tests, and further learning. Becoming a good reader means acquiring the skills that effective readers have. One important skill is to read selections more than one time. Every time you read a selection, read for a different purpose. The first time through a passage, do not read it line by line. Instead, look for an overview of the topic. In other words, try to understand the general subject area and get a quick indication of the main idea of the selection. This skill is called viewing ahead, or previewing.

EXERCISE 3 **Using a prereading strategy**

Preview Reading Selection 1 by completing these steps:

> Step 1: Read the headings and subheadings.
> Step 2: Read the first and last sentence of each of the three paragraphs.
> Step 3: Use any knowledge you have about the subject to help you make predictions about the main idea of the paragraphs.

Then answer these previewing questions:

1. What is the main topic or focus of this selection?
2. In looking at the title, how does studying sociology give breadth and depth? What will you read about in the rest of the chapter?

Now read the complete selection. Read every line in order to understand the main idea and supporting ideas of the text. Read every line, but do not expect to understand every word. After you complete the selection, you will be asked to answer some comprehension questions.

Reading Selection 1

STUDYING SOCIOLOGY FOR BREADTH AND DEPTH

By John Avery

Studying in American Colleges and Universities

1 When attending a college or university in the U.S., students usually major in one subject area and take other classes which meet their "distribution requirements." This means they have to take a lot of classes in one main or academic "major" subject and many other classes in different areas of study such as science, math, humanities, English, and the social sciences. The idea behind this system is for students to develop breadth and depth. The breadth comes from having some education in a number of areas and the depth comes from concentrating, or majoring, in just one. Each college or university has its own requirements, but most students are required to take some courses in the social sciences. To fulfill the distribution requirement for social science, students may take a sociology course.

> ### A Dictionary Definition of Sociology
>
> The study of human social behavior, especially the study of the origins, organization, institutions, and development of human society.*
>
> *Source: Editors. (2002). *American Heritage Dictionary of the English Language.* Boston: Houghton Mifflin, p. 1350.

What Is Sociology?

2   Sociology is one of the main social sciences. Anthropology, economics, geography, political science, and psychology are other social sciences. In the textbook *Introduction to Sociology*, authors Ethel Wood and Judith Lloyd Yero explain sociology by giving us a quotation and some definitions.

Here are some of the authors' key points.

- According to Auguste Comte, a Frenchman who was the first to use the term sociology (in 1824), sociology means "the study of society."
- "Sociologists . . . study social behavior in human groups and look for patterns." (p. 2)
- Sociologists look at how social relationships affect group behavior. (p. 2)

3   The subject of sociology covers a large number of topics, such as race and ethnicity. In this chapter, you will read about these topics and respond by discussing the subject in your class. If you attend a college or university and major in sociology, you will acquire a great deal more depth in this subject. To major in a subject means you will take a lot of classes in that area so you will have more knowledge about it than you will about other subjects. For now, you will read about two topics in sociology and gain some breadth of understanding about an important field of study.

○ Assessing Your Learning

Demonstrating Comprehension

EXERCISE 4 Focusing on "Studying Sociology"

Answer these questions about Reading Selection 1 by circling the correct response. After answering the questions, go back to the selection and check your answers.

1. What is an academic major?

   a. It is a subject area of concentration for students.

   b. It is one of the distribution requirements.

   c. It is a requirement to be completed before entering college.

   d. It is all the distribution requirements together.

2. How do students gain depth of study in college?

   a. by studying only subjects of personal interest

   b. by taking a number of distribution requirements

   c. by studying an academic major

   d. by meeting all the requirements for entry into college

3. Which of the following is an example of a subject that sociologists might study?

   a. the stages of child development

   b. the political systems of Asian countries

   c. Irish immigration to the United States in the 1800s

   d. relationships within groups

4. What was the purpose of this selection?

   a. to introduce students to the subject of sociology

   b. to introduce students to American colleges and universities

   c. to explain how sociology can be studied for breadth and depth

   d. to convince students to major in sociology if they attend college in the United States

EXERCISE 5 **Writing short-answer responses**

Many college instructors give quizzes and tests that require students to respond with short definitions and written answers. Respond to these requests for information in writing. Your answer should be longer than a sentence but no longer than one paragraph. Write your answer in the space provided below.

1. Use your own words to define depth and breadth of academic study in colleges and universities.
2. Define distribution requirements, and give examples of classes you might take from at least three areas of study. You may want to look at a college catalog for ideas.

_____

_____

_____

_____

_____

_____

_____

_____

_____

_____

_____

_____

_____

_____

_____

_____

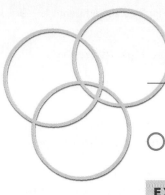

Reading Assignment 2

UNDERSTANDING RACE AND ETHNICITY

○ Getting Ready to Read

EXERCISE 6 Previewing and learning key terms

Study these key sociology terms to prepare for reading the second selection. The italicized sentences contain examples of the words as they are used in Reading Selection 2. Use a dictionary as needed to help you understand these terms.

sociologists *n.* People who study and research in the field of sociology. "*Sociologists are not interested in the biology of race. They are interested in race as it relates to the social structure.*"

norm *n.* A standard, model, or pattern regarded as typical: *the current middle-class norm of two children per family.* "*The dominant group establishes the values and **norms** of the society.*"

power *n.* A person, group, or nation having great influence or control over others. In sociology, power always relates to the influence an individual or group has in society. "*In a society, the group of people that has the **power** . . . is the dominant group.*"

dominant group *n.* The group of people in a society that has the power. The rulers and leaders. "*A nation's history identifies its **dominant group**.*"

minority group *n.* The group of people in a society that doesn't have power. They often do not have all the privileges and rights that the dominant group possesses. "*Groups in a society that have been overpowered by the dominant group . . . make up **minority groups**.*"

characteristic *n.* A major feature of a culture or group that is used to define or describe that culture or group. "*Some cultures are known because of their religion. Sociologists identify minority groups by four **characteristics**.*"

repressed *v. (past)* To hold back one group in order to favor another group. "*In history minorities are often **repressed** by the dominant group.*" **repression** *n.*, **repressed** *adj.*

Use what you have learned about the key terms above to complete these sentences. The first one is done as an example.

1. In India, the Brahmins are a *dominant group* as they have control over the people in lower castes.

2. African, Hispanic, and Asian Americans are examples of _____ _____ in the United States.

3. _____ differ from psychologists because they study the behavior of people in groups.

4. Eating with a knife, fork, and spoon versus using chopsticks is an example of a _____ that changes from one culture to another.

5. Dedication to Islam is a _____ of most Arab societies.

6. Nelson Mandela was _____ by the government of South Africa when they kept him in jail.

○ Reading for a Purpose

In preparation for reading the first selection, you learned to read the text more than once in order to read for different purposes.

Preview Reading Selection 2 by completing these steps:

Step 1: Read the headings and subheadings.
Step 2: Read the first and last sentence of each section.
Step 3: Try to predict what you think the main idea of the selection might be. Use any knowledge you have about the subject to help you make your prediction.

As you read these elements, use a highlighter pen to mark any text you think expresses the main idea of the selection. The main idea is *not* directly expressed at the beginning of this selection. Think of the main idea as coming from the most general sentences in a selection that state the author's point in writing the passage. You can sometimes find the main idea by turning a heading into a question. For this selection, the title, "Understanding Race and Ethnicity," becomes *What are race and ethnicity, and how can we understand them?* Can you answer this question?

STRATEGY

Scanning

Scanning is a skill that readers use to find specific information quickly. When readers scan, they look for keywords or parts of the text that stand out. Readers want to find the key information for a specific purpose. Sometimes readers just want to find a telephone number, for example, and thus they look in a telephone book for just one number.

EXERCISE 7   Scanning for supportive evidence

In this exercise, you will practice scanning to find numbers, words, or phrases that support the main ideas of the passage. Once you locate this information, you will be better able to find and understand the main ideas when you read. You will also be able to understand a basic organization pattern used in this selection. For now, complete the following exercise.

Scan Reading Selection 2 to find these indicators of supporting evidence. Write the paragraph number where the indicators can be found. (See paragraphs 11–17.)

Indicators of Supporting Evidence   **Paragraph Number**

1. Expressions used to give examples, "in actual practice"
    "***In actual practice***, *the Census Bureau invites people to check one of dozens of categories to identify their race.*"   11

2. Numbers
    "*. . . there were about **60** different racial combinations recognized for non-Hispanics and another **60** for Hispanics.*"   _____

3. Percentages
    "*In the United States, about **30** percent of the population is non-white.*"   _____

4. Dates
"*If current trends continue, by* **2050** *almost half of the U.S. population will be non-white.*"   _____

Indicators of Supporting Evidence   Paragraph Number

5. Example
"*Asian Americans* comprise *a minority group that includes many different national groups. Japanese Americans not only speak a different language from Korean Americans, but they have different customs and political and social beliefs as well.*"   _____

6. "In fact" elaborations
"***In fact****, the term ethnic comes from the Greek word ethnos, meaning "people" or "nation.*"   _____

EXERCISE 8   **Identifying indicators of supportive evidence**

In academic texts, authors often make a general statement (or theory) and then support that statement with facts and examples. Check the items you think will indicate if the phrase or sentence contains facts or examples to support the main ideas in a selection.

_____ Numbers and percentages   _____ "In actual practice . . ."

_____ Dates   _____ Example(s)

_____ "In the United States . . ." _____ "In fact . . ."

If you checked all these indicators, you are correct. They all indicate (tell us) that a fact or example is being used to provide evidence to support a theory. As you read through the second reading selection, be aware of these indicators and the theories or main ideas they support. After reading, you will complete an exercise in which you make the connection between theory and support.

Reading Selection 2

UNDERSTANDING RACE AND ETHNICITY

Racial and Ethnic Minorities

1   The oldest human records speak of minorities and raise the question of how they should be treated. There were minorities in ancient Egypt and Babylon, and the Hebrew Scriptures furnish complete descriptions of numerous minority groups. How do sociologists view this aspect[1] of human society?

Dominant Groups

2   In a society, the group of people that has the power—whose members include the rulers, lawgivers, and religious, military, and educational leaders—is the dominant group. A nation's history identifies its dominant group.

Example:

3   In Spain, the dominant group is the group whose power dates from the time of Ferdinand and Isabella and their European ancestors. These 15th-century rulers expelled and persecuted Jews and Muslims and established a white, Roman Catholic nation with Castilian Spanish as its official language.

---

1. **as•pect** (ăs′pĕkt) *n.* A way in which something can be viewed by the mind; a feature.

Minority Groups

4   Groups in a society that have been overpowered by the dominant group—such as American Indians in the United States—or have come in after the dominant group's power is established— immigrants in the United States other than the English—make up minority groups.

5   The dominant group establishes the values and norms of the society. It creates a social structure that operates in its favor. Minority groups have to live by the rules set by the dominant group, which usually means they don't have the same privileges[2] and must accept inferior[3] housing and jobs and are often treated differently by the justice system.

6   A common misconception[4] about minority groups is that they are always numerically smaller than the majority group in a society. That may be true, but a minority group is better defined as any recognizable group in a society that suffers some disadvantage due to prejudice or discrimination by the dominant group. In some nations of the world, religion distinguishes a minority group. Major minority groups in the United States are identified by race and ethnicity.

Racial Groups

7   The concept of race is based on observable physical differences among people resulting from inherited biological traits. It divides people into groups based on skin color and ancestral origin. Traditionally, English-speaking people have talked in terms of three races with their origins from three of the world's continents:

1. Africa.
2. Asia.
3. Europe.

8   Centuries of racial mixing—through migration,[5] exploration, and invasion—have resulted in a great intermingling of races. We cannot accurately categorize individuals as "black" or "white." Sociologists are not interested in the biology of race. They are interested in race as it relates to the social structure.

2. **priv•i•lege** (prĭv´ ə-lĭj) *n.* A special advantage, right, or permission given to an individual or group.
3. **in•fe•ri•or** (ĭn-fîr´e- ər) *adj.* Low or lower in quality, value, or estimation.
4. **mis•con•cep•tion** (mĭs´kən-sĕp´shən) *n.* A mistaken thought, idea, or notion; a misunderstanding.
5. **mi•gra•tion** (mī-grā´shən) *n.* A move from one country or region to settle in another.

9   In order to make the gathering of data uniform, sociologists rely on the categories of race that the Census Bureau uses or on the definition of race that individuals give themselves or others.

10   If you read a U.S. Census Bureau report, you might find data divided among the following five groups:

1. White, not Hispanic.
2. Black.
3. Hispanic.
4. Asian and Pacific Islander.
5. American Indian, Eskimo, and Aleut.

11   In actual practice, the Census Bureau invites people to check one of dozens of categories to identify their race. In the 2000 census, there were about 60 different racial combinations recognized for non-Hispanics and another 60 for Hispanics. Census forms were available in English, Spanish, Chinese, Korean, Vietnamese, and Tagalog, the language of the Philippines. Guides for the census takers were written in 49 languages. As you can see, race in the United States is a matter of culture, and is not easy to define.

12   In the United States, about 30 percent of the population is non-white. African Americans make up the largest racial minority group. However, in the near future the Hispanic population is expected to outnumber the black population. If current trends continue, by 2050 almost half of the U.S. population will be non-white.

Ethnic Groups

13   While racial groups are based on physical characteristics, ethnic groups are based on such cultural factors as national origin, religion, language, norms, and values. As with the concept of racial groups, there is great variety within broad ethnic categories.

Examples:

14   Asian Americans comprise[6] a minority group that includes many different national groups. Japanese Americans not only speak a different language from Korean Americans, but they have different customs and political and social beliefs as well.

15   Jews, although they are racially diverse and live in many countries around the world, are bound together by their common religious beliefs, customs, and values.

6. **com•prise** (kəm-prīz´) *tr.v.* To consist of one or more elements; include.

16   Within the United States, nationality groups often settle in the same neighborhoods and retain separate identities. Poles, Ukrainians, Mexicans, Puerto Ricans, Italians, and Germans who live in the United States may vary in the strength of their ethnic identities, but national heritage often sets such groups apart.

17   Ethnic groups retain[7] their separate identities as long as they pass their cultural beliefs and practices from generation to generation. A common ancestry is usually—but not necessarily—shared by group members. In groups with strong ethnic identities, members are encouraged to form friendships with and to marry only others of the same ethnicity. In fact, the term ethnic comes from the Greek word ethnos, meaning "people" or "nation." The special feeling of "my people" sets the group apart from others and discourages members from forming close ties with "outsiders."

Characteristics of Minority Groups

18   Sociologists identify minority groups by four characteristics, in addition to their receiving unequal treatment in society:

   a. **Shared Physical or Cultural Characteristics.** Members of a minority group are identified by a wide array of physical and/or cultural differences, including race, religion, ancestry, language, and customs. The foods served, the celebrations observed, the ways in which people choose their spouses—these are often similar among members of an ethnic group.

   b. **Ascribed[8] Statuses.** Membership in a minority (or dominant) group is not voluntary. People are born into the group; race and ethnicity are ascribed statuses.

   c. **Group Solidarity.**[9] When a group is the object of long-term prejudice or discrimination, the feeling of "us *versus* them" often becomes intense. Members of ethnic groups stick together when they feel under attack from the dominant group or from other minority groups.

---

7. **re•tain** (rĭ-tān´) *tr.v.* To keep something.
8. **a•scribe** (ə-skrīb´) *tr.v.* To attribute to a specified cause, source, or origin.
9. **so•li•dar•i•ty** (sŏl´ĭ-dăr´ĭ-tē) *n.* A union of interests, purposes, or sympathies among members of a group.

d. **Endogamy.** Members of a minority generally marry others from the same group, a practice known as endogamy. Two factors account for this: (1) the unwillingness of members of the dominant group to marry into, and thus in some way join, a lower level of society; and (2) a minority group's sense of solidarity, which encourages marriages within the group.

Patterns of Repression and Response

19   Societies vary in the degree to which racial and ethnic minority groups participate in mainstream society. Minorities respond to their situation with behaviors ranging from submission and acceptance to agitation and violence. In history, repression of minorities by the dominant group has taken four forms:

a. **Forced Removal**—in which a minority population is transferred to a separate geographic location.

Example: The Trail of Tears removal of the Cherokee from Georgia to Oklahoma in 1838.[10]

b. **Segregation**—in which a minority group is kept separate from the dominant population in the same location. It can be *de jure*, based on laws, or *de facto*, based on informal norms.

Example: Earlier laws in the South that kept blacks and whites from attending the same schools (*de jure*); the discriminatory practice of sellers, real estate agents, and mortgage lenders in the North that kept African Americans from living in neighborhoods with whites (*de facto*).

c. **Subjugation**—maintaining control over the minority population by force.

Example: The Israeli use of curfew laws and troops with guns and tanks to punish the Palestinian minority following acts of terrorism by militant individuals.

d. **Annihilation**—the destruction of a targeted minority population. Also called genocide.

Example: In Rwanda, the efforts of the Hutu rebels against the Tutsis. In April 1994, hundreds of thousands of Tutsis were murdered by Hutu rebels in the central African country of Rwanda in an attempt to annihilate the Tutsis.

10. The **Cherokee** are a group of Native Americans whose ancestors were moved from their homelands in Georgia to unwanted land in Oklahoma by the U.S. government.

20   Minority groups have often responded to these negative forms of treatment in three ways:

    a. **Submission and Acceptance**—deferring to members of the dominant culture and learning ways of "getting along."

    b. **Withdrawal**—avoiding contact with the dominant culture through self-segregation.

    c. **Agitation and Violence**—protesting minority status and unequal treatment or organizing a revolt against the dominant group.

Assimilation—Melting Pot or Cultural Salad

21   Society in the United States has tried to encourage most of its immigrant minority groups, particularly those that are white, to join (assimilate) mainstream society. Historically, it has done this in two ways, described by figures of speech:

    a. **The Melting Pot** (from the container in which metals are melted to make such alloys as steel) is a term for American society that suggests the people of different nations have given up their distinctive ways to become members of the dominant culture through assimilation, the process by which people become like others around them, taking their norms on as their own.

    b. **The Salad Bowl** refers to the idea of cultural pluralism[11] in which mainstream society acknowledges there is value in preserving the uniqueness of the subcultures that comprise it. Minority groups are encouraged to maintain unique identities within the larger culture, and society accepts diversity as part of its own definition.

---

11. **plu·ral·ism** (plo͞or′ ə-lĭz′ əm) *n.* A condition in which numerous distinct ethnic, religious, or cultural groups are present and tolerated within a society.

○ Assessing Your Learning

Demonstrating Comprehension

You can increase your understanding of this reading selection by studying how it is organized. In the "Reading for a Purpose" section, Exercises 7 and 8, you saw how academic authors often use a standard organizational pattern. This pattern happens when an author gives general statements and then provides support for those generalizations. The support is often in the form of examples or facts.

EXERCISE 9   Outlining with supporting evidence

Complete the following outline of Reading Selection 2. Fill in the generalizations and support used by the authors. Reread the passage and complete all the lines in the outline. You do not need to use the exact words from the passage. In fact, it is better for your comprehension if you try to express the concepts in your own words. Share your outline with a partner when you have completed the exercise.

I. **Introduction**—Human records speak of *minorities* and how they

should be *treated*. Sociologists have a *view* on this subject.

II. **Dominant Groups**

Definition: The group of people in society that has the power is the

_____ .

Example

_____

_____

III. **Minority Groups**

Definition: Groups in a _____ that have been

_____ by the dominant group make up

_____ groups.

Example

_____

_____

IV. Racial Groups

Definition: The concept of _____ is based on

observable _____ differences among people

resulting from inherited biological _____ .

Three major traditional groups for English-speaking people based on origin from three of the world's continents.

1. _____

2. _____

3. _____

Sociologists are interested in race as it relates to the

_____ .

Sociologists rely on the _____ of race that the

Census Bureau uses. You can find five groups in a census report.

1. _____

2. _____

3. _____

4. _____

5. _____

In actual practice, the Census Bureau invites people to check one

of dozens of _____ to _____

their race.

V. Ethnic Groups

Definition: While racial groups are based on _____ characteristics, _____ groups are based on such _____ factors as national origin, religion, language, _____, and values.

Examples

1. _____

   _____

2. _____

   _____

Ethnic groups retain their separate _____ as long as they pass their _____ beliefs and practices from generation to generation.

VI. Characteristics of Minority Groups

Sociologists identify _____ groups by four characteristics, in addition to their receiving _____ treatment in society:

1. _____

2. _____

3. _____

4. _____

VII. **Patterns of Response and Repression**

Repression   In history, _____ of minorities by the

_____ group has taken four forms:

1. Forced Removal

Definition: _____

_____

Example

_____

_____

2. Segregation

Definition: _____

_____

Example

_____

_____

3. Subjugation

Definition: _____

_____

Example

_____

_____

4. Annihilation

Definition: _____

_____

Example

_____

_____

Response Minority groups have often ———————————— to

these ———————————— forms of ———————————— in

three ways:

1. Submission or ————————————————

Definition: ——————————————————————————

———————————————————————————————————

2. Withdrawal

Definition: ——————————————————————————

———————————————————————————————————

3. Agitation and ————————————————

Definition: ——————————————————————————

———————————————————————————————————

VIII. Assimilation—Melting Pot or Cultural Salad

Society in the United States has tried to encourage most of its

———————————— minority groups, particularly those that are

————————————, to join ———————————— mainstream

society. Historically, it has done this in two ways, described by

figures of speech:

1. The ———————————— **Pot**

Definition: ——————————————————————————

———————————————————————————————————

2. The ———————————— **Bowl**

Definition: ——————————————————————————

———————————————————————————————————

Understanding Patterns of Academic Writing: Repetition, Explanation, and Extension

Authors often use patterns when writing academic texts. By understanding these patterns, we can better understand their texts. The authors of *Introduction to Sociology* use a pattern several times to introduce a concept and then give an explanation about that concept. The pattern has two sentences. In the first sentence, the authors introduce the concept; in the second sentence, the authors use synonyms and pronouns to give more information about the subject and the concept. The authors may also extend the concept with an additional phrase.

EXERCISE 10   **Understanding elaboration patterns**

Follow these steps:

1. Read paragraph 5. The first two sentences contain the pattern we are studying.
2. Read the chart, which shows how the author uses the pattern.
3. Read the explanation of what the second sentence teaches us.

Example 1

Step 1: Read this paragraph.

The dominant group establishes the values and norms of the society. It creates a social structure that operates in its favor. Minority groups have to live by the rules set by the dominant group, which usually means they don't have the same privileges and must accept inferior housing and jobs and are often treated differently by the justice system.

Step 2: Study the pattern of the first two sentences.

The Pattern

In the first sentence, the author provides a definition. In the second sentence, the author restates that definition and gives more information about the topic.

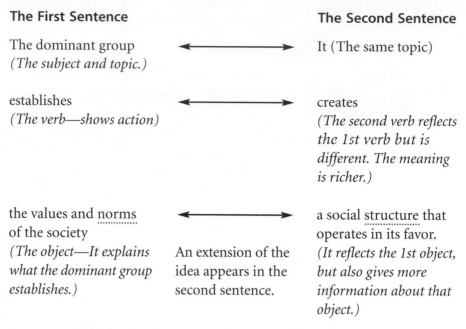

The First Sentence		The Second Sentence
The dominant group *(The subject and topic.)*	⟷	It (The same topic)
establishes *(The verb—shows action)*	⟷	creates *(The second verb reflects the 1st verb but is different. The meaning is richer.)*
the values and <u>norms</u> of the society *(The object—It explains what the dominant group establishes.)*	An extension of the idea appears in the second sentence.	a social <u>structure</u> that operates in its favor. *(It reflects the 1st object, but also gives more information about that object.)*

Step 3: Read this explanation.

What the second sentence tells us. **We learn that . . .**

- *creates* is similar to *establishes*.
- the values and norms of a society are its social structure, its form and definition.
- the social structure (or the values and norms) operate in favor of the dominant group.

This pattern deepens our understanding of the topic.

Example 2

Now study this second example, and complete the explanation of what the second sentence teaches us.

Step 1: Read this paragraph.

The concept of race is based on observable physical differences among people resulting from inherited biological traits. It divides people into groups based on skin color and ancestral origin. Traditionally, English-speaking people have talked in terms of three races with their origins from three of the world's continents:

1. Africa.
2. Asia.
3. Europe.

Step 2: Study the pattern of the first two sentences.

The First Sentence	The Pattern Used by the Author	The Second Sentence
The concept of race	⟷	It
is based on	⟷	divides
observable physical differences among people resulting from inherited biological traits.	⟷	people into groups based on skin color and ancestral origin.

Step 3: Write your explanation of what the second sentence tells us:

- _____

  _____

- _____

  _____

- _____

  _____

Example 3

Now study this third example. Draw arrows which match parts of the first sentence to similar parts in the second sentence. Also complete the explanation of what the second sentence teaches us.

Step 1: Read this paragraph.

Society in the United States has tried to encourage most of its immigrant minority groups, particularly those that are white, to join (assimilate) mainstream society. Historically, it has done this in two ways, described by figures of speech: the melting pot and the salad bowl.

Step 2: Draw arrows to link similar parts of each sentence. (See the examples above.)

The First Sentence	**The Second Sentence**
Society in the United States	It
has tried to encourage most of its immigrant minority groups,	has done this
to join (assimilate into) mainstream society.	in two ways, described by figures of speech: a melting pot and a salad bowl.

Step 3: Describe any additional understanding you gain about assimilation from the second sentence.

- _____

- _____

- _____

This exercise shows just one kind of writing pattern found in academic texts. Authors use many other patterns. As you read, look for other patterns. They will help you understand the material in textbooks.

○ Focusing on Sociology

In the first selection of this chapter, you read,

> Sociology is one of the main social sciences . . . Sociologists . . . study social behavior in human groups and look for patterns . . . Sociologists look at how social relationships affect group behavior.

The author writes that "sociology is a social science." It is social because it is concerned with human relationships, particularly group relationships. It is a science because it follows the rules of science on how to observe and analyze information, or data. In the following exercise, you look at some ways that sociologists observe and analyze social relationships.

EXERCISE 11 **Understanding concepts from sociology**

Reread these paragraphs from Reading Selection 2 on pages 14–19, and then answer T–F questions that follow. Do this exercise individually first, and then work in small groups to check your answers with your classmates.

Circle True or False to indicate if these statements are accurate according to the sections above. On separate paper, rewrite the false sentences to make them true.

1. Race is generally related to physical differences among people. True False

2. Physical differences come from biological traits. True False

3. Skin color is the only physical indication of race. True False

4. English-speaking people group races into three categories. True False

5. The categories for race of English-speaking people are accepted by all. True False

6. The races have remained separate over time. True False

7. Races can accurately be divided into just black and white. True False

8. Sociologists do not use biology to identify races. True False

9. Sociologists use social relationships to identify races. True False

10. Sociologists use uniform data to be scientific. True False

11. The Census Bureau data cannot be trusted by social scientists. True False

12. The Census Bureau identifies only five races. True False

13. For a sociologist, race is related to culture. True False

14. The definition of race is very complicated for a sociologist. True False

EXERCISE 12 Checking comprehension

Choose the best answer for each multiple-choice question. Base your answers on information in Reading Selection 2.

1. Why are sociologists not interested in the biology of race?

    a. They cannot agree on how to define race in the same way.

    b. They look for social relationships, not biological relationships.

    c. They have not yet established a definition of race, as sociology is a new science.

    d. They study economic differences, not physical differences.

2. What kind of data do sociologists use to base their understanding of race?

    a. Inherited biological traits and physical differences

    b. Traditional definitions and skin color

    c. Officially used categories and self-reporting by individuals

    d. Ancestral origins from three continents

3. In its practice of categorizing census data, the U.S. Census Bureau uses

    a. the three traditional categories of English-speaking people.

    b. a simplified set of five groups.

    c. dozens of categories.

    d. both b and c.

4. The U.S. Census Bureau prints census forms in many languages to

    a. ensure that all people can be counted.

    b. show the world that Americans use many languages.

    c. make all the people happy.

    d. increase the minority population.

5. A sociologist

    a. defines race as a biologist does.

    b. defines race as it is related to culture.

    c. defines race in a simple and easy-to-understand manner.

    d. defines race as a mixing of individuals.

EXERCISE 🔢 **Discussing a key question**

Reread paragraphs 13–17, and then answer the following question.

How do sociologists define race differently from ethnicity?

Selection 2 that you studied earlier in the chapter is from a chapter in a textbook written for students preparing to enter college. This chapter on race and ethnicity helps students understand these terms from the perspective of a sociologist. To learn more, go to http://esl.college.hmco.com/students.

Wood, E., & Yero, J. L. (2002). *Introduction to Sociology.* Evanston, IL: McDougal Littell.

 S T R A T E G Y

Summarizing What You Read

A written summary is a brief statement of the main points of a longer reading. Summaries are used in academic work for many purposes. One use of summaries is to help you understand and remember what you have read.

> **EXERCISE 14**   Summarizing what you read

For this exercise, follow the steps to summarize the material on the characteristics of minority groups. Your summary will be a short paragraph that includes all the main points of the original selection.

Step 1: Reread the following selection about the characteristics of minority groups.

Characteristics of Minority Groups

18   Sociologists identify minority groups by four characteristics, in addition to their receiving unequal treatment in society:

   a. **Shared Physical or Cultural Characteristics.** Members of a minority group are identified by a wide array of physical and/or cultural differences, including race, religion, ancestry, language, and customs. The foods served, the celebrations observed, the ways in which people choose their spouses—these are often similar among members of an ethnic group.

   b. **Ascribed Statuses.** Membership in a minority (or dominant) group is not voluntary. People are born into the group; race and ethnicity are ascribed statuses.

   c. **Group Solidarity.** When a group is the object of long-term prejudice or discrimination, the feeling of "us *versus* them" often becomes intense. Members of ethnic groups stick together when they feel under attack from the dominant group or from other minority groups.

   d. **Endogamy.** Members of a minority generally marry others from the same group, a practice known as endogamy. Two factors account for this: (1) the unwillingness of members of the dominant group to marry into, and thus in some way join, a lower level of society; and (2) a minority group's sense of solidarity, which encourages marriages within the group. *(This original consists of 197 words.)*

Step 2: Recall the four characteristics of minority groups. Use the subheadings.

1. <u>Shared physical or cultural characteristics</u>

2. _____

3. _____

4. _____

Step 3: Now complete this sentence. Notice the use of a synonym replacing the word characteristics.

The four aspects of minority groups are shared physical or cultural

features, _____, _____, and

_____.

Step 4: Now summarize a key point about each of these characteristics (aspects). Use the main idea, but do not give all the information included in the original version. The first two are done for you as examples. Write the third and fourth summary sentences.

   a. Minorities share physical and cultural similarities such as race and customs.

   b. People do not choose to join a minority. Instead they are born into it.

   c. _____

      _____

      _____

   d. _____

      _____

      _____

Step 5: On separate paper, write your summary in paragraph form. Then, count the number of words you used and compare that number with the original count of 197 words. Finally, answer the questions below about summaries.

   1. What is a summary? Give your own definition. _____

      _____

      _____

   2. How can writing a summary help you to understand a textbook

      better? _____

      _____

      _____

3. How can writing a summary help you to prepare for a test?

_____

_____

_____

⭘ Questions for Review

EXERCISE 15 **Writing short-answer responses**

Just as you did after the first selection, write short answers for the following questions. Write these as a means to prepare for a test on Reading Selection 2. Write or type them on separate paper. Your instructor may have you share these answers with your classmates and/or submit your responses.

1. What is sociology? Give a brief definition and compare it to other social sciences.
2. Define and contrast dominant groups and minority groups. Give examples of each.
3. Define race as a sociologist perceives race. Support your answer with information from the second reading.
4. What are some cultural factors that define an ethnic group? Give examples from your own ethnic group or a group you know well.
5. How do ethnic groups keep (retain) their identities? Give examples from the text and/or your own experience.
6. Name and discuss the four characteristics of minority groups. Why are these characteristics important in defining a minority group?

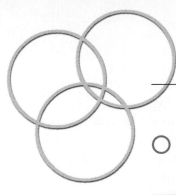

Reading Assignment 3

○ **Getting Ready to Read**

STRATEGY

Previewing Introductory Elements

Notice the introduction to Reading Selection 3, Life as an Alien. You can recognize it as an introduction because it is printed before the story and in *italic type*. Textbooks often use special type (or formatting) such as italics, a special font size, and underlining to tell the reader that one part of a section is different from another. An effective reading strategy is to pay attention to these formatting differences as you read textbooks.

EXERCISE 16 Answering warm-up questions

Read the introduction to Life as an Alien on p. 37, and then answer these background questions based on your reading of that part only. Check your answers with your classmates.

1. Who is the author? _____

2. What is the story about? _____

3. When was the story written? _____

4. Where does the story take place? _____

5. Why did the author write this story? _____

_____

⚪ Reading for a Purpose

Social science classes often include reading assignments with stories of individuals or groups that reflect the main sociological themes in the class and textbook. The next reading selection is connected to the previous reading selection in this way. It is about a woman from a minority group. Notice how her story illustrates some of the concepts you have learned about race and ethnicity. Also notice how your reading process may differ as you read this narrative, in contrast with the reading the second selection.

EXERCISE 17   Applying the prereading strategy

Preview Reading Selection 3 by completing these steps:

Step 1: Review the introductory paragraph (*in italics*), and read the complete first paragraph.

Step 2: Read the first and last sentence of each paragraph, and the complete final paragraph.

Step 3: Try to predict what you think is the main idea of the selection. Use any knowledge you have about the subject to help you make your prediction.

Then answer these questions. Base your answers on your preview.

1. What is this woman's country of origin?
2. To which minority group does this woman belong?
3. How is that minority group defined?
4. What repression do you think she may have experienced as a member of that group?
5. How do you think she would have responded to repression?

⭕ Reading the Selection

Read the following selection completely. Pay particular attention to how the concepts from the sociology passages you have read so far are reflected in the story of Meri Nana-Ama Danquah.

Reading Selection 3

LIFE AS AN ALIEN

By Meri Nana-Ama Danquah

The immigrant experience frequently brings with it a "half and half" feeling of not fully belonging to either the culture of the new country or the old. With one foot in each culture, immigrants are distanced from people that they grew up with. The process of adjusting completely to their new lives is often slow and difficult. In the following selection written in the 1990s, Meri Nana-Ama Danquah, an African immigrant from Ghana who was living in Los Angeles, explores her life as an "alien" and contemplates the emotional effects of living in the United States for many years without becoming a citizen.

1   I don't know where I come from. When people ask me, I have to stop and wonder what it is they really want to know about me. Do they want to know where I was born, where I grew up, where I have lived as an adult, where I live now? It troubles me to be so scattered,[1] so fragmented, so far removed from a center. I am all and I am nothing. At the same time. Once, a long time ago, when I believed that answers were as easy as smiles, someone told me that home is where the heart is. Perhaps this is true. Love has always been a magnet.[2] It is half the sky, the raggedy part that needs to be held up and saved. It is a name as long as history with enough vowels for each of its children to claim. It is the memory of wearing open-toed shoes in December.[3]

2   Love is a plate of steamed white rice and pig's-feet stew. As a child, this was my favorite meal. I would sit at the dining table, my legs swinging back and forth, and hum as I scooped the food into my mouth with my hand. I always ate the rice first, saving the meat in a towering heap on the side for last. Then I would greedily dig into the pile of pork and choose the largest piece. When my teeth had grazed all the flesh off the bone, I would hold the pork to my lips and suck it dry of its juice. I would bite down hard until it broke in half and I could touch the marrow with the tip of my tongue. Right then, right there, I knew my world was complete.

3   Several years ago, in what I can only assume was a temporary loss of sanity;[4] I decided to become a vegetarian.[5] Swept into the New Age organic, fat-free health obsessions of Los Angeles, the city in which I live, I vowed to never again eat another piece of meat. Not fish, not chicken, and certainly never pork. It felt strange to not eat meat anymore; nothing I took in seemed to fill me. "You'll get used to the change," a friend promised. We were at an Indian restaurant celebrating my newfound diet. When my dinner arrived, a gentle nostalgia[6] descended upon me. The food—a creamy stew of chopped spinach—resembled kontumare, a Ghanaian dish I very much enjoy.

1. **scat•ter** (skăt′ ər) *v.* Separate and go in different directions; disperse.
2. **mag•net** (măg′nĭt) *n.* A person, a place, an object, or a situation which exerts a powerful attraction.
3. The author is using poetic language to describe love. Study the last four sentences to see how these different descriptions or images give the reader different aspects or understandings of love.
4. **san•i•ty** (săn′ĭ-tē) *n.* Soundness of mind, judgment, or reason.
5. **veg•e•tar•i•an** (vĕj′ĭ-târ′ē-ən) *n.* A person who eats only plants and plant products, or one who eats plants, plant products, and eggs and dairy products.
6. **nos•tal•gi•a** (nŏ-stăl′jə) *n.* A longing for the past.

Except there was no meat. And that absence left me feeling so cheated out of an integral[7] part of the experience I was having that before returning to my apartment I stopped by an uncle's house and begged the leftover remains of his curried goat dinner.

4   My attempt to be an herbivore was but one in a long list of numerous attempts I have made to create or "try out" a new identity. In my twenty-four years of living in America, I have adapted to all sorts of changes. I have housed many identities inside the one person I presently call myself, a person I know well enough to admit that I don't know at all. Like a chameleon, I am ever changing, able to blend without detection into the colors and textures of my surroundings, a skill developed out of a need to belong, a longing to be claimed. Once, home was a place, perhaps the only place, where I imagined that I really did belong, where I thought myself whole. That is not so anymore, at least not in the home that I grew up believing was mine. That word, "home," and all it represents, has shifted in meaning too many times.

5   From the age of six, when I left Ghana and arrived in Washington, D.C., to be with my mother who had been in the States already for three years, it was quite clear that someday we would return. There was always talk of going back. There were always plans being made, sentences being spoken that began with words like "When I go home . . ." Even after my father joined us, America was just a place of temporary existence, not home. And in consideration of our imminent departure, assimilation was frowned upon. My parents tried to fan the flames of our culture within me, in hopes that they would grow into a raging fire and burn fully any desire I had to become an American.

6   The split between the me who lived in [our] apartment and the me who had to learn how to survive outside it was immediate. It had to be. Initially, I suppose that I viewed that split simply as an external divide, straight and pronounced, like the threshold of our front door, marking the point of separation between two distinct realities. On one side was America, on the other was Ghana. And I didn't know how to bring them together, how to make one make sense *to*, let alone *in*, the other.

7. **in•te•gral** (ĭn′tĭ-grəl) *adj.* Essential or necessary for completeness.

7   Newness is easy to detect, especially with immigrants. Everything about you is a dead giveaway. And people constantly watch and stare through the scrutinizing lens of curiosity. That was a foreign thing for me, being questioned, being eyed. From top to bottom, the eyes would travel. From top to bottom, taking a silent inventory of the perceived differences: the way I wore my hair wrapped with thread as thick as an undiluted accent, or in small braids intricately woven like a basket atop my head; my clothing, a swirl of bright, festive colors dyed on fabric much too thin for the shivery East Coast climate.

8   Being black made the transition from Africa to America extremely difficult because it introduced another complex series of boundaries. The one place where I found acceptance was in the company of other immigrants. Together, we concentrated[8] on our similarities,[9] not our differences, because our differences were our similarities. Still, I secretly envied the other foreign kids because I believed that their *immigrant* experience was somehow more authentic than mine. Unlike me, they were not caught in the racial battlefield of black and white, their *ethnicity* was visible. Mine invariably[10] faded to black. They spoke languages that were identifiable. Everybody's heard of Spanish, Korean, Chinese, even Arabic. The few people who had heard of Ga and Twi colonially labeled them dialects, not languages.

9   When I [lost] my accent, I suddenly internalized[11] the divide, blurred the lines between continents and allegiances. There was no middle ground anymore, no threshold, no point of distinction[12] between one reality and another. I had strayed so far away from the place I called my home that I could not find my way back. From that point on, every culture I made contact with seeped in to create one fluid geography within me. Yet as much as I imagined that I could claim them all, I still belonged to none of them. I didn't even belong to the one in which my family resided,[13] the one that had once

8. **con•cen•trate** (kŏn´sən-trāt´) *v.* Keep or direct one's thoughts, attention, or efforts on a common center; focus.

9. **sim•i•lar•i•ty** (sĭm´ə-lăr´ĭ-tē) *n.pl.* Related in appearance or nature; alike but not exactly the same.

10. **in•var•i•a•ble** (ĭn-vâr´ē-ə-bəl) *adj.* Not changing or subject to change; constant.

11. **in•ter•nal•ize** (ĭn-tûr´nə-līz´) *tr.v.* Take in and make an integral part of one's attitudes or beliefs.

12. **dis•tinc•tion** (dĭ-stĭngk´shən) *n.* The condition of being dissimilar or different; difference.

13. **re•side** (rĭ-zīd´) *intr.v.* Live in a place permanently or for an extended period.

provided me the safety of a home base. Like everywhere else, I became the "other" there, unable to fully <u>expand</u> and unfold the many selves I now had, unable to ever again feel completely whole.

10   As the result of a recent <u>incident</u>[14] with my six-year-old daughter, Korama, I began, for the first time, to accept myself, my history of traversal.[15] I began to <u>create</u> a <u>context</u> for the cross-<u>cultural</u> life that I have led.

11   For whatever reason, in the course of one of Korama's kindergarten conversations, she let it be known that my favorite television program is *The X-Files.* That afternoon when I picked her up from school, she told me about the disclosure. "Oh. Okay, Korama," I said. "Mo-o-m," she whined, "it's not okay. They said you like that show because you're an alien. I tried to tell them, that you weren't, but Hugo said I was wrong. He said that you're not from America, and that everyone who's not from here is an alien. Is that true? Are you an alien?" She stared at my head as if antennae[16] would pop out at any time. I wasn't sure how to reply, but with the shrewdness that parenthood teaches you, I tried to figure out a way to answer her question without <u>volunteering</u> too much information that might, ultimately, confuse her. While I was mulling it over, she and I walked side by side in silence. With each step, I felt a distance growing between us.

12   For a moment, her stare was as disempowering as those of the American children whom I had <u>encountered</u>[17] as a child, her questions as offensive. I wanted to arm myself against the pain of being reminded that I was "other." I wanted to beg that little girl before me to try, to just try to accept, if not love—me for who I was, the way I was—no matter how different that seemed from the way she was. But I knew I didn't have to, because she already did. "Yes," I <u>finally</u> said to Korama, "I am." I explained to her that in addition to creatures from outer space, the word "alien" was used to refer to human beings from other countries. I expected her to be a bit

14. **in•ci•dent** (ĭn′sĭ-dənt) *n.* An unusual occurance that interrupts normal routines.
15. **tra•verse** (trə-vûrs′) *n.* To travel or pass across, over, or through.
16. **an•ten•nae** (ăn-ten′ē) *n.pl.* A pair of long, slender structures growing on the head of an insect or a crustacean such as lobster that are sensitive to touch or odors.
17. **en•coun•ter** (ĕn-koun′tər) *tr.v.* Meet, especially unexpectedly; come upon.

confused, but she didn't appear to be. She nodded, reached out for my hand as we approached[18] the street we had to cross to get to our apartment, and the distance disappeared.

13 When I tucked her into bed that evening, she raised the subject again. "Mom, will you always be an alien?" she asked. And, again, I tried to find a straightforward,[19] uncomplicated response, this time to a question I had been trying unsuccessfully to answer for over twenty years. "No," I told her. "Not if I become an American." Up until the second I said that, I had never so much as considered becoming a United States citizen. In the belief that I would one day return to the country of my birth, I had never made a commitment[20] to being in the country where I have spent the better part of my life. I had always thought of naturalization[21] as nothing more than a piece of paper one received after passing a test. If that's the case, I could live or die without that slip of paper, that change of nationality. It wouldn't make a difference one way or the other. I have lived my life as an alien, an outsider trying to find a way and a place to fit in. And it is only through that experience that I have come to think of myself not as a citizen of one country or another but, rather, of an entire world.

18. **ap·proach** (ə-prōch′) *v.* To come near or nearer in place or time.
19. **straight·for·ward** (strāt-fôr′wərd) *adj.* Direct; honest and frank.
20. **com·mit·ment** (kə-mĭt′mənt) *n.* A promise or an obligation to keep certain beliefs or to follow a certain course of action; the state of being emotionally or mentally bound to another person or to a course of action.
21. **nat·u·ral·i·za·tion** (năch′ər-ə-lĭ-zā′shən) *n.* The act of granting full citizenship to one of foreign birth; to become a citizen.

○ **Assessing Your Learning**

Demonstrating Comprehension

EXERCISE 18 **Matching activity**

Write in the letter representing the correct word or words to complete these statements.

Statements	Completions
1. Meri Nana-Ama Danquah's home country was _____.	a. identity
2. Danquah emigrated to the city of _____ in the 1970s as a child.	b. accent
3. Danquah made many tries to construct a new _____.	c. temporary
4. Danquah now lives in _____.	d. country
5. Danquah saw America as a _____ place to live.	e. accept
6. Recently, Danquah has begun to feel that America is her _____ home.	f. alien
7. In her eating habits, she tried to become a _____.	g. American
8. Eventually, she returned to being a _____ in her eating habits.	h. permanent
9. People knew she was a _____ because of her accent, hairstyle, and clothing.	i. Ghana
10. Danquah felt comfortable with other _____.	j. vegetarian
11. To fit into America, Danquah learned to speak without an _____.	k. meat eater
12. Because of a situation with her daughter, Korama, she began to _____ herself.	l. Washington, D.C.
13. Korama wanted to know if Meri Danquah was an _____.	m. newcomer
14. Korama didn't know that one meaning of the word *alien* is to be from another _____.	n. Los Angeles
15. Korama's questions led Meri Danquah to consider becoming an _____.	o. immigrants
16. Danquah considers herself a citizen of _____.	p. the world

EXERCISE **19** **Answering discussion questions**

The following discussion questions are about the "Life as an Alien" selection, as well as about its connection with Reading Selection 2 on race and ethnicity. Terms from the sociology textbook are indicated with **bold type***. You may want to review them now. Work in groups of three or four classmates. Answer the following questions together, and then be prepared to share your answers with the class. Elect a spokesperson who can report to the whole class from your group.*

1. What in the story gives us details of Meri Nana-Ama Danquah's cultural background?
2. What **characteristics of her minority group** are mentioned in the story?
3. How does her detailed description about eating fit into the rest of the story? Why does she include that information?
4. What **group solidarity** does Danquah describe?
5. How did Danquah experience **segregation** and **subjugation** in America?
6. What kinds of **responses** did she have to these **forms of repression**?
7. In paragraph 5, Danquah tells us her parents "tried to fan the flames of culture within me, in hopes that it would grow into a raging fire and burn fully any desire I had to become an American." Why would immigrant parents want to discourage their children from assimilating in America?
8. In the reading, Danquah considers becoming an American. If she does take that step, will her joining American society be an example of **the melting pot** or **the salad bowl**? Give reasons for your response.

○ Learning Vocabulary

EXERCISE 20 Reviewing academic vocabulary

Scan Reading Selection 3 for AWL words with the <u>dotted underlines</u> *in the same way you did for Selection 2. Write the paragraph number next to the word the first time it appears. The first two are done for you. As you work with these words, keep a list of those that are new for you in your reading journal. In Chapter 3, you will learn about making word cards. You will come back to these and other words to make study cards. Words that you study and use are words that you will remember.*

1. adult   _1_

2. assume   _3_

3. temporary   ___

4. integral   ___

5. shifted   ___

6. survive   ___

7. distinct   ___

8. constantly   ___

9. encountered   ___

10. commitment   ___

○ Assessing Your Learning at the End of a Chapter

Revisiting Objectives

Return to the first page of this chapter. Think about the chapter objectives. Put a check mark next to the ones you feel secure about. Review material in the chapter you still need to work on. When you are ready, answer the chapter review questions in Exercise 21.

◯ Practicing for a Chapter Test

Check your comprehension of main concepts, or ideas, in this chapter by preparing answers for the following questions in a small study group. These questions will help you review all three reading selections in this chapter. Work in groups of three or four classmates. Discuss possible answers, select a group spokesperson, and be ready to share your answers with the whole class. Take notes of your own group's answers, as well as those of the other groups. Your notes will assist you in preparing for a test on this chapter.

EXERCISE 21 Reviewing comprehension

Prepare a response for each item. Distribute the items among group members to prepare, and then take turns explaining each one. Work together.

1. What makes sociology a social science?

2. Why are sociologists interested in race and ethnicity?

3. Are minority groups always numerically smaller than majority groups in society? Why or why not? Give examples to support your answer.

4. How does dominant society repress minority groups? Give examples from the text or from the current situation in the world.

5. What are the three ways minorities have responded to repression? Give examples.

6. What are two models for assimilation? How are they similar and different?

7. How is Meri Nana-Ama Danquah representative of other immigrants who are members of minority groups?

8. Would Danquah's experience be different if she were of a different racial group?

○ Linking Concepts

STRATEGY

Keeping a Reading Journal

Researchers tell us that students who are aware of how they learn are more effective learners. These students can understand more, remember more, and use more English than other students. One of the best ways to become more aware of your own learning is to keep a reading journal. As you work with this book, we recommend that you keep a reading journal. Write the date every time you put something in the journal. Keep the following information in your journal:

- New words you have learned from reading, especially words from the Academic Word List (AWL words).
- Notes on organizational patterns that authors use. See exercises throughout this book for examples.
- Reading strategies that work for you. You may want to note, for example, what kind of reading process works best for you. You can also keep notes on the following types of questions. Does it help to preview and outline? Does it help to read a text more than once and for different purposes? What kind of review helps you to remember information and to use it for a test? What techniques have you developed to learn and remember vocabulary?
- Notes on learning preferences you may have, such as the right time and place to read. Also, do you like to read in a quiet place or one where there is music?
- Take notes on your reading speed and what kind of information you should and can read faster versus which material you need to read more carefully.

Learning is an individual process. As you discover more about your own learning process, you can become an even better learner. Trust yourself and give yourself permission to develop your own rules that work best for you.

EXERCISE 22   Answering questions about learning

The following are questions about learning and reading and the sociological topic of race and ethnicity. You can respond to these questions in three possible ways.

1. Write responses in your reading journal.
2. Discuss these questions in groups and as a whole class.
3. Provide short written answers to share with your classmates and/or your instructor.

Your instructor can provide specific instructions on how to respond to these questions.

Reflections on Learning

1. Describe the process you follow when you read academic textbooks. Do you preview the text? Do you look for the organization of the text? How many times do you read the chapter, and what do you do each time you read?
2. What three strategies can you use to remember new vocabulary?
3. In Exercise 8 on p. 13, you learned about scanning for keywords that indicate support for theory. How will your scanning skills help your comprehension of a passage?
4. You studied about a pattern that authors use to clarify an explanation. In the pattern you studied, the authors used a second sentence to explain the first sentence. Did you notice any other writing patterns in this chapter? If so, describe them.
5. What is the Academic Word List? How can it help you in your studies?
6. How can summarizing a textbook chapter help you comprehend and remember the information in the chapter?

Reflections on Race and Ethnicity

1. What are the dominant and minority groups in the country in which you were born?

2. Did you consider yourself a member of a dominant group or a minority group in your home country?

3. Do you consider yourself a member of a dominant group or a minority group in America?

4. Are all immigrants members of a minority group? If so, what characteristics of a minority group do immigrants share?

5. Have you ever been subject to repression? Explain the situation or tell a story.

6. Sociologically speaking, do you think your experience as an immigrant will be different from the experience of your children? Explain your answer.

7. What questions do Americans sometimes ask immigrants that may indicate some attempt to subjugate the immigrants?

8. Have you been questioned in ways that you thought were supposed to make you feel inferior?

9. How do you view America? Is it a melting pot or a salad bowl?

EXERCISE 23 **Reviewing academic vocabulary**

Here is a multiple-choice quiz on some academic vocabulary you found in this chapter. Take the quiz and check your answers on the website for this book. Review any words you missed. Keep the AWL words in your reading journal.

Circle the correct answer:

1. The social group that sets the rules for society is called the _____ group.

   a. minority   **b.** majority   **c.** dominant   **d.** subjugated

2. Facts and studies are examples of _____ sociologists use when building support of a theory.

   a. data   **b.** definitions

   c. categories   **d.** norms

3. National origin, religion, language, and norms and values are examples of _____ used to identify ethnic groups.

   a. physical characteristics   **b.** cultural factors

   c. trends   **d.** norms

4. Black and white American children in the 1950s used to attend different schools. This was an example of _____.

   a. forced removal   **b.** annihilation

   c. withdrawal   **d.** segregation

5. When members of a minority group do not accept the treatment of the dominant group, the minority group members might _____, which means they would avoid contact with the dominant group members.

   a. agitate   **b.** submit   **c.** withdraw   **d.** segregate

These words will be useful for learning in many academic areas. Study them and the other AWL words by clicking on the Web study link below to help you review your words.

WEB POWER

Go to **http://esl.college.hmco.com/students** to view more readings about race and ethnicity, plus exercises that will help you study the selections and the academic words in this chapter.

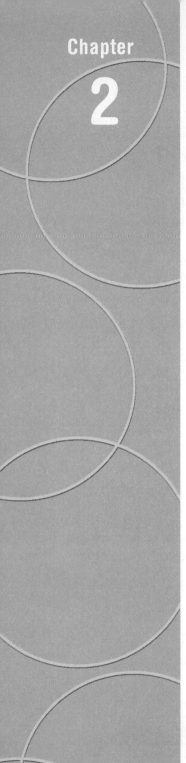

Stress and Adaptation

ACADEMIC FOCUS: PSYCHOLOGY

Psychology: The Science of Behavior and Mental Processes

Psychologists study what we do and what we think, feel, dream, sense, and perceive. They use scientific methods to investigate behavioral and mental processes.

Academic Reading Objectives

After completing this chapter, you should be able to:

✓ Check here as you master each objective.

1. Preview readings using survey techniques and prediction ☐
2. Develop vocabulary learning strategies using context and dictionary resources ☐
3. Interpret charts and graphs ☐
4. Outline a text's organizational structure ☐
5. Identify common style elements in scientific passages ☐
6. Recognize and scan for citation sources ☐

Psychology Objectives

1. Define stress ☐
2. Identify sources of stress ☐
3. Discuss the three stages of the body's reaction to stress ☐
4. Define acculturative stress ☐
5. Relate new knowledge about stress to personal experiences ☐

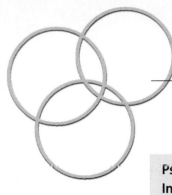

Reading Assignment 1

THE BODY'S RESPONSE TO STRESS— THE GENERAL ADAPTATION SYNDROME

Psychology classes are popular in U.S. colleges and universities. Introduction to Psychology classes are often in the top five courses taken by students starting their college studies. This chapter provides an introduction to one of the subjects psychologists study: stress. You will read about the causes and effects of stress on people.

○ Getting Ready to Read

EXERCISE 1 Recognizing word family members

Match the forms of the word psychology *with the correct definitions. The first one has been done for you as an example.*

Word form	Definition
Psychologist	1. The science that deals with mental processes and behavior.
Psychological	2. An adjective form of the base word meaning of or relating to psychology.
Psychology	3. The treatment of psychological problems by encouraging communication of and insight into conflict.
Psych	4. A person trained and educated to perform psychological research, testing, and therapy.
Psychotherapy	5. The short or abbreviated form of the word *psychology*. It is often used in college course schedules to list psychology classes.

EXERCISE 2 **Using correct word forms**

Complete these sentences by writing in the correct member of the psychology word family from the table in Exercise 1.

1. The alarm stage is accompanied by strong physiological and

   _____ arousal.

2. The science of behavior and mental processes is

   _____ .

3. Lyudmilla and Tran just registered for _____ 101

   for next fall.

4. _____ study what we do and what we think, feel,

   dream, sense, and perceive.

5. To overcome his fear of crowds, Peter decided to undergo

   _____ for treatment.

EXERCISE 3 **Defining psychology**

To prepare for Reading Selection 1, read the definition of psychology *in the box below, and then check the topics you think psychologists study. Discuss your answers with other students and with your instructor.*

Psychologists study . . .	What is psychology?
_____ the ways people learn. _____ the mental and personal growth of children. _____ how to help people with mental health problems. _____ human social behavior. _____ different types of people and their behavior. _____ the evolution and physical development of humans.	1. The science that deals with mental processes and behavior. 2. The emotional and behavioral characteristics of an individual, group, or activity.

○ Focusing on Psychology

Read the following text about stress, and then complete the activities that follow.

AN INTRODUCTION TO STRESS

The author of the reading selections included in this chapter writes that psychologists define stress as "pressures or demands placed upon an organism to adjust or adapt to its environment." An organism is any living thing; for this chapter, we only discuss the organisms called human beings. Stress is something humans experience that puts pressure or a requirement on us. That pressure means we have to adjust (change) to our new situation or environment. Stress can last for a short period, as when a driver has to act to avoid having an accident, or it can last for longer periods of time, as when a woman is told she has a medical problem and thus must change her diet or daily routine in order to become well again. Another example of a situation that causes stress is being an immigrant. When people immigrate to a new country, they often experience great stress in adjusting to their new cultural and economic situations. Stress comes both from everyday events and from the "big" events in our lives, such as buying a home, which are often positive in nature but still stressful. Some stress is useful to keep us challenged and involved with life, but too much stress can cause problems.

We all experience stress in different ways. Some people experience stress as just a nervous or busy feeling. Other people experience stress so strongly that it may cause them to seek professional help at a hospital. Still other people may die from experiencing so much stress that it leads to heart disease or other serious heath-related problems. Sometimes these health-related problems are physical, and other times they are psychological (mental or behavioral). Some people have a personality type (often referred to as a "Type-A personality") that causes them to experience stress more than others. These people are often impatient, competitive, and aggressive and are always short on time.

Stress is part of life and can be experienced for different reasons and have different effects. By being aware of stress and how we adjust to it, we can act to control its impact on our health and our lives.

EXERCISE 4 **Understanding stress**

Consider the two examples given in the above passage about stress. In one, a person is faced with an emergency while driving. In the second, a woman is faced with a serious medical problem. Both situations are stressful and cause a person to adjust to the environment of the situation. Read the following quotes from the passage, and circle the synonyms that best match the meaning of the key vocabulary words in bold type.

1. "Stress is something humans experience that puts **pressure**, or a requirement on us."

   *Circle the three most accurate synonyms for the kind of **pressure** that stress places on a person:*

   strain   weight   anxiety   energy   importance   influence   tension

2. "Psychologists define stress as "pressures or demands placed upon an organism to **adjust** or adapt to its environment."

   *Circle the three most accurate synonyms for the word **adjust** as it is used in this context.*

   vary   conform   contrast   alter   differ   change   modify

Place a check mark next to situations that are stressful.

_____ hearing of the death of a friend or relative

_____ moving to a new house

_____ getting married

_____ doing your daily exercise routine

_____ going through divorce

_____ being stuck in heavy traffic

_____ experiencing the birth of a child

_____ having a regular breakfast

_____ listening to your favorite music

_____ giving a speech

_____ immigrating to a new country

_____ having an aggressive personality

Choose the correct words to complete the following sentences by writing your selections on the lines provided for your answers.

1. Stress can happen _____ situations.

   a. only in negative
   b. only in positive
   c. in both negative and positive

2. Stress _____ .

   a. can be totally avoided
   b. is a natural part of life
   c. always causes health problems

3. Stress has an impact on us. In response, we can _____

   _____ .

   a. only feel nervous and unhealthy
   b. learn to adjust and stay healthy
   c. avoid any situation that is stressful

○ Learning Vocabulary

Think about the introductory passage you read. Can you answer the following questions: What is **stress**? When does it occur? What might some of its causes be? Who might feel stress more than others? When have you felt stress?

Stress is defined as follows in this chapter:

> Stress results from pressure or demands placed on an organism to adjust or adapt to its environment.

In the remaining part of this chapter, you will read two passages from a college textbook on psychology. The first passage uses the word *stress* in phrases. Learning how a word functions inside phrases is an important part of learning new vocabulary.

EXERCISE **5**   **Previewing phrases with *stress***

Work with these phrases to better understand how the word stress *is used in the text passages. The phrases have been grouped together. Work with other students to answer these questions. Some questions have been completed for you as examples.*

Phrases with *stress*	
Group one	**Questions**

the body's response to stress
 	
exposure to stress
 	
relentless intense stress
 	
during times of stress
 	
persistent stress
 	
the stresses of contemporary life
	1. Is *stress* used as a noun, verb, or adjective in these phrases?
	
	_____
	
	2. List the three adjectives that describe stress.
	
	   ● *relentless*
	
	   ●
	
	   ●
	
	3. From these phrases, can you tell if stress happens once or repeatedly?
	
	_____

Group two	**Questions**
a stress-related disorder	1. Is *stress* used as a noun, verb, or adjective in this phrase? _____ 2. *Stresss* is used to describe the word *disorder*. What more do we know about the meaning of *stress* from this phrase? _____

Phrases with *stress* (cont.)	
Group three	**Questions**
the famed stress researcher …	**1.** Is *stress* used as a noun, verb, or adjective in this phrase? _____ **2.** What does it mean to be a stress researcher? _____
Group four	**Questions**
specific stressors response to a stressor the stressor continues the stressor persists responds to various stressors	**1.** Is *stressor(s)* used as a noun, verb, or adjective in these phrases? _____ **2.** What does the stressor do? _It continues. It persists._____ _____
Group five	**Questions**
stressful experiences a stressful event	**1.** Is *stressful* used as a noun, verb, or adjective in these phrases? _____ **2.** List three stressful events or experiences. • _learning to drive_ • •

○ Reading for a Purpose

STRATEGY

Understanding Charts

Concept charts are graphic illustrations that help readers understand the ideas, theories, or concepts presented in a text. Previewing charts before you read a selection can increase your background knowledge. You can first locate the subject of a chart by reading the chart title. Then notice how charts are made of rows and columns. The rows read from left to right; they are horizontal. The columns read from top to bottom; they are vertical. Each column has a heading, which tells you the kind of information contained in the column. As you read down each column, a different aspect of the subject of the chart is described.

EXERCISE 6   Understanding charts

The following concept chart gives more information about the sources of stress on an individual. Preview the chart, and answer these questions.

1. The heading for the first column is *Source*. That is a brief title for a longer term. What is the longer term? (*Hint.* Look at the title of the chart.)

   _____

2. The heading for the second column is *Description*. What is being described? Give an example.

   _____

3. The heading for the third column is *Key Points*. A key point is the important idea you should remember about the subject of that row. What do you learn from the information under *Key Points* that you do not learn from the information under *Description*?

   _____

Sources of *stress*		
Source	**Description**	**Key points**
hassles	Common annoyances of everyday life	The accumulation of a large number of daily hassles may contribute to chronic stress, which can impair psychological and physical well-being.
life events	Changes in life circumstances, either positive or negative, that place demands on us to adjust	A greater number of life change events is associated with poorer psychological and physical health outcomes, but cause-and-effect relationships are difficult to tease out.
frustration	A state of negative arousal brought about by the thwarting of one's efforts to attain personal goals	We feel frustrated when obstacles placed in our path prevent us from achieving our goals or when we set unattainable goals for ourselves.
conflict	The state of tension that occurs when we feel torn between two opposing goals	Conflicts are most stressful when opposing goals are equally strong and no clear resolution appears in sight.
traumatic stressors	Sudden, life-threatening events such as natural or technological disasters, combat experiences, accidents, or physical or sexual assault	Traumatic events can tax our coping abilities to the limit. Many survivors of trauma go on to develop a type of psychological disorder called post-traumatic stress disorder (PTSD).
Type A behavior pattern (TABP)	A behavior pattern characterized by impatience, competitiveness, aggressiveness, and time urgency	The TABP is linked to a higher risk of coronary heart disease. While Type A "hares" are not likely to become "tortoises," they can learn to reduce their Type A behavior.
acculturative stress	Pressures imposed on immigrant people to adapt to the cultural and linguistic demands of the host country	Complex relationships exist between acculturation status and psychological adjustment. Adjustment depends on many factors, including economic opportunities, language proficiency, ethnic identification, and a supportive social network.

From Nevid, J. (2003). *Psychology Concepts and Applications*. Boston: Houghton Mifflin Company, p. 599.

EXERCISE 7   **Extending a chart**

The concept chart in Exercise 6 gives readers much useful information about the sources of stress. It identifies different sources, describes the stress, and gives important (key) information about the sources. Now add a fourth column in which you list a real-life example of a stress source. If appropriate, use examples from your own life or from someone you know well.

Sources	Examples
Hassles	Rush-hour traffic
Life events	
Frustration	
Conflict	
Traumatic stressors	
Type A behavior pattern	
Acculturative stress	

EXERCISE 8 Previewing to identify the topic

Earlier in this chapter, you read an introduction to the topic of stress. In Reading Selection 1, you will read about how the body responds to stress. Read the first paragraph of the selection, and then answer the following questions.

1. Who is "Dr. Stress"? _____

2. What did he discover about the body's reaction to different kinds of stress? _____

3. What did he call that reaction? _____

4. What is the acronym for this reaction? _____

EXERCISE 9 Previewing headings

Look ahead at the passage, and complete the following brief outline by filling in the rest of the section headings.

The Body's Response to Stress—The General Adaptation Syndrome
I. Introduction

II. The Alarm Stage

III. _____

IV. _____

V. Conclusion

○ Reading the Selection

Academic writing often follows a pattern of organization where a topic is described through definition, explanation, and exemplification. As you read this selection, look for a more detailed pattern or organization that uses definitions, explanations, and examples in these paragraphs. You will complete a post-reading exercise on the organization of the passage.

As you read, also keep in mind that common academic words (AWL words) are marked in the reading selections in this textbook with dotted underlines.

Reading Selection 1

THE BODY'S RESPONSE TO STRESS—THE GENERAL ADAPTATION SYNDROME

1   Much of what we know about the body's response[1] to stress is the result of pioneering research by Hans Selye (1907–1982), the famed stress researcher known affectionately as "Dr. Stress." Selye found that the body responds in a similar manner to various stressors—cold, noise, infectious agents, pressures on the job, or mental stress in the form of worry or anxiety. He recognized that specific stressors, such as an invading virus, do elicit specific reactions in the body. But layered over these specific responses is a more general response to stress, which he called the general adaptation[2] syndrome (GAS) (also called the stress response). The general adaptation syndrome consists of three stages, each of which we consider below.

Alarm Stage

2   The alarm[3] stage is the body's first stage of response to a stressor, during which its defenses prepare for action. Suppose a car ahead of you on the road suddenly veers out of control. This is an immediate stressful event. Your heart starts pounding faster, speeding the flow of blood to your extremities and providing muscles with the oxygen and fuel they need to take swift action, such as performing an emergency maneuver to avoid a collision. The body's response during the alarm stage is called the fight-or-flight[4] response because it is characterized by biological changes that prepare the body to deal with a threat by either fighting it off or fleeing from it.

3   The alarm stage is accompanied by strong physiological[5] and psychological arousal. Our hearts pound, our breathing quickens, sweat pours down our foreheads, and we are flooded with strong emotions such as terror, fright, anxiety, rage, or anger.

1. **re•sponse** (rĭ-spŏns´) *n.* A reaction that an organism may have in response to a specific cause, mechanism, or stimulus.
2. **ad•ap•ta•tion** (ăd´ăp-tā´shən) *n.* A change or adjustment to meet new conditions.
3. **a•larm** (ə-lärm´) *n.* Sudden fear caused by a sense of danger.
4. **fight-or-flight** *adj.* Relating to a set of physiological (body) changes, such as increase in heart rate, initiated by the nervous system to mobilize body systems in response to stress.
5. **phys•i•o•log•i•cal** (fĭz´ē-ə-lŏj´ĭ-kəl) *adj.* Related to the physical processes, activities, and functions of a living organism.

4   Different stressful events may trigger[6] the alarm stage of the GAS. The threat may be physical, as in an attack by an assailant, or psychological, as in an event that induces fear of failure (a professor handing out an examination, for example). In some people, the alarm is triggered whenever they meet a new person at a social gathering; they find themselves sweating heavily and feeling anxious, and they may become tongue-tied. In others, the body alarm system is activated whenever they visit the dentist. Whether the perceived threat is physical or psychological, the body's response is the same.

5   The alarm stage is like a "call to arms" that is prewired into the nervous system. This wiring is a legacy[7] inherited[8] from our earliest ancestors who faced many potential threats in their daily lives. A glimpse of a suspicious-looking object or a rustling sound in the bush might have cued them to the presence of a predator, triggering the fight-or-flight response, which helped prepare them to defend themselves against a threat. But the fight-or-flight response didn't last long. If they survived the immediate threat, their bodies returned to their normal state. If they failed, they simply perished.[9]

Resistance Stage

6   Death may occur within the first few hours or days of exposure[10] to a stressor that is so damaging (such as extreme cold) that its persistence is incompatible[11] with life. But if survival is possible and the stressor continues, the body attempts to adapt to it as best it can. Selye called this part of the GAS the resistance[12] stage (also called adaptation stage). During this stage, the body attempts to return to a normal biological state by restoring spent energy and

6. **trig•ger** (trĭg´ ər) *tr.v.* Cause.
7. **leg•a•cy** (lĕg´ ə-sē) *n.* Something handed down from an ancestor. In this case it is a genetic trait.
8. **in•her•it** (ĭn-hĕr´ ĭt) *v.* To acquire (characteristics) by genetic transmission from one's parents or ancestors.
9. **per•ish** (pĕr´ ĭsh) *intr.v.* To die or be destroyed.
10. **ex•po•sure** (ĭk-spō´zhər) *n.* The condition of being exposed, especially to severe weather or other forces of nature so as to cause harm.
11. **in•com•pat•i•ble** (ĭn´kəm-păt´ə-bəl) *adj.* Not able to exist together with something else at the same time. Extreme stress can cause death.
12. **re•sis•tance** (rĭ-zĭs´təns) *n.* A force that tends to oppose or slow down an opposing force or motion.

repairing damage. Yet arousal[13] remains high, though not as high as during the alarm reaction. This prolonged bodily arousal may be accompanied by such emotional reactions as anger, fatigue, and irritability.

Exhaustion Stage

7   If the stressor persists, the body may enter the final stage of the GAS—the exhaustion[14] stage. Heart rate and respiration now decrease to conserve bodily resources. Yet with continued exposure to stress, the body's resources may become seriously depleted and the individual may develop what Selye called "diseases of adaptation"— stress-related disorders such as kidney disease, heart disease, allergic conditions, digestive disorders, and depression. Some people are hardier than others, but relentless, intense stress can eventually exhaust anyone. The figure on page 78 shows the changes that occur in the body's level of resistance across the three stages of the GAS.

8   A sensitive alarm system may have helped our ancient ancestors survive many of the physical threats they faced. Yet the alarm reaction was designed not to last very long. Our ancestors either escaped a predator or fought it off; within seconds, minutes perhaps, the threat was over and their bodies returned to their normal, pre-aroused state. The stresses of contemporary life are more persistent. Our ancestors didn't need to juggle[15] school and jobs, fight daily traffic jams, or face the daily grind of working a double shift to make ends meet. The reality for many of us today is that the stressful demands of everyday life may repeatedly activate[16] our alarm reaction day after day, year after year. Over time, persistent stress may tax our bodies' resources to the point where we become more susceptible to stress-related disorders.[17]

From Nevid, J. S. (2003). *Psychology Concepts and Applications*. Boston: Houghton Mifflin Company, pp. 598–600.

13. **a•rous•al** (ə-rou´zəl) *n.* The act or state of being excited.
14. **ex•haus•tion** (ĭg-zôs´chən) *n.* The state of being very tired; extreme fatigue; lacking any energy or ability to resist.
15. **jug•gle** (jŭg´əl) *v.* To have difficulty holding or balancing something; to keep more than two activities in progress at one time.
16. **ac•ti•vate** (ăk´tə-vāt´) *tr.v.* To make something active; start in motion.
17. **dis•or•der** (dĭs-or´dər) *n.* A sickness that affects the function of the mind or body.

○ Assessing Your Learning

Demonstrating Comprehension

EXERCISE 10 **Understanding reactions to stress**

Answer these questions about the passage on "The Body's Reaction to Stress" by circling the correct response.

1. According to the text, Hans Selye based his writings about general adaptation syndrome on
   a. his personal experience with stress.
   b. the experience of one of his patients with stress.
   c. his research on stress.
   d. the ideas of important psychologists.

2. Which of the following is an example of a response during the alarm stage?
   a. Adapting to the pressures of work
   b. Running away from a wild animal
   c. Developing heart disease
   d. Feeling calm and relaxed

3. Which of the following is an example of a response during the resistance stage?
   a. Adapting to the pressures of work
   b. Running away from a wild animal
   c. Developing heart disease
   d. Feeling calm and relaxed

4. Which of the following is an example of a response during the exhaustion stage?
   a. Adapting to the pressures of work
   b. Running away from a wild animal
   c. Developing heart disease
   d. Feeling calm and relaxed

5. According to the text,
   a. people in past times were always in a state of arousal.
   b. we experience less stress than people in past times.
   c. we experience stress more continuously than people in past times.
   d. we experience heavy stress, but then we have a chance to relax.

> **POWER GRAMMAR**
>
> ### Verbs for Describing Research
>
> 1. The verb that presents research findings is called a reporting verb. In scientific writing, the reporting verb is often in the past tense, and it is frequently followed by a "that phrase" with a subject + present verb, or modal verb form. Using present tense for the second part makes the ideas feel close or immediately relevant to a current situation. Consider these two examples:
>
>   > He found that the body responds in a similar manner to various stressors.
>   > He recognized that specific stressors elicit specific reactions in the body.
>
> 2. For discussions and generalizations, as well as for statements of theory resulting from research, scientific writers use other tenses, but they rely particularly on the present form. Also, they often use a modal verb, particularly the modal verb *may* and will frequently use the passive voice. Examine these examples:
>
>   > The general adaptation syndrome consists of three stages . . .
>   > The alarm stage is the first stage . . .
>   > Different stressful events may trigger the alarm stage of the GAS.

EXERCISE **11** **Analyzing sentences about research**

At the beginning of Reading Selection 1, we learn, "Much of what we know about the body's response to stress is the result of pioneering research by Hans Selye (1907–1982), the famed stress researcher known affectionately as 'Dr. Stress.'"

In this sentence, we learn three important pieces of information:

A. The research topic is "the body's response to stress."
B. Much of our understanding of this subject comes from the work of Hans Selye.
C. Selye's knowledge came from his research.

With this information about Hans Selye, the reader should expect a discussion of his research. Each item below begins with a sentence about research from Reading Selection 1. Analyze the sentences carefully in order to respond.

1. "Selye **found** that the body responds in a similar manner to various stressors—cold, noise, infectious agents, pressures on the job, or mental stress in the form of worry or anxiety."

   The word found *in this sentence is a reporting verb. Listed below are several definition entries for this word. Analyze how* found *is used in this sentence. Place a check mark next to the correct definition from* The American Heritage English as a Second Language Dictionary.

   _____ Came upon somebody or something, often by accident: *found a quarter on the sidewalk.*

   _____ Came upon or discovered after a search: *found the leak in the pipe.*

   _____ Perceived somebody or something to be, after observation or experience: *found her interesting.*

   _____ Experienced or felt: *found comfort in her smile.*

   _____ Decided on and made a declaration about somebody or something: *The jury deliberated and found a verdict of guilty. All the jurors found him guilty.*

2. "He [Selye] **recognized** that specific stressors, such as an invading virus, do elicit specific reactions in the body."

   The word recognized *in this sentence is a reporting verb. Listed below are several definition entries for this word. Analyze how* recognized *is used in this sentence. Place a check mark next to the correct definition.*

   _____ Knew to be something that had been percieved before: *recognized a face.*

   _____ Knew or identified from past experience or knowledge: *recognized hostility.*

   _____ Showed awareness of, approved of: *recognized services rendered.*

   _____ Exhibited recognition for (an antigen or a substrate, for example).

3. "But layered over these specific responses is a more general response to stress, which he called the general adaptation syndrome (GAS) (also called the stress response)."

Analyze how the word called *is used in this sentence. Listed below are several definition entries for this word. Place a check mark next to the correct definition.*

_____ Said something in a loud voice; announced: *called my name from across the street; called out numbers.*

_____ Asked or sent for somebody to come: *called the children to dinner; call the police.*

_____ Gave a name to: *What have you called the discovery?*

_____ Lured (prey) by imitating the characteristic cry of an animal: *called ducks.*

4. "The general adaptation syndrome **consists** of three stages, each of which we consider below."

Analyze how the word consists *is used in this sentence. Listed below are several definition entries for this word. Place a check mark next to the correct definition.*

_____ To be made up of or composed of: *New York City consists of five boroughs.*

_____ To have a basis; reside or lie: *The beauty of the artist's style consists in its simplicity.*

_____ To be compatible; accord: *The information consists with her account.*

EXERCISE **12** **Filling in the blanks**

Complete the sentences below by using these academic verbs (find, consist, call, recognize) *in the correct tense form.*

1. George Vancouver discovered a beautiful mountain near Seattle and

   _____ it Mt. Rainier.

2. Water _____ of hydrogen and oxygen.

3. Muscle weakness is now _____ as an uncommon

   though serious complication of steroid therapy.

4. Through his experiments, Louis Pasteur _____ that

   microorganisms reproduce and can cause diseases.

EXERCISE **13** **Analyzing writing style**

As a class, discuss the following questions.

1. As explained in the Power Grammar box, which elements of expository writing style can you find throughout Reading Selection 1?
2. Can you find examples of the present passive voice in this selection?
3. How does knowing about the elements of scientific writing styles help you comprehend this piece of writing?

○ Learning Vocabulary

One important challenge in reading is learning to be an efficient reader. An efficient reader gets the most out of a reading passage and reads it more quickly than a beginning reader. Difficult vocabulary can present a major roadblock to becoming an efficient reader because students often stop reading the text and turn to a dictionary to find the meanings of words.

STRATEGY

Understanding Vocabulary in Context

You can become a more efficient reader by staying with the original text and using it to help you comprehend words you do not know. This is called understanding vocabulary in context.

EXERCISE 14   **Using context clues**

Each item below begins with a sentence from the reading selection and includes an academic vocabulary word in context. The sentences are followed by a "think through" explanation about understanding the word from its context. Imagine someone is talking to you through the meanings of these words. After the explanation, apply your understanding of the academic words in a new context. In addition to answering the questions in the exercise, make notes in your reading journal on how these techniques can be helpful for you.

1. Paragraph 1 focus academic term: *layered over*

   > "He recognized that specific stressors, such as an invading virus, do elicit specific reactions in the body. But layered over these specific responses is a more general response to stress, which he called the general adaptation syndrome (GAS) (also called the stress response)."

   Talking you through . . . The author is explaining the body's response to stress. In this part of the text, layered over is in a sentence starting with the word *but*. The author is contrasting "specific responses" with a "more general reaction" in this sentence. The general reaction is not specific; it applies to all situations. Thus, layered over is a two-word verb that tells us a response to stress can be spread across or layered over many situations. The general reaction to stress applies to all stressful situations. We all feel this response every time we feel stress.

   A new context . . . Think about how the term *layered over* might apply to this situation:

   > An engineer was having difficulty in designing a set of wheels for trains. The trains had to work in different climates. One set of wheels became rusty in wet climates, and another set became too overheated in deserts. Finally, the engineer invented a new type of wheel using a new material. This was his solution:

   Write a sentence to describe the engineers' solution. Use the term layered over.

   _____

   _____

As you read and responded using the term *layered over*, what did you learn about using context to help you comprehend the meaning of new words and terms?

_____

_____

2. Paragraph 6 focus academic word: *persistence*

> "Death may occur within the first few hours or days of exposure to a stressor that is so damaging (such as extreme cold) that its persistence is incompatible with life."

Talking you through . . . The author uses the term *its persistence*. The *its* refers to the persistence of a stressor (such as extreme cold). Thus, persistence is a characteristic of the stressor. We also know from the sentence that a stressor (which has persistence) is also damaging (it causes harm) and it is incompatible with life (it can kill). That means a stressor harms us and because it has persistence, can kill us. The persistence of the stressor means it is more damaging; it makes the harm worse.

A new context . . . Think about how the term *persistence* might apply to this situation:

> "Our ancestors didn't need to juggle school and jobs, fight daily traffic jams, or face the daily grind of working a double shift to make ends meet. The reality for many of us today is that the stressful demands of everyday life may repeatedly activate our alarm reaction day after day, year after year."

Write a sentence to describe the kind of stress many of us feel today. Use a form of the word persist.

_____

_____

As you read and responded using the term *persistence*, what did you learn about using context to help you comprehend the meanings of new words and terms?

_____

_____

○ **Demonstrating Comprehension**

For the previewing exercise before the reading selection, you looked at passage section headings in order to understand the author's text organization. This section and exercise will assist you in improving your ability to read academic passages as you explore the organization of the text. By recognizing organizational structure, you can better understand academic writing.

The author introduces and defines the subject, General Adaptation Syndrome or GAS, in the first paragraph. He also gives a predictor of the remainder of the passage when he writes in the last sentence that "The general adaptation syndrome consists of three stages. . . ." This sentence allows the reader to predict the subtopics and organizational structure of the remaining paragraphs.

Master Student Tip

I.   An Introduction—defines the subject and often uses a predictor to divide it into subtopics

II. The Body—each of the subtopics is discussed

III. The Conclusion—it often contains a summary, a statement indicating the importance of the information, and a transition to the next section

The text—Paragraph 1	Its elements
Much of what we know about the body's response to stress is the result of pioneering research by Hans Selye (1907–1982), the famed stress researcher known affectionately as "Dr. Stress." Selye found that the body responds in a similar manner to various stressors—cold, noise, infectious agents, pressures on the job, or mental stress in the form of worry or anxiety. He recognized that specific stressors, such as an invading virus, do elicit specific reactions in the body. But layered over these specific responses is a more general response to stress, which he called the general adaptation syndrome (GAS) (also called the stress response). The general adaptation syndrome consists of three stages, each of which we consider below.	An introduction to the topic A predictor—it tells what is coming in the rest of the passage. It divides the subject into subtopics.

EXERCISE 15 Finding the text organization

Look back at the rest of the passage, and write the three stages or subtopics below.

1. Subtopic One: _____

2. Subtopic Two: _____

3. Subtopic Three: _____

The text—Paragraph 2	Its elements
The alarm stage is the body's first stage of response to a stressor, during which its defenses prepare for action. Suppose a car ahead of you on the road suddenly veers out of control. This is an immediate stressful event. Your heart starts pounding faster, speeding the flow of blood to your extremities and providing muscles with the oxygen and fuel they need to take swift action, such as performing an emergency maneuver to avoid a collision. The body's response during the alarm stage is called the fight-or-flight response because it is characterized by biological changes that prepare the body to deal with a threat by either fighting it off or fleeing from it.	The topic sentence. It contains a definition of the subtopic. An example is introduced. The example is followed by an explanation. The explanation gives many details. It helps the reader draw a mental picture to understand the subtopic, the alarm stage. The summary contains the significance of the information about the subtopic, the alarm stage, and makes a transition to the next paragraph.

> The third and fourth paragraphs give further details about the alarm stage. The third paragraph explains how the alarm stage is triggered. The fourth paragraph restates the concept of the alarm stage being the first response to stress. It also contrasts surviving and not surviving the initial alarm and starts the transition to the next stage, the resistance stage, which is continued in paragraph 6.

Make notes on the elements of paragraph 6 in the following chart. Use the notes written above for paragraphs 1 and 2 as an example. Look for the same elements. Look for and identify a transition, a definition, an example, and an explanation, and the significant elements in the paragraph. Not all elements may be in this one paragraph.

The text—Paragraph 6—The Resistance Stage	Your notes about its elements
Death may occur within the first few hours or days of exposure to a stressor that is so damaging (such as extreme cold) that its persistence is incompatible with life. But if survival is possible and the stressor continues, the body attempts to adapt to it as best it can. Selye called this part of the GAS the resistance stage (also called adaptation stage). During this stage, the body attempts to return to a normal biological state by restoring spent energy and repairing damage. Yet arousal remains high, though not as high as during the alarm reaction. This prolonged bodily arousal may be accompanied by such emotional reactions as anger, fatigue, and irritability.	

Discuss the other paragraphs in Reading Selection 1. Work in small groups.

1. *Compare your answers about the organization of paragraph 6 with members of your group. Discuss any differences you may have.*
2. *Read paragraphs 7 and 8. Find the organizational elements of those paragraphs. Discuss with your group what you find.*

EXERCISE 16   Finding the total organizational structure

Use your work so far to help you complete this outline of the passage.

The Body's Response to Stress—The General Adaptation Syndrome

I. Introduction

    a. Research basis by Hans Selye

    b. Definition of GAS

    c. Introduction of the stages

II. The Alarm Stage

    a. Definition

    b. Example

    c. Explanation

    d. Additional physiological and psychological factors

    e. Triggers of stress

    f. Summary and significance of initial response to stress

III. The Resistance Stage

    a. _____

    b. _____

    c. _____

    d. _____

IV. The Exhaustion Stage

    a. _____

    b. _____

    c. _____

    d. _____

       _____

STRATEGY

Looking Closely at Graphs

Graphs are drawings or diagrams that authors use to illustrate relationships. In textbooks, they are usually labeled as figures. For example, "Figure 15.2" means that a graph is the second figure found in chapter 15 of a textbook. Captions with concise explanations are usually found above or below figures. A longer explanation about the information in the graph can often be found in the reading passage somewhere close to graphs. Lines on the sides of graphs are labeled for readers to quickly see the focus of relationships.

The figure following Exercise 17 explains the information found in paragraphs 2 through 7 of Reading Selection 1. It is a useful example because it combines three types of graphic elements into one figure. The figure can be seen as a whole, or it can be divided into three main parts. The first part is an actual graph that compares two factors. The second is a series of drawings to give a pictorial idea of the impact of stress on a person. The third is a series of comment boxes that follow the progression of the stages of response to stress. In each box, more information is given to help the reader understand the stages.

EXERCISE 17   **Understanding graphs**

Paragraph 7 contains a reference to the graph shown on the next page. The text reads, "Figure 15.2 shows the changes that occur in the body's resistance across the three stages of GAS." Scan the graph, and answer the following questions. Circle Yes or No.

1. Is significant <u>new</u> information included in the graph?   Yes   No
2. Is its main purpose to support the information in the text?   Yes   No
3. Does it help you understand the text better?   Yes   No
4. Does it give you a picture of the effects of stress?   Yes   No
5. Did it make you remember a stressful time you have experienced?   Yes   No

Level of Resistance During the Stages of the General Adaptation Syndrome

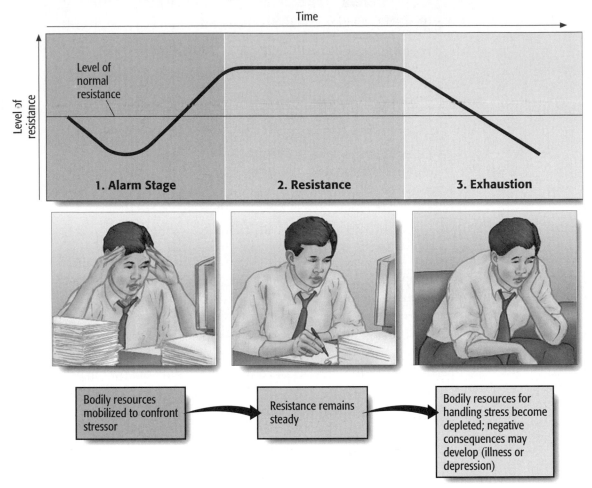

The body's resistance to stress first dips during the alarm stage, as the impact of the stressor takes a toll, but then increases as the body mobilizes its resources. Resistance remains steady through the resistance stage as the body attempts to cope with the stressor. But if the stressor persists, exhaustion eventually sets in as bodily reserves needed to resist stress become dangerously depleted.

From Nevid, J. (2003). *Psychology Concepts and Applications.* Boston: Houghton Mifflin Company, p. 601.

EXERCISE 18   **Reading graphs**

Using the information in this graph, answer the following questions.

1. Look at the top and the left side of the graph. Some labels are written over the arrows. List the two labels:

   _____

   _____

2. Why are the arrows used? Why is it important that the arrows go in only one direction?

   _____

   _____

   _____

3. Consider the whole figure. What are the three main divisions that run from the top to the bottom?

   _____

   _____

   _____

4. How is color used in the figure?

   _____

   _____

   _____

5. What do you understand better about the body's reaction to stress that you didn't know before studying this graph?

   _____

   _____

   _____

Reading Assignment 2

ACCULTURATIVE STRESS

○ Getting Ready to Read

EXERCISE 19 Interviewing classmates

Make two lists of students in your class. (This can be done as a whole-class activity on the board.) Label one category "more recent immigrants" and the other category "immigrated more than one year ago". Then make pairs of class members. Pair recent immigrant students with those who have been in the country for a longer period of time. Partners should then interview each other using the questions below. Answer the questions on the basis of your own experiences or the experiences of others you know, such as family members.

1. Tell me a little about your own experience with immigration.
2. What changes happen when a person immigrates to a new country?
3. How is immigration stressful for an individual or for a family?
4. Does the stress from being an immigrant ever cause serious mental or physical problems?
5. What helps people overcome the stress of immigration?
6. Who would experience more stress, a new adult immigrant or teenage children of recent immigrants? Explain the reasons for your answer.

As a class, share what you learned from your interviews. How were your answers similar or different? Write your response below.

_____

_____

_____

_____

_____

_____

EXERCISE 20 **Previewing vocabulary**

Look up the following words in a dictionary. Write out a definition, and include the part of speech (noun, verb, adjective, or adverb). Then write down any other word forms. Note the part of speech for each word form. Discuss your answers with your classmates. The first one has been done for you as an example.

1. Acculturate: *(v.)* To cause (a society, for example) to change by the process of acculturation.

   Acculturation *(n.)* ac·cul·tur·a·tion (ə-kŭl´chə-rā´shən) *n.*

   The modification of the culture of a group or individual as a result of contact with a different culture.

   Other forms: ac·cul·tur·a·tion·al *(adj.)* and ac·cul·tur·a·tive *(adj.)*

2. Linguistic: _____

   _____

   _____

   _____

3. Customs: _____

   _____

   _____

   _____

4. Dominant: _____

   _____

   _____

   _____

EXERCISE 21   **Previewing the first paragraph**

*Read the first paragraph only of Reading Selection 2, "Acculturative Stress."
Then provide a short written answer to the following questions. Base your
answers on the information in that paragraph. Check your answers with
another classmate.*

1. The title of the selection is "Acculturative Stress." Think about the
   meaning of those words, and restate the title in your own words.

   _____

   _____

   _____

2. Describe the causes of stress for immigrants.

   _____

   _____

   _____

3. Describe a custom associated with the dominant culture in the United
   States. Compare that custom with one from a nondominant culture in
   America.

   _____

   _____

   _____

4. Predict what the rest of the selection will be about. Write your
   prediction below.

   _____

   _____

   _____

○ **Reading the Selection**

Reading Selection 2

ACCULTURATIVE STRESS

1   For immigrants, the demands of adjusting to a new culture can be a significant[1] source of stress. Establishing a new life in one's adopted country can be a difficult adjustment, especially when there are differences in language and culture and few available jobs or training opportunities. One significant source of stress is pressure[2] to become acculturated[3]—to adapt to the values, linguistic preferences, and customs of the host or dominant culture. How does acculturative stress, which results from this pressure, affect psychological health and adjustment?

2   What we've learned is that relationships between acculturation and psychological adjustment are complex[4] (Escobar & Vega, 2000). Some researchers find that acculturated Hispanic Americans are more likely to develop psychological disorders than their less acculturated counterparts (Ortega et al., 2000). Others find that Mexican Americans born in the United States tend to show higher rates of psychological problems than recent immigrants from Mexico (Escobar, Hoyos Nervi, & Gara, 2000). But still other researchers link lower acculturation status among Hispanic Americans to higher risks of depression[5] and anxiety (Neff & Hoppe, 1993; Salgado de Snyder, Cervantes, & Padilla, 1990; Zamanian et al., 1992).

3   In attempting to understand these mixed findings, we should note that the process of adjusting successfully to a new society depends on a number of factors. For example, stress associated with economic hardship is a major contributor to adjustment

---

1. **sig•nif•i•cant** (sĭg-nĭf´ĭ-kənt) *adj.* Having or likely to have a major effect; important.
2. **pres•sure** (prĕsh´ər) *n.* A condition of physical, mental, social, or economic distress.
3. **ac•cul•tur•at•e** (ə-kŭl´chə-rāt´) *v.* To be changed or modified as a result of contact with a different culture.
4. **com•plex** (kəm-plĕks´) *adj.* Involved or intricate, as in structure; complicated.
5. **de•pres•sion** (dĭ-prĕsh´ən) *n.* The condition of feeling sad and sorrowful.

problems in immigrant groups, as it is for members of the host culture. And difficulties faced by poorly acculturated immigrants in gaining an economic foothold[6] in the host country may lead to anxiety and depression. Not surprisingly, a study of immigrant Chinese children in the United States showed more adjustment problems among those living in more economically stressful situations (Short & Johnston, 1997). Yet acculturation can lead to an erosion[7] of traditional family networks, which in turn may increase vulnerability[8] to psychological disorders in the face of stress (Ortega et al., 2000).

4   All in all, factors such as economic opportunity, language proficiency, and connections to a social network of people whom one can identify[9] with and draw support from may underlie the psychological adjustment of immigrant groups. Maintaining a sense of ethnic identity may also buffer[10] the effects of stress (Ryder et al., 2000; Thompson et al., 2000). Studies of Asian Americans show that establishing contacts with the majority culture while maintaining one's ethnic identity generates less stress than withdrawal and separation (Huang, 1994). Withdrawal fails to prepare the individual to make the necessary adjustments to function effectively in a multicultural society. But we should not be surprised by evidence showing that Asian American adolescents with a stronger sense of ethnic identity tend to be better psychologically adjusted and to have higher self-esteem[11] than their less affiliated[12] counterparts (Phinney & Alipuria, 1990; Huang, 1994).

---

6. **foot•hold** (fŏŏt´hōld´) *n.* A firm or secure position from which it is possible to advance.
7. **e•ro•sion** (ĭ-rō´zhən) *n.* Deterioration or disappearance; a wearing away; To gradually eliminate something that people have relied upon. An eroded family network no longer works as it used to do.
8. **vul•ner•a•ble** (vŭl´nər-ə-bəl) *adj.* Being open to danger and attack or of being harmed or injured. Being in a situation where a person can be physically or emotionally harmed.
9. **i•den•ti•fy** (ī-dĕn´tə-fī´) *tr.v.* To be or feel closely associated with a person or thing.
10. **buff•er** (bŭf´ər) *tr.v* To protect by stopping or lessening negative pressures or influences. "A sense of humor . . . may have served as a buffer against the . . . shocks of disappointment." (James Russell Lowell)
11. **self-es•teem** (sĕlf´ĭ-stēm´) *n.* Pride in oneself; self-respect.
12. **af•fil•i•ate** (ə-fĭl´ē-at´) *v.* Closely connect or associate with.

○ Assessing Your Learning

Demonstrating Comprehension

EXERCISE 22   **Scanning for information**

Scan Reading Selection 2 for the following items. On the blank, write the number of the paragraph where you find each item.

1. The term *dominant culture*   paragraph: _____

2. Studies about Mexican Americans   paragraph: _____

3. A study of immigrant Chinese children   paragraph: _____

4. Studies about Asian Americans   paragraph: _____

STRATEGY

Information on Sources and Citations

Sources and citations in reading passages credit the work of researchers an author has studied before writing. Sources are used and "cited" in almost every academic piece of writing. *Citing* means giving in a citation the name of the researcher and the date the research was published. Look for citations as you read academic works. Full citations are usually included in a bibliography at the end of articles or books. You may want to look up some original research sources as you study subjects in more depth. You will also learn to provide citations in your writing classes. They are an essential part of academic reading and writing.

EXERCISE 23   Locating sources

Scan Reading Selection 2 to find the names of researchers. Write the correct source after each citation. The bracketed number after each quotation indicates the paragraph location. The first one is done for you as an example.

1. "Some researchers find that acculturated Hispanic Americans are more likely to develop psychological disorders than their less acculturated counterparts." [2]

   Ortega et al., 2000
   _____

   _____

2. "What we've learned is that relationships between acculturation and psychological adjustment are complex." [2]

   _____

   _____

3. "... [O]ther researchers link lower acculturation status among Hispanic Americans to higher risks of depression and anxiety." [2]

   _____

   _____

4. "... [A] study of immigrant Chinese children in the United States showed more adjustment problems among those living in more economically stressful situations." [3]

   _____

   _____

5. "Maintaining a sense of ethnic identity may also buffer the effects of stress." [4]

   _____

   _____

⚪ **Learning Vocabulary**

EXERCISE 24   **Using academic words**

Match the bold words in the following phrases with the best definition of the word as it is used in Selection 2. The bracketed numbers after the words indicate the paragraph where each word can be found. Put the letter of the correct definition in the blank.

Vocabulary items	Definitions
1. _____ customs *to adapt to the values, linguistic preferences, and* ***customs*** *of the host or* <u>dominant</u> *culture* [1]	**a.** Exercising the most influence or control
2. _____ dominant *to adapt to the values, linguistic preferences, and customs of the host or* ***dominant*** *culture* [1]	**b.** A causal, parallel, or reciprocal relationship; a correlation
3. _____ link *But still other researchers* ***link*** *lower acculturation status* [2]	**c.** Detachment, as from social or emotional involvement
4. _____ contributor *stress associated with economic hardship is a major* ***contributor*** [3]	**d.** A practice followed by people of a particular group or region
5. _____ withdrawal *generates less stress than* ***withdrawal*** *and separation* [4]	**e.** A person or factor helping bring about a result

○ Focusing on Psychology

EXERCISE 25   **Participating in group discussion**

Complete this exercise about acculturative stress with your classmates.
Refer to Reading Selection 2 to support your point of view.

1. Describe some factors that contribute to acculturative stress.
2. Contrast the different findings by researchers about psychological problems for acculturated versus non-acculturated Hispanic Americans. (paragraph 2)
3. Describe some difficulties immigrants might face when they become acculturated.
4. Identify some factors that can lead to an acculturation experience with less stress and better psychological adjustment.

○ Assessing Your Learning at the End of a Chapter

Revisiting Objectives

Return to the first page of this chapter. Think about the chapter objectives.
Put a check mark next to the ones you feel secure about. Review material in
the chapter you still need to work on. When you are ready, answer the
chapter review questions on the next page

○ Practicing for a Test

Check your comprehension of main concepts, or ideas, in this chapter by
preparing answers for the following questions in a small study group. These
questions will help you review the complete chapter. Work in groups of three
or four classmates. Discuss possible answers. In your discussion, you may
sometimes agree or disagree with others in your group. In either case, base
your opinion on your knowledge and understanding of psychology, and be
prepared to explain your opinions by giving examples of both psychological
theory and research. Elect one group member as a discussion leader and
another as a reporter. It is the responsibility of each participant to
contribute to the discussion. It is the responsibility of the discussion leader
to ensure that all members are encouraged and prompted to participate and
to not allow any one student to take over the conversation. The reporter
should report back to the whole class on the results of your discussion.

EXERCISE 26   **Reviewing comprehension**

Prepare a response for each item. Distribute the items among group members to prepare, and then take turns explaining each one. Work together.

Chapter Review Questions

1. Define stress. Recall the textbook definition, and then paraphrase that definition in your own words.
2. Identify the causes of stress. Generate examples of stressful situations, and assess how stressful each situation might be.
3. Contrast a major cause of stress from a minor cause. Explain why one situation might be a major cause and another might be a minor cause.
4. Explain why some stress might be helpful to an individual.
5. Describe a Type-A personality. Give examples of people you know who might have that personality type.
6. Stress often has a negative affect on people. Discuss ways people can manage that affect.
7. Name the stages of the body's response to stress. Identify the main characteristics of each of these stages.
8. Psychological researchers often conduct experiments with laboratory animals. Design a hypothetical experiment that might cause stress for laboratory animals such as mice. Determine what would be stressful for the animals and how you would evaluate the stages of stress the animals would experience. In other words, how would you know when the mice are feeling stress?
9. Refer back to the first "Getting Ready to Read" section at the beginning of this chapter (p. 54). You learned the different forms of the word *psychology*. Use the same vocabulary learning strategy for the word *anthropology*. Complete these sentences by writing in the correct member of the anthropology word family.
   a. The scientific study of the origin, the behavior, and the physical, social, and cultural development of humans is _____.
   b. A person who studies anthropology is an _____.
   c. The adjective form of *anthropology* is _____.
   d. The abbreviation for anthropology classes is _____.

○ Linking Concepts

EXERCISE 27 **Writing reflections in your reading journal**

In your journal, write reflections on the following questions.

Reflections on learning

1. How do you preview a reading selection?

2. What can you learn by previewing a reading?

3. How does finding the organizational structure of a passage help you understand its contents?

4. Give examples of past tense reporting verbs an author might use to write about discoveries from scientific research.

5. Give an example of a present tense generalization an author might write about a psychological theory.

6. Identify a new word you learned recently from context. Explain where you found the word and how the context helped you.

7. What is a citation?

Reflections on Stress and Adaptation

1. Describe stressful experiences you have had. Interpret those experiences now that you know more about stress. Detail the stages of response you experienced and how you would adapt now that you have a greater understanding of stress.

2. Define acculturative stress as the kind of stress experienced by immigrants or by people who experience living in other cultures. Give examples of acculturative stress you may have experienced, and explain how you adapted to the new situation.

EXERCISE 28 **Reviewing academic vocabulary**

Listed in the box are some of the academic words used in this chapter. Identify which words you know and which words you need to review. Study those words in the text or a dictionary. When you are ready, use the words from the box to fill in the blanks in the sentences below.

potential	designed	intense	eventually
physical	induces	survive	survived
trigger	normal	stress	psychological

1. A sensitive alarm system may have helped our ancient ancestors _____ many of the physical threats they faced.

2. Yet the alarm reaction was not _____ to last very long.

3. Our earliest ancestors faced many _____ threats in their daily lives.

4. The presence of a predator could _____ the fight-or-flight response.

5. When they _____ the immediate threat, their bodies returned to their _____ state quickly.

6. In today's society, a threat may be _____ , such as in an attack by an assailant, or, _____ , such as in an event that _____ fear of failure (a professor handing out an examination, for example).

7. Some people are hardier than others, but relentless, _____ _____ can _____ exhaust anyone.

WEB POWER

Go to **http://esl.college.hmco.com/students** to view more readings about stress and adaptation, plus exercises that will help you study the selections and the academic words in this chapter.

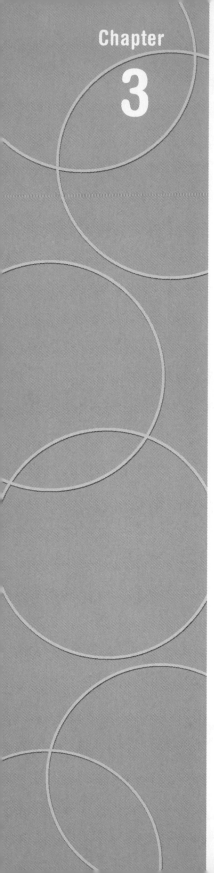

Managing a New World

ACADEMIC FOCUS: BUSINESS MANAGEMENT

Academic Reading Objectives

After completing this chapter, you should be able to:

✓ Check here as you master each objective.

1. Create vocabulary study cards ☐
2. Analyze a complex definition of a business concept ☐
3. Outline, summarize, and paraphrase to analyze and clarify the meaning ☐
4. Understand figures with graphic elements ☐
5. Classify business-specific terminology ☐

Business-Management Objectives

1. Restate a comprehensive definition of business management ☐
2. Compare management theory with real-life business practices ☐
3. Explore business websites and evaluate indicators of diversity ☐
4. Develop a perspective on diversity ☐
5. Evaluate the use of business plans with positive social-advancement objectives guiding management decisions ☐

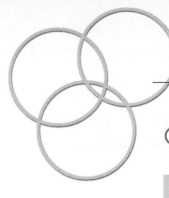

Reading Assignment 1

○ Getting Ready to Read

EXERCISE 1 Participating in group discussion

Look at the photograph at the beginning of this chapter. With your classmates, discuss this picture and the excerpt from a textbook on management below. Which of the key truths mentioned in the text can you see in the photograph? How can you see these realities in this photograph?

> We present four key truths of managing today:
> 1. The only certainty today is change. Management requires that leaders be able to change and to lead others to be open to change.
> 2. Speed, teamwork, and flexibility are very important as managers plan and carry out their plans.
> 3. Managers at all levels need to pay attention to the customer. If a company wants to have customers, it has to offer high-quality products and services.
>
> To make economic progress, individuals and organizations must be continuously improving and always be learning.
>
> Adapted from Kreitner, R. (2004). *Management* (9th ed.). Boston: Houghton-Mifflin Company, p. 4.

○ **Learning Vocabulary**

Master Student Tip

▼ **Key Terms**

A key term is an important word or group of words used in a chapter. Knowing key terms can help you unlock the meaning of a chapter.

Using Word Study Cards

Word study cards are useful tools for learning and reviewing important academic vocabulary or key terms. The cards should contain the essential information you need to understand the new words. Here is a list of information that should be on the cards:

On the front of the card

1. The **vocabulary word** you are learning.
2. The **part of speech** for the word. Words have different forms. A word can be a noun in one sentence and a verb in another. The part of speech you put on a word card should match how the word is used in the passage you are studying.
3. The **pronunciation** of the word. This pronunciation should match the part of speech you list in item #2. The word *process*, for example, is pronounced (prŏs´ĕs´) when it is used as a singular noun or as a transitive verb. However, it can be used as an intransitive verb, such as in the sentence "They will process from the door to the stage." In this case, the word is pronounced (prə-sĕs´).

On the back of the card

1. The **word in use**. The word-in-use line gives the word in a sentence as it is used in the chapter you are studying. This section is very important as words change not only their form but also their meanings, depending on how they are used in sentences. You need to search the text to find the word in context and then write the sentence on the card.
2. A **definition**. The definition you use should match the word as it is used in the chapter. Match the meaning and the grammatical form of the word.
3. **Word family members**. The word family members give the other forms of the key term. It is useful to learn to recognize word family members. This knowledge can help you notice recurrences of vocabulary across passages and in other readings from your studies. Family members include forms representing different parts of speech and different grammatical forms. They may be pronounced differently. You can find the family members in English-only dictionaries.

4. **Collocations**. Sample collocations are sentence elements or phrases containing words that commonly go together with the key terms you are studying. Knowing collocations can guide you to use these words as native English speakers do when you speak and write in English. You can find some of these collocations in English-English dictionaries. Look at the examples, which are often in italic print, to find collocations.

A sample vocabulary card

Work with 3" × 5" or 4" × 6" index cards. Refer to this model card as you make your vocabulary cards. For practice, use the words in the next section, which come from this chapter's readings on management.

The front of your vocabulary card
VOCABULARY WORD: **process**
Part of Speech: noun singular
Pronunciation and stress: prŏs'ĕs'

The back of the card

Word in use: "Management is the **process** of working with and through others to achieve organizational objectives in a changing environment."
A definition: A series of actions, changes, or functions leading to a desired result.
    Word family members:
    plural noun: proc·ess·es
    transitive verb: proc·essed, proc·ess·ing, proc·ess·es
    other nouns: pro·ces·sion, pro·ces·sion·al, proc·es·sor
    Collocation: "Obtaining an immigration visa is a lengthy process."

EXERCISE **2** **Preparing vocabulary cards**

Listed below are academic words from Reading Selection 1. Use the information provided to start creating your own word cards. You will need to research the words more by using a dictionary or Web links from http://esl.college.hmco.com/students. Definitions for some of these words can be found in the reading selection's footnotes. The bracketed number next to each word indicates the paragraph in the reading selection where you can find it.

1. Keyword   process [1]

   Definition   *n.* A series of actions, changes, or functions leading to a desired result.

   Word in Use   "Management is the **process** of working with and through others to achieve organizational objectives in a changing environment."

2. Keyword   achieve [1]

   Definition   *tr.v.* To succeed in completing, producing, or gaining something; to be successful.

   Word in Use   "Ghosn's goal-oriented approach strives to inspire and energize Nissan's employees to **achieve** greater organizational success."

3. Keyword   environment [1]

   Definition   *n.* The social and cultural conditions affecting the nature of a person or community.

   Word in Use   "Management is the process of working with and through others to achieve organizational objectives in a changing **environment**."

4. Keyword   resources [1]

   Definition   *n. pl.* Things that can be used for support or help.

   Word in Use   "Efficiency enters the picture when the **resources** required to achieve an objective are weighed against what was actually accomplished."

5. Keyword

components [2]

Definition

n. The parts that make up a whole.

Word in Use

"Five **components** of this definition require closer examination. . . ."

6. Keyword

interact [4]

Definition

intr.v. To act on or affect each other.

Word in Use

"Aspiring managers who do not **interact** well with others hamper their careers."

7. Keyword

conclusion [4]

Definition

n. A judgment or decision reached by reasoning.

Word in Use

"This was the **conclusion** two experts reached following interviews with 62 executives."

8. Keyword

derailed [4]

Definition

v. Came to or brought to a sudden halt.

Word in Use

"Each of the executives was asked to describe two managers whose careers had been **derailed**."

9. Keyword

involve [5]

Definition

v. To contain something as a part; include.

Word in Use

"Significantly, the first and third shortcomings **involve** failure to work effectively with and through others."

10. Keyword

perceived [5]

Definition

tr.v. To achieve understanding of (the way a person is seen or viewed by others).

Word in Use

"They were **perceived** as manipulative, abusive, untrustworthy, demeaning, overly critical, not team players and poor communicators."

Continue creating word cards until you have one for each word on this list. Evaluate your word knowledge with the checklist.

Academic vocabulary words	I always know this word.	I usually know it.	I need to study it.
1. process [1]			
2. achieve [1]			
3. environment [1]			
4. resources [1]			
5. components [2]			
6. interact [4]			
7. conclusion [4]			
8. derail [4]			
9. involve [5]			
10. perceived [5]			
11. manipulative [5]			
12. objective [8]			
13. attained [8]			
14. challenging [8]			
15. goals [9]			
16. margin [9]			
17. approach [10]			

Academic vocabulary words (cont.)	I always know this word.	I usually know it.	I need to study it.
18. effectiveness [11]			
19. efficiency [11]			
20. experts [15]			
21. approximately [17]			
22. economics [18]			
23. factors [18]			
24. globalization [19]			
25. ethical [19]			
26. revolution [19]			
27. evolution [19]			

EXERCISE **3** **Completing vocabulary learning activities**

Here are additional classroom vocabulary-learning activities to try.

1. Review the words individually. Shuffle the words and go through the deck.
2. Quiz a classmate on the words. Quiz for all the information on the cards.
3. Create sentences that include two or more of the words in the same sentence.
4. In small groups or pairs, have a speaking competition trying to use as many of the words as possible in a conversation. Each group should have a judge, who can check off whenever one of the words is used. The group that uses the greatest number of words wins the game.
5. Go to *http://esl.college.hmco.com/students* for a Web link to create a crossword puzzle with these words.

○ Reading for a Purpose

EXERCISE **4**   **Previewing with a definition**

Here is the definition of **management** *from paragraph 1 of Reading Selection 1. Read it, and then answer the questions that follow. Discuss your answers with your classmates.*

> Management is the process of working with and through others to achieve organizational objectives in a changing environment. Central to this process is the effective and efficient use of limited resources.

1. Management is called a **process** in this definition. In the vocabulary card exercise, you learned that a process is "a series of actions, changes, or functions leading to a desired result." What words in this paragraph mean the same as the expression "to bring about"?

    _____

2. According to the definition, what is the goal of the management process?

    _____

3. Identify a business environment. What factors might make that environment change?

    _____

4. How can a manager work **with** others?

    _____

5. How can a manager work **through** others?

    _____

6. How are *effectiveness* and *efficiency* opposite terms, and how can they be complementary (work together) in management?

    _____

7. Give examples of resources that might be limited.

    _____

8. Describe a management situation in business or government. Then discuss how the definition above applies or doesn't apply to that situation. Examples: a fast-food restaurant, a clothing store, an insurance company, the post office, the military.

_____

_____

_____

EXERCISE 5 **Matching definition parts to subheadings**

This definition of management sets the stage for the whole passage. Here is the definition in a table. Segments of the definition are given on the left side of the table. Scan Reading Selection 1, and then complete the right side of the table by writing in subtitles to match each part. (Notice that the order of subheading presentation varies slightly from the definition word order.) The first item has been completed as an example.

A definition of management	List subtitles from the chapter
Management is the process of working with and through others . . .	1. _Working with and Through Others_
to achieve organizational objectives	2.
in a changing environment.	5.
Central to this process is the effective and efficient . . .	3.
use of limited resources.	4.

⃝ Reading the Selection

Effective readers use the whole organization of a passage to build comprehension. One way to see the whole organization is to scan for outline structure. The subtitles you wrote in Exercise 5 serve this purpose. As you read, also notice that these same subtopic categories can be found in a numbered list at the end of paragraph 2. The author's organizational structure is very direct: 1, 2, 3 . . . He believes that management is a series of steps that includes specific elements. Having the subtitle organizational structure in mind before and as you read provides a context that can help you understand the vocabulary and concepts in the chapter. Keep this outline structure in mind as you read. We return to it after you complete your first reading of the chapter.

Now read the selection. Read every line in order to understand the main idea and supporting ideas of the text. Read carefully, but do not expect to understand every word. After you complete the selection, answer the questions that follow.

⃝ Focus on Management

Reading Selection 1

Management Defined

¹To begin with, we need to define management in order to highlight the importance, relevance, and necessity of studying it. Management is the process¹ of working with and through others to achieve² organizational objectives in a changing environment.³ Central to this process is the effective and efficient use of limited resources.⁴

---

1. **pro•cess** (prŏs´ĕs´) *n.* A series of actions, changes, or functions leading to a desired result.
2. **a•chieve** (ə-chēv´) *tr.v.* To succeed in completing, producing, or gaining something; to be successful.
3. **en•vi•ron•ment** (ĕn-vī´rən-mənt) *n.* The social and cultural conditions affecting the nature of a person or community.
4. **re•sour•ces** (rē´sôrs´) *n pl.* Things that can be used for support or help.

2   Five components[5] of this definition require closer examination:
(1) working with and through others, (2) achieving organizational
objectives, (3) balancing effectiveness and efficiency, (4) making the
most of limited resources, and (5) coping with a changing
environment.

Working with and Through Others

3   Management is, above all else, a social process. Many collective
purposes bring individuals together—building cars, providing
emergency health care, publishing books, and on and on. But in all
cases, managers are responsible for getting things done by working
with and through others.

4   Aspiring managers who do not interact[6] well with others
hamper their careers. This was the conclusion[7] two experts reached
following interviews with 62 executives from the United States,
United Kingdom, Belgium, Spain, France, Germany, and Italy. Each
of the executives was asked to describe two managers whose
careers had been derailed.[8] Derailed managers were those who had
not lived up to their peers' and superiors' high expectations. The
derailed managers reportedly had these shortcomings:

- Problems with interpersonal relationships.
- Failure to meet business objectives.
- Failure to build and lead a team.
- Inability to change and adapt during a transition.

5   Significantly, the first and third shortcomings involve[9] failure
to work effectively with and through others. The derailed managers
experienced a number of interpersonal problems; among other
things, they were perceived[10] as manipulative,[11] abusive,
untrustworthy, demeaning, overly critical, not team players and
poor communicators.

---

5. **com•po•nents** (kəm-pō′nənt) *n.pl.* The parts that make up a whole.
6. **in•ter•act** (ĭn′tər-ăkt′) *v.* To act on or affect each other.
7. **con•clu•sion** (kən-kloo′zhən) *n.* A judgment or decision reached by reasoning.
8. **de•railed** (dē-rāl′) *v.* Came to or brought to a sudden halt.
9. **in•volve** (ĭn-vŏlv′) *v.* To contain something as a part; include.
10. **per•ceived** (pər-sēv′) *tr.v.* To achieve understanding of (the way a person is seen or viewed by others).
11. **ma•nip•u•la•tive** (mə-nĭp′yə-lə′tĭv) *adj.* Acting in a way to influence or manage people in a way that gets something from them without their knowledge or full agreement.

6 Even managers who make it all the way to the top often have interpersonal problems, according to management consultant Richard Hagberg. His study of 511 executive officers led to this conclusion about why managers often fail to inspire loyalty in employees:

7 *Many are also hobbled by self-importance, which keeps them from hearing feedback about their own strengths and weaknesses. The head of one large company told me he and his wife recently were waiting in line to get his driver's license renewed. He was frustrated at how long it was taking and grumbled to his wife, "I have a lot to do. Don't they know who I am?" She replied, "Yeah, you're a plumber's son who got lucky." Her remark really got to him. It drove home how far he had gotten caught up in his sense of self-importance.*

Achieving Organizational Objectives

8 An objective[12] is a target to be strived for and, one hopes, attained.[13] Like individuals, organizations are usually more successful when their activities are guided by challenging,[14] yet achievable, objectives. For an individual, scheduling a course load becomes more systematic and efficient when a student sets an objective, such as graduating with a specific degree by a given date.

9 Although personal objectives are typically within the reach of individual effort, organizational objectives or goals[15] always require collective action. A master of powerful organizational objectives is Carlos Ghosn, the Brazilian-born CEO of Nissan. When France's Renault bought a controlling interest in Nissan in 1999 and put Ghosn in charge, the Japanese automaker was a real money loser. Thanks to Ghosn's bold Nissan Revival Plan, based on lots of employee input, Nissan is turning a profit. Now comes the next step: Ghosn has laid out what he calls the "180 Plan" for Nissan. The "1" in the 180 Plan means Nissan intends to sell 1 million more vehicles a year worldwide than it does now. The "8"

---

12. **ob·jec·tive** (əb-jĕk′tĭv) *n.* A goal; a purpose.
13. **at·tained** (ə-tān′) *tr.v.* Gained, accomplished, or achieved something by effort.
14. **chal·leng·ing** (chăl′ənj) a*dj.* Requiring the full use of one's abilities or skills.
15. **goals** (gōl) *n. pl.* The purposes toward which one is working; objectives.

refers to the target of 8% profit margin,[16] roughly double what's typical. The "0" means the debt-burdened automaker wants no debt. The goals are to be accomplished before the end of 2005.

10 Thus, Ghosn's goal-oriented approach[17] strives to inspire and energize Nissan's employees to achieve greater organizational success.

Balancing Effectiveness and Efficiency

11 Distinguishing between effectiveness[18] and efficiency[19] is much more than an exercise in semantics. The relationship between these two terms is important and it presents managers with a never-ending dilemma. Effectiveness entails promptly achieving a stated objective. Swinging a sledgehammer against the wall, for example, would be an effective way to kill a bothersome fly. But given the reality of limited resources, effectiveness alone is not enough. Efficiency enters the picture when the resources required to achieve an objective are weighed against what was actually accomplished. Although a sledgehammer is an effective tool for killing flies, it is highly inefficient when the wasted effort and smashed walls are taken into consideration. A fly swatter is both an effective and an efficient tool for killing a single housefly.

12 Managers are responsible for balancing effectiveness and efficiency (see Figure 1.1). Too much emphasis in either direction leads to mismanagement. On the one hand, managers must be effective, although those who waste resources in the process flirt with bankruptcy.

13 On the other hand, managers need to be efficient by containing costs as much as possible and conserving limited resources. But managers who are too stingy with resources may not get the job done.

16. **prof•it mar•gin** (prŏf´ĭt mär´jĭn) *n.* The amount of money left after the costs of producing an item have been subtracted; the money a producer can keep.
17. **ap•proach** (ə-prōch´) *n.* A way or method of dealing or working with somebody or something.
18. **ef•fec•tive•ness** (ĭ-fĕk´tĭv) *n.* The capability of a person or a process to produce a desired result or effect.
19. **ef•fi•cien•cy** (ĭ-fĭsh´ən-sē) *n.* The ratio of the effective or useful output to the total input in any system; using resources to create the greatest amount of production possible.

Making the Most of Limited Resources

14   We live in a world of scarcity. Those who are concerned with such matters worry not only about running out of nonrenewable energy and material resources but also about the lopsided use of those resources. The United States, for example, with about 5 percent of the world's population, currently uses about 25 percent of the world's annual oil production and creates 23 percent of the greenhouse gases linked to global warming.

15   Although experts[20] and non-experts alike may argue over exactly how long it will take to use up our nonrenewable resources or come up with new technological alternatives, one bold fact remains. Our planet is becoming increasingly crowded.

16   Demographers who collect and study population statistics tell us the Earth's human population is growing by 8,741 people every hour (as the result of 15,020 births and 6,279 deaths.) The present world population of 6.1 billion people is projected to reach 9 billion within 70 years. Meanwhile, our planet's carrying capacity is open to speculation.

17   Approximately[21] 83 percent of the world's population in the year 2020 will live in relatively poor and less-developed countries. Developed and industrialized nations, consequently, will experience increasing pressure to divide the limited resource pie more equitably.

18   "Because of their common focus on resources, economics[22] and management are closely related. Economics is the study of how limited resources are distributed among alternative uses. In productive organizations, managers are the trustees of limited resources, and it is their job to see that the basic factors[23] of production-land, labor, and capital-are used efficiently as well as effectively. Management could be called "applied economics."

20. **ex•perts** (ĕk´spûrt) *n. pl.* Persons with great knowledge or skill in a particular field.
21. **ap•prox•i•mate•ly** (ə-prŏk´sə-mĭt) *adv.* Very similar; be nearly the same as; closely resembling.
22. **ec•o•nom•ics** (ĕk´ə-nŏm´ĭks) *n.* The study of the ways in which goods and services are produced, transported, sold, and used.
23. **fac•tors** (făk´tər) *n. pl.* Things that help cause a certain result; an element or ingredient.

Coping with a Changing Environment

19   Successful managers are the ones who anticipate and adjust to changing circumstances rather than being passively swept along or caught unprepared. Employers today are hiring managers who can take unfamiliar situations in stride. Successful managers doing business in the twenty-first century will need to be able to adjust to five overarching sources of change: globalization,[24] the evolution[25] of product quality, environmentalism, an ethical[26] reawakening, and the Internet revolution.[27]

Source: Kreitner, R. (2004). *Management* (9th ed.). Boston: Houghton-Mifflin Company, pp. 5–10.

○ Assessing Your Learning

Demonstrating Comprehension

EXERCISE 6   Checking comprehension

Circle the correct response to answer these questions about Reading Selection 1.

   1. How must managers do their work?
      a. With and through others
      b. Only with groups of people
      c. Only with individuals
      d. Only by themselves

   2. What happens to managers who do not work well with others?
      a. They succeed at personal relationships.
      b. They meet business objectives.
      c. They fail to build and lead a team.
      d. They are able to change and adapt during transitions.

24. **glob·al·i·za·tion** (glō′bə-līz′) *v.* To make global or worldwide in scope or application.
25. **ev·o·lu·tion** (ĕv′ə-lo͞o′shən) *n.* A gradual process by which something develops or changes into a different and often a more complex or better form.
26. **eth·i·cal** (ĕth′ĭ-kəl) *adj.* Following accepted standards of behavior or conduct; morally right.
27. **rev·o·lu·tion** (rĕv′ə-lo͞o′shən) *n.* A sudden and important change.

3. Which of the following are *not* examples of interpersonal problems?
   a. Being manipulative
   b. Being abusive
   c. Being a team player
   d. Being a poor communicator

4. Which of the following is *not* a synonym of the term "an objective."
   a. A target
   b. A goal
   c. A hope
   d. An effort

5. Carlos Ghosn, the CEO of Nissan, is given as an example of
   a. an effective manager.
   b. a derailed manager.
   c. a goal-oriented manager.
   d. an efficient manager.

6. Using a sledgehammer to kill a fly is given as an example of
   a. an effective means to reach an objective.
   b. an efficient means to reach an objective.
   c. an effective but inefficient means to reach an objective.
   d. an efficient but ineffective means to reach an objective.

7. Good management will
   a. emphasize effectiveness over efficiency.
   b. emphasize efficiency over effectiveness.
   c. control all costs and conserve all resources.
   d. balance effectiveness and efficiency.

8. Using oil for energy production is an example of using a
   a. non-renewable resource.
   b. renewable resource.
   c. current technological alternative.
   d. source to decrease greenhouse gases.

9. We are fairly sure that by 2020
   a. the United States will be the largest country on Earth.
   b. the world's population will be smaller than it is now.
   c. most people will live in non-industrialized countries.
   d. industrialized countries will use most of the world's resources.

    10. Successful managers will do all of the following except
       a. be always ready for a changing world.
       b. be ready to adjust to globalization.
       c. follow current management methods.
       d. respond to environmental challenges.

EXERCISE 7 **Outlining to increase comprehension**

    In the prereading exercise, you saw Reading Selection 1 outlined by subheadings as follows:

Management Defined

    1. Working with and Through Others
    2. Achieving Organizational Objectives
    3. Balancing Effectiveness and Efficiency
    4. Making the Most of Limited Resources
    5. Coping with a Changing Environment

To practice building deeper comprehension, write a more extensive outline of one section, part 3, "Balancing Effectiveness and Efficiency." Complete the outline that follows. You are given some information at the start and will have to provide more information toward the end of this outline. Fill in the blanks.

Management Defined

  1. Introduction—The relationship of effectiveness and _____.

  2. _____ and efficiency

    a. Effectiveness = _____ objectives

    b. _____ = Complete _____ with few

      _____

  3. Managers _____ to _____ effectiveness and

    efficiency

    a. Avoid _____

    b. But not _____

    c. Get _____ _____.

EXERCISE 8   **Developing understanding**

Respond to the items below. Base your answers on your more detailed knowledge of the information in this section. Discuss your responses with your classmates.

1. Define effectiveness.

   _____

   _____

2. Define efficiency.

   _____

   _____

3. What is the danger of being too effective?

   _____

   _____

4. What is the danger of being too efficient?

   _____

   _____

5. Describe another example of a business management situation in which a manager must balance effectiveness and efficiency.

   _____

   _____

EXERCISE 9 **Summarizing what you read**

In Chapter 1, you learned the steps for creating a summary. This exercise will guide you through a shortened version of those steps for writing a summary on the section of the management chapter about effectiveness and efficiency.

Step One: Reread Section 3, and think about your outline from Exercise 7. Section 3 is 201 words. Your job will be to shorten that while still capturing the meaning of the section.

Step Two: Create statements that summarize a key point from each major part of the outline. Use the main idea but do not give all the information of the original. The first sentence is done for you as an example. Fill in words in the second and third sentences, and use information from the outline to write the final sentences.

Summary for section three

Distinguishing between the relationship of effectiveness and efficiency is important and a never-ending dilemma for managers. Effectiveness _____ promptly achieving a _____ objectives. Efficiency means _____ the _____ _____ to _____ an objective against the _____ accomplishment.

_____

_____

_____

_____

Now count the total number of words in this summary and compare it with the original.

The original = <u>201 words</u>   My summary = _____ words

EXERCISE **10** **Developing understanding**

Respond to the items below. Base your answers on your more detailed knowledge of the information in this section. Discuss your responses with your classmates.

1. What is the relationship between effectiveness and efficiency?

2. How are the two terms similar, and how are they different?

3. What would happen if a manager ignored the balance between these two responsibilities?

4. As a student, you manage your own studying. How are you effective and efficient?

◯ Linking Concepts

 **STRATEGY**

Paraphrasing What You Read

What is a paraphrase? The *American Heritage College Dictionary** defines a paraphrase as follows:

1. A restatement of a text or passage in another form or other words.

2. The restatement of texts in other words as a studying or teaching device.

According to these definitions, a student writes a paraphrase for two reasons: to clarify the meaning of a text, and to aid in studying (remembering and recalling) that text.

*Editors. (2002). *The American Heritage College Dictionary* (4th ed.) Boston: Houghton Mifflin Company, p. 1009.

Paraphrases help your reading

Both of the reasons in the strategy box on the previous page show how a paraphrase can help a reader understand and reuse information from a passage.

Paraphrases help your writing

Paraphrases can also be valuable in your academic writing. When you write a paraphrase, you use ideas you have read about from your studies. Remember that, as a writer, you must always give credit when you paraphrase (this is called citing your sources). When you use the meaning of the text but write it in similar yet different words, you will be better able to fit the original meaning into your papers than if you just use long quotes from one author after another. Effective academic student writers are able to bring the contributions of other writers into their own work in a way that connects the ideas while keeping the student's own style of writing. In full academic writing, you will paraphrase (and cite) many sources. It is impossible to overemphasize how careful you need to be in citing your sources. When you write academic essays and papers, your instructors will always expect you to carefully cite the sources. If you do not, you may fail an assignment or even a course because the instructor may think you are trying to say that another person's writing is your own. For this lesson, you will work only to paraphrase this one source, since the main purpose of this book is to assist students in paraphrasing so you may learn an effective reading strategy.

How Do I Write a Paraphrase?

In writing a paraphrase, a student changes part of an original text.

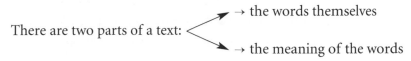

There are two parts of a text: → the words themselves
→ the meaning of the words

As much as is possible, keep the meaning of the words consistent while changing the words themselves. The meaning of a text is contained in the information and ideas the author gives the reader. Usually, a paraphrase is written directly from the original text. First, find the important information and ideas in the original text; then, work at writing a paraphrase.

EXERCISE 11 **Practicing with paraphrasing**

For this exercise, you will write a paraphrase of the author's ideas found in paragraph 11. Follow the steps as indicated.

Step 1: First, reread the paragraph. It is copied here for you.

Balancing Effectiveness and Efficiency

Distinguishing between effectiveness and efficiency is much more than an exercise in semantics. The relationship between these two terms is important and it presents managers with a never-ending dilemma. Effectiveness entails promptly achieving a stated objective. Swinging a sledgehammer against the wall, for example, would be an effective way to kill a bothersome fly. But given the reality of limited resources, effectiveness alone is not enough. Efficiency enters the picture when the resources required to achieve an objective are weighed against what was actually accomplished. Although a sledgehammer is an effective tool for killing flies, it is highly inefficient when the wasted effort and smashed walls are taken into consideration. A fly swatter is both an effective and an efficient tool for killing a single housefly.

Step 2: Review the first part of the outline you completed in Exercise 7. It is copied here for you.

Management Defined

1. Introduction—The relationship of effectiveness and efficiency
2. Effectiveness and efficiency
   a. Effectiveness = achieving objectives
   b. Efficiency = Complete job with few resources

Step 3: Review the summary you wrote for Exercise 9. Notice how the summary included many words taken directly from the text.

Step 4: Study the chart on p. 115 of possible substitutions for original words the author, Robert Kreitner, chose to use. These synonyms may help you start generating ideas for your paraphrase.

Original word	Synonym
distinguishing between	understanding the difference
important	essential
never-ending	ongoing
dilemma	situation
entails	requires
promptly	quickly
achieving	accomplishing
stated	declared
objective	goal
acheive	accomplish
against	in contrast to
actual	real

Step 5: Write a paraphrase of paragraph 11 on the lines below. Keep the same meaning that was in the original. Say the same information, but in words and sentences that come from you. This is a worthwhile exercise because it causes you to work with the meanings of the words as they make sense to you. The material you are using comes from the following source: Kreitner, R. (2004). *Management* (9th ed.). Boston: Houghton Mifflin Company, pp. 5–10.

Management Defined—A Paraphrase

According to Robert Kreitner, _____

_____

_____

_____

_____

_____

_____

_____

_____

_____

What do you see in this passage now, that you didn't see before writing the paraphrase? In other words, how did writing the paraphrase increase your understanding of the original source?

○ Focusing on Management

EXERCISE **12** **Writing short-answer responses**

In Chapter 1, you learned about writing short definitions and written answers for quizzes and tests. Respond to the following questions in writing. Each answer should be longer than a sentence but no longer than one paragraph. Each question comes from a different section of Reading Selection 1. Write your responses in the space provided. Use extra pages if needed.

Working with and Through Others

1. Describe the working skills of managers that the author believes are essential for successful managers. What would happen if a manager does not have these skills?

_____

_____

_____

Achieving Organizational Objectives

2. Define what an objective is, and discuss how having a set of objectives is important for an organization. You may use examples from the chapter.

_____

_____

Balancing Effectiveness and Efficiency

3. Why is the relationship between effectiveness and efficiency "a never-ending dilemma" for managers?

_____

_____

Making the Most of Limited Resources

4. According to the author, "managers are the trustees of limited resources." To be a trustee means being a person who takes care of something. How are managers supposed to take care of resources, and why is that important for a successful manager?

_____

_____

Coping with a Changing Environment

5. What kinds of changes must a manager deal with in a changing world?

_____

_____

6. Overall, how would you define the challenge of managing an organization? What knowledge, skills, and perspectives must a modern manager have in order to be successful?

_____

_____

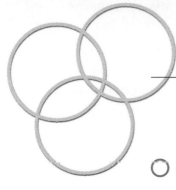

Reading Assignment 2

FIGURE 1.1—BALANCING EFFECTIVENESS AND EFFICIENCY

○ Getting Ready to Read

When you read textbooks, you will often find charts and graphs included as figures in the chapters. They support the main information and concepts in the text.

EXERCISE 13 **Previewing and reviewing to connect**

Prepare to read this selection by previewing it and connecting it with ideas from Reading Selection 1.

1. Read the title of the chart. Find the main idea.
2. Reread the section in Reading Selection 1 that refers to this chart. It is found in paragraph 12.

○ Reading the Selection

Study Figure 1.1 carefully. Read every sentence, and look carefully at the graphics as well as the words. Think about how the bar chart elements visually illustrate the written ideas. Complete the following sentence.

Figure 1.1 illustrates the information in paragraph 12 by showing. . .

Reading Selection 2

FIGURE 1.1: BALANCING EFFECTIVENESS AND EFFICIENCY

Balancing Effectiveness and Efficiency

Effectiveness
The job gets done, but...

Efficiency
Limited resources are wasted

Too much emphasis on effectiveness

Efficiency
Available resources are underutilized

Effectiveness
The job does not get done, because...

Too much emphasis on efficiency

Effectiveness
The job gets done, and...

Efficiency
Limited resources are not wasted

Balanced Emphasis on Effectiveness and Efficiency

Kreitner, R. (2004). *Management* (9th ed.). Boston: Houghton Mifflin Company, p. 9.

○ Assessing Your Learning

EXERCISE **14** **Understanding figures with graphic elements**

Answer these questions about the parts of Figure 1.1:

Part 1

1. According to this figure, what has been achieved?

   _____

   _____

   _____

   _____

2. What is not good?

   _____

   _____

   _____

   _____

3. What is out of balance in this figure?

   _____

   _____

   _____

   _____

Part 2

Effectiveness
The job does not
get done, because...

Efficiency
Available resources
are underutilized

Too much emphasis on efficiency

Answer these questions.

1. According to this figure, what happened to the achievement?

   _____

   _____

   _____

   _____

   _____

2. What does "available resources are underutilized" mean?

   _____

   _____

   _____

   _____

3. What is out of balance in this figure?

   _____

   _____

   _____

   _____

Part 3

Effectiveness	Efficiency
The job gets done, and...	Limited resources are not wasted

Balanced Emphasis on Effectiveness and Efficiency

Answer these questions.

1. According to this figure, what has been achieved?

   _____

   _____

   _____

   _____

2. Why has achievement occurred?

   _____

   _____

   _____

   _____

3. What is in balance in this figure?

   _____

   _____

   _____

   _____

4. What more did you learn from Figure 1.1 that was not covered in Reading Selection 1?

   _____

   _____

   _____

   _____

Reading Assignment 3

○ Getting Ready to Read

**Master
Student Tip**

▼ **Making
Connections with
Symbols and
Themes**

Textbook authors often draw your attention to special features by using unique symbols or colors to indicate focus elements in the books. The symbols used in a textbook are usually explained in the introductory part of the book.

In his textbook on management, Robert Kreitner uses a sun symbol to mark the pages dealing with a theme of **diversity**. He uses a sun (see below) to show that a section is approaching the topic from the diversity theme. Other symbols are used to present the themes of global management and management ethics. We read in the preface that these themes are ones the Association to Advance Collegiate Schools of Business suggests should be part of the education of business and management students. That means this textbook, instructors, and schools will be stressing these themes.

The next reading selection includes both a theme section on diversity and a case study. It discusses how a real company, Allstate, has served its community better, as well as made more money, by caring about diversity.

Master Student Tip

Making Connections with Case Studies

Case studies are another familiar part of a modern textbook. Case studies are examples or situations from real life. Authors use case studies with some subjects more than others. In the fields of business and management, case studies are very popular. They help students apply the theories they are studying. When you read about real-life situations, you are better able to understand the text material.

EXERCISE 15 **Previewing a title**

The title for Reading Selection 3 is "Diversity Boosts Allstate's Bottom Line." Research a definition and a synonym(s) for each word in the title of this reading. Use a dictionary, a thesaurus, or Web resources you can find at http://esl.college.hmco.com/students. Then respond to the items that follow.

1. diversity

   Definition: _____

   _____

   Synonym(s): _____

2. boosts

   Definition: _____

   _____

   Synonym(s): _____

3. bottom line

   Definition: _____

   _____

   Synonym(s): _____

4. Rewrite the title as a sentence using the definitions and synonyms. Start with the subject.

   The Allstate Insurance Company . . . _____

   _____

   _____

5. I expect to read about . . . _____

   _____

   _____

   _____

○ Reading the Selection

Reading Selection 3

DIVERSITY BOOSTS ALLSTATE'S BOTTOM LINE

1 A number of progressive companies that had a head start in elevating diversity to a strategic priority are starting to see the results, from better customer satisfaction to increased sales. Allstate Insurance Co. is one of those leaders (www.allstate.com). Since 1993, the Northbrook, Illinois, insurance company has been managing diversity as a central business issue closely connected to its overall corporate objectives. The focus is to drive greater levels of employee and customer satisfaction by taking an integrated approach to diversity in the workplace and the market.

2 Joan Crockett, Senior Vice-President for human resources at Allstate, stresses that the company's diversity initiative isn't a nice-to-do, social conscience program. "It's a compelling business strategy," she says. . . .

An Integrated Approach

3 Diversity at Allstate is rooted in the company's culture, which has embodied inclusiveness and equal opportunity since the 1960s. But it wasn't until 1993 that it became a strategic initiative. Today, for Carlton Yearwood, Director of Diversity Management, the question thus becomes: "How do you take this workforce of differences and bring them together in a more powerful way so that it can impact business results?"

4 The answer was to incorporate differences into all business processes, such as decision-making and product innovation. Once Allstate began this process, it started to see an increase in its customer base and greater levels of customer satisfaction as well.

5 "Diversity has become an initiative that has clear business outcomes," Yearwood says. "If you start by having customers say they want to interact with knowledgeable workers who are like themselves, that gives the customers the absolute best services and products. Through the diversity initiative, we demonstrate our commitment to a diverse marketplace."

6   Just as a company would inject <u>financial goals</u> in daily operations, Allstate is resolved to penetrate its day-to-day <u>functions</u> with the concept of diversity. A number of processes have been <u>established</u> to bring the concept and <u>strategy</u> alive. These processes go beyond recruiting a <u>diverse</u> mix of employees to encompass a proactive retention strategy, <u>ongoing</u> training and <u>education</u>, a rigorous <u>feedback</u> mechanism, and community outreach.

Sensitivity to Customers

7   Allstate's leading position in market share among <u>minorities</u> reflects its commitment to local communities <u>consisting</u> of many <u>ethnic</u> backgrounds. The key to success is that local agents have learned over the years how to relate to the specific needs of their respective communities.

8   Allstate's director of relationship marketing, Andre Howell, says that learning from customers is the best way to develop products and services which serve their specific needs. "Education, education and education will be my <u>primary</u> lead," he says. "We need to be continuously in a learning <u>mode</u> from customers."

9   Howell works with a <u>team</u> of six to create a community outreach program whose <u>ultimate</u> aim is to capture a larger market share. These programs include financial and <u>expert contributions</u> to ethnic, local, and other organizations.

10   The company also works with community groups and homeowner associations to accelerate urban revitalization <u>projects</u> through its Neighborhood <u>Partnership</u> Program (NPP). By <u>establishing</u> a good relationship with residents of the communities, Allstate has been able to accelerate its customer <u>aquisitions</u>. In many cases, the company's businesses in inner cities that used to lose money are now profitable, says Ron McNeil, senior vice president for product operations.

11   "Our <u>diverse</u> workforce has allowed us to <u>establish</u> relationships in communities and allowed us to shorten the <u>acquisitions</u> curves for new customers," he says. The partnership program in Philadelphia, for example, boosted Allstate's market share in the city from 7.3 <u>percent</u> in 1993 to 33 percent in 1997.

○ Assessing Your Learning

Learning Vocabulary

Words change meaning from one subject to another. The world of management uses a special vocabulary that can be called "business speak." If you can think like a business person, you will be better able to understand business speak. With Reading Selection 3, it can help to relate certain words and phrases to three key terms: a **plan**, a **process**, and **profit**. Study these terms to put business vocabulary in context.

1. A business **plan** has to do with setting goals or objectives. When a business person plans, he or she maps out a way to reach an objective or outcome. Plans will include a list of proposed steps.

2. A business **process** includes the steps or approaches a business person actually uses to reach a goal. The steps may involve carrying out a short-term plan or a long-term strategic plan. Hopefully, the result of the process is a profit.

3. A **profit** is a gain for the business person. The gain is often financial, but it can also be a non-financial gain like providing customer satisfaction.

EXERCISE 16   Classifying business-related expressions

Read the list of expressions in the following chart. They come directly from Reading Selection 3 and follow its sequence. Indicate if you believe the expression relates to a plan, a process, or a profit by checking one of the boxes on the right. Return to the selection to understand how the author uses the terms in the business management context.

Classifying Business-related Expressions			
Business expressions	Plan	Process	Profit
1. strategic priority			
2. customer satisfaction			
3. increased sales			
4. corporate objectives			
5. drive levels of satisfaction			
6. take an integrated approach			
7. a compelling business strategy			
8. increase a customer base			
9. daily operations			
10. penetrate day-to-day functions			
11. proactive retention strategy			
12. rigorous feedback mechanism			
13. community outreach			
14. boosted market share			
15. accelerate urban revitalization			
16. accelerate customer acquisitions			
17. shorten acquisition curve			

Check over your answers in class, and then read the selection again. This time, think about how the expressions relate to a plan, a process, or profit. Doing so will provide you with a global understanding of the passage.

○ Demonstrating Comprehension

EXERCISE 17 Discussing in small groups

Answer the following questions about Reading Selection 3. The bracketed number following each question refers to the paragraph in which you can find information needed for the answer. Work in small groups, and discuss your answers with your classmates.

1. Why did Allstate elevate diversity to a strategic priority? [¶ 1]
2. Joan Crockett, Allstate's Senior Vice-President, says her "company's diversity initiative isn't a nice-to-do, social conscience program." It is a "business strategy." What is a social conscience program, and how is it usually different from a business strategy? [¶ 2]
3. What does it mean to "incorporate differences into all business practices"? [¶ 4]
4. What are some ways that Allstate's diversity initiative was incorporated into how it deals with its own employees? [¶ 6]
5. What are some ways that Allstate has reached out to a diverse base of customers? [¶ 7–10]
6. What benefits has Allstate realized because of its diversity initiative? [¶ 10–11]

○ Linking Concepts

EXERCISE 18 Investigating diversity in corporate America

Select three insurance companies to research on the Internet from the list in the box. Your investigation will be guided by the questions below to focus on evaluating each company's commitment to diversity. You can find these company websites by checking our site http://esl.college.hmco.com/students for links, or you could look for each company name with a search engine such as Google. Discuss your findings with your classmates.

Allstate	Farmers	State Farm	Prudential Financial
Metropolitan Life	Safeco	Travelers	

1. Do you see pictures of people from different backgrounds?
2. Are there any case studies or personal stories? If so, do the stories represent people from different racial and ethnic groups?

3. How friendly is their customer service? Does it accommodate people with diverse backgrounds?
4. Do they provide information in any language besides English? If so, what information?
5. Do any agents or customer service people speak other languages?
6. Do their job recruiting policies reflect a commitment to diversity?
7. Are any community service or grants to the community mentioned? If so, do they reach out to the whole community, or just part of it?

◯ Assessing Your Learning at the End of a Chapter

Revisiting Objectives

Return to the first page of this chapter. Think about the chapter objectives. Put a check mark next to the ones you feel secure about. Review material in the chapter you still need to work on. When you are ready, answer the chapter review questions in Exercise 19.

◯ Practicing for a Chapter Test

EXERCISE 19 Reviewing comprehension

Check your comprehension of this chapter's main concepts or ideas by answering the following questions. Work in groups of three or four. Discuss possible answers, and select a group spokesperson who will be ready to share your answers with the class. Take notes of your own group's answers, as well as those of other groups.

1. What is the primary goal of management?
2. How do managers achieve that goal?
3. What are some dangers managers must be aware of that might derail them in reaching their goals?
4. What are some standard principles of management? What must a manager do to be effective?
5. People in business are often concerned about change. What kinds of changes do they see as possible?
6. Why do business people seem more concerned about change than other professionals?

7. Have you ever worked with a manager? Describe the situation. Was that manager effective according to the description given in this chapter?

8. Describe the management challenge for the Allstate executives. What made their situation unique and challenging?

9. What are some interview questions that Allstate executives might ask management candidates in a hiring process?

10. Why might some managers not want to work for Allstate?

11. What additional benefits might a manager gain in working for Allstate that he or she wouldn't receive in working for a company that does not stress diversity?

12. Allstate mixes achieving desirable social policy with its business practice. What are the pluses and minuses of such an approach to business? Explain your answer.

13. Does Allstate's approach to its insurance business lead you, as a customer, to want to buy insurance from it or go to a different company?

○ Linking Concepts

EXERCISE 20 **Responding to questions**

The following questions are about learning and reading and business management. You can respond to these questions in three possible ways:

1. Write your responses in your reading journal.
2. Discuss these questions in groups and as a whole class.
3. Provide short written answers to share with your classmates or your instructor.

Your instructor can provide specific instructions on how to respond to these questions.

Reflections on Learning

1. Describe the steps in making academic vocabulary cards. What information is included?
2. You should have been reviewing your vocabulary cards during the period you have been studying this chapter. Answer these questions about your reviewing.
    a. When did you review the cards?
    b. Were some words easier to remember than others?
    c. What helped you the most to remember the words—making the cards or reviewing the information?
    d. Did you see any of the words in this chapter's readings or in other readings you have done?
    e. Did you use any of the words in your speech or writing? Give details.
3. What have you learned about management from this chapter that will help you in reading about this topic in the future?

Reflections on Management

1. According to the author, what are components of management?
2. Here is a definition of management from the chapter:

    Management is the process of working with and through others to achieve organizational objectives in a changing environment. Central to this process is the effective and efficient use of limited resources.

    How has your understanding of management increased after reading? In other words, what do you know about management that you didn't know before studying this chapter?
3. Based on the case study from the Allstate Insurance Company, what are some practical concerns managers must think about when putting management theory into practice?

EXERCISE 21 Reviewing academic vocabulary

Here is a multiple-choice quiz on some of this chapter's academic vocabulary. Take the quiz, and check your answers on the website for this book. Review any words you missed. Keep the AWL words in your reading journal.

Circle the correct answer:

1. When you reach your objectives, you _____ them.

    a. begin   **b.** end   **c.** achieve   **d.** process

2. The five _____ of a definition are its parts.

    a. components   **b.** plans   **c.** approaches   **d.** goals

3. Effective managers must _____ well with employees.

    a. hamper   **b.** manipulate   **c.** derail   **d.** interact

4. A manager's career can be _____ when it runs into a serious problem.

    a. perceived   **b.** derailed   **c.** attained   **d.** achieved

5. When you get to the end of a project, you reach a _____.

    a. conclusion   **b.** involvement   **c.** evolution   **d.** component

These words will be useful for learning in many academic areas. Study them and the other AWL words by going to http://esl.college.hmco.com/students to help you review your words.

WEB POWER

Go to http://esl.college.hmco.com/students to view more readings about business management, plus exercises that will help you study the selections and the academic words in this chapter.

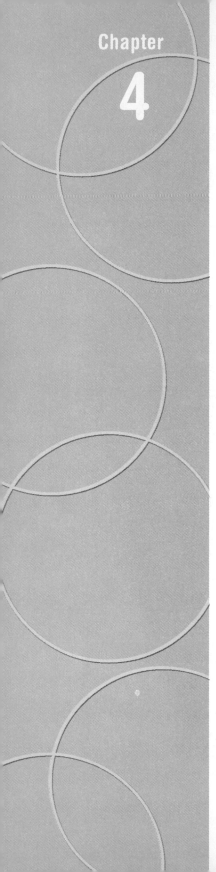

Global Obesity

ACADEMIC FOCUS: NUTRITION

Academic Reading Objectives

After completing this chapter,
you should be able to . . .

✓ Check here as you
master each objective

1. Ask significant questions before reading ☐
2. Identify and use nouns and noun phrases from
   informational academic texts ☐
3. Make plausible inferences when reading ☐
4. Analyze the use of statistics to support
   statements ☐
5. Identify audience and purpose in a reading ☐

Nutrition Objectives

1. Study key terms in nutrition and health-related
   disciplines ☐
2. Examine the steps in the scientific method
   of research in nutrition ☐
3. Examine your eating habits by using information
   about nutrition and health ☐

Reading Assignment 1

OBESITY AND BEING OVERWEIGHT

○ Getting Ready to Read

Obesity is spreading across the globe. In fact, the World Health Organization has coined a new word to describe it: *globesity*. This serious health concern is also a major topic of study in nutrition and other health fields such as dietetics, medicine, nursing, and biology.

○ Focusing on Nutrition

EXERCISE 1 Previewing nutrition

Prepare for the chapter readings by studying the definition of nutrition in the box below. Then, check the topics you think nutritionists study. Discuss your answers in a group.

What is Nutrition?
1. The process of nourishing, especially the process by which a living organism uses food.
2. The study of food and nourishment.
3. Nourishment; diet.

Nutritionists study . . .

_____ basic nutrients in food

_____ weather and air pollution

_____ worldwide hunger and malnutrition

_____ vegetarianism

_____ food labels on processed food

_____ mental disorders

_____ anatomy and physiology

_____ stress management

_____ exercise programs

EXERCISE 2 **Examining eating habits**

On separate paper, make notes about what you eat and drink in a typical day, from the beginning to the end of the day. Describe your main meals, plus anything you typically eat or drink between meals. Include the type and amount of each item you eat—for example, one slice of pepperoni pizza *and* a medium cup of coffee with sugar and milk.

Chapter 4 explores nutrition around the world. Many countries use graphics to depict their dietary guidelines. The following three versions of the U.S. Food Guide Pyramid are examples. The pyramid shape is designed to show people that they should eat less of some foods (the top of the pyramid) and more of other types of foods (the base of the pyramid). Descriptive captions next to each food category indicate the numbers of servings that people should eat daily. Study the U.S. Food Pyramids below.

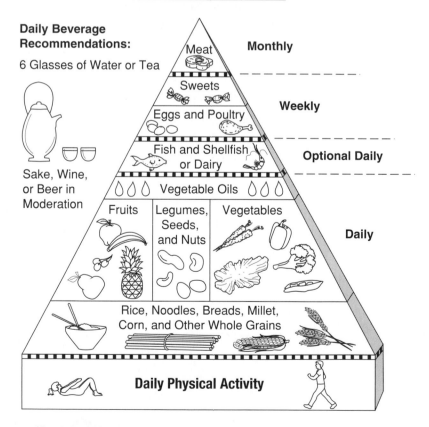

Source: www.oldwayspt.org/pyramids

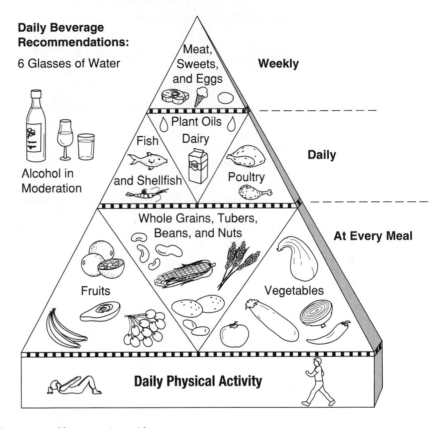

The Traditional Healthy Latin American Diet Pyramid

Source: www.oldwayspt.org/pyramids

Make notes on the lines below to highlight special elements that differentiate each pyramid:

Asian Diet Pyramid: _____

_____

_____

Latin American Pyramid: _____

_____

_____

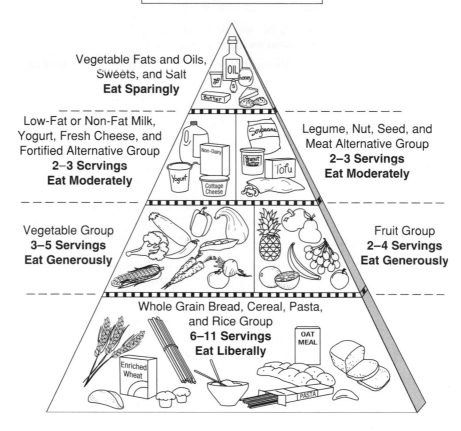

The Vegetarian Food Pyramid
(Daily Amounts)

Vegetable Fats and Oils, Sweets, and Salt
Eat Sparingly

Low-Fat or Non-Fat Milk, Yogurt, Fresh Cheese, and Fortified Alternative Group
2–3 Servings
Eat Moderately

Legume, Nut, Seed, and Meat Alternative Group
2–3 Servings
Eat Moderately

Vegetable Group
3–5 Servings
Eat Generously

Fruit Group
2–4 Servings
Eat Generously

Whole Grain Bread, Cereal, Pasta, and Rice Group
6–11 Servings
Eat Liberally

Source: www.vegsource.com/nutrition/pyramid.htm

Make notes on the lines below to highlight special elements that differentiate the Vegetarian pyramid from the other pyramids:

Vegetarian Diet Pyramid:

_____

_____

_____

EXERCISE 3 **Participating in group discussion**

Using your notes from Exercise 2, fill in this blank pyramid labeled "My Food Pyramid." Show your own eating habits in a typical day. Use drawings or names of food types in your pyramid. Indicate which food types you eat in greater or lesser quantities by the location in your pyramid. Compare your food pyramids in a group. Discuss your eating habits.

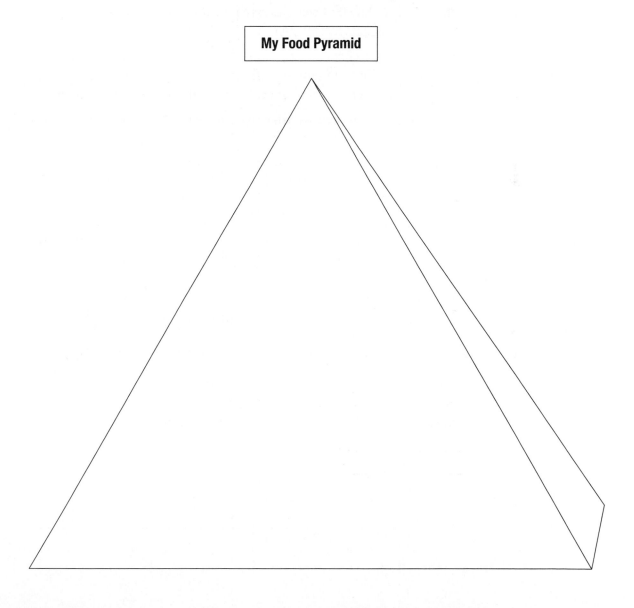

My Food Pyramid

POWER GRAMMAR

Word Families

As you learned in Chapter 2, English words belong to families. Word "members" of the family perform a variety of functions in sentences. Common functions are *subject*, *verb*, and *object*. Words can also be identified by the parts of speech *noun*, *verb*, *adjective*, and *adverb*. When a word's function changes, its form, or ending, changes.

Read the following sentences, focusing on the italicized members of the word family of *diet*. Pay attention to the ending of each italicized word.

Dieters have to watch what they eat. Some people *diet* for a few weeks, but then they quit their *diets*.

Dietetics is the study of nutrition as it relates to health. *Dieticians* recommend *dietary* guidelines for maintenance of good health.

The word family of *diet* has many members, as the chart below indicates. A word family may consist of more than one part of speech and none of another part. You can study word families by using a dictionary.

Noun	Verb	Adjective	Adverb
diet	diet	dietary	dietarily
dietetics		dietetic	dietetically
dieter			
dietician			

EXERCISE **4**   **Focusing on word forms of key terms**

Study the list of key terms in nutrition and other health disciplines below.
Put a check mark next to the words you know.

1. obesity ____

2. hypertension ____

3. nutrient ____

4. carbohydrate ____

5. insulin ____

6. hormonally ____

7. kidney ____

8. chronic ____

9. consumption ____

10. undernourished ____

11. colon ____

12. epidemic ____

13. stroke, *n.* ____

14. cholesterol ____

15. metabolic ____

16. gallbladder ____

17. cardiovascular ____

18. disability ____

19. clinically ____

20. triglycerides ____

21. respiratory ____

22. prostate ____

23. puberty ____

24. calorie ____

25. infertility ____

26. endometrium ____

27. morbidities ____

Use a dictionary to find definitions of unfamiliar words. Then test your
knowledge of different forms of these terms by circling the appropriate word
to complete the following sentences from Reading Selection 1. Check your
answers by finding the sentences in the reading selection.

1. Globally, there are more than 1 billion overweight adults, at least
   300 million of them (obese / obesity).

2. The health consequences range from increased risk of premature
   death, to serious (chronically / chronic) conditions that reduce the
   overall quality of life.

3. . . . [R]ecent studies have shown the people who were (undernourished / undernourishment) in early life and then become obese in adulthood, tend to develop conditions such as high blood pressure, heart disease and (diabetic / diabetes) at an earlier age . . . .

4. The non-fatal, but debilitating health problems associated with obesity include (respire / respiratory) difficulties, chronic musculoskeletal problems, skin problems and (infertility / infertile).

5. The more life-threatening problems fall into four main areas: cardiovascular disease problems; conditions associated with insulin resistance such as type 2 diabetes; certain types of cancers, especially the (hormonally / hormonal) related and large-bowel cancers; and gallbladder disease.

6. Confined to older adults for most of the 20th century, this disease now affects obese children even before (pubertal / puberty).

7. Childhood (obese / obesity) is already epidemic in some areas and on the rise in others.

8. [Obesity] is also one of the key risk factors for other (chronic / chronically) diseases.

9. Key elements include mounting a (clinical / clinically) response to the existing burden of (obese / obesity) and associated conditions.

STRATEGY

Asking Questions before Reading

Asking questions about the reading topic before you read enables you to focus your reading on finding specific information. Especially in readings from academic textbooks, the textbook titles, headings, and subheadings can provide topics for prereading questions. Then, as you read, try to answer the questions.

EXERCISE 5 **Asking questions before reading**

With a partner, use the title of Reading Selection 1 and its headings, listed below, to write questions about the topics in the reading. Some of the headings are already in question form, but write at least one additional question based on each heading. Share your questions with your classmates. As you read, look for the answers to the questions.

1. Title: "Obesity and Being Overweight"

   Questions: *Is obesity a bigger problem in some places more than in others? Am I considered overweight?*

2. Heading: "Why is this happening?"

   Additional Question: _____

   _____

   _____

3. Heading: "How do we define obesity and being overweight?"

   Additional Question: _____

   _____

   _____

4. Heading: "The Extent of the Problem"

   Questions: _____

   _____

   _____

5. Heading: "How does excess body fat impact health?"

   Questions: _____

   _____

   _____

6. Heading: "What can we do about it?"

   Additional Question: _____

   _____

   _____

EXERCISE **6** **Previewing the text introduction**

As you learned in Chapter 2, readings may begin with a short introduction. Reading Selection 1 begins with a bulleted list of important facts. Read the list, printed below, and discuss the following questions with a group of classmates.

● Globally, there are more than 1 billion overweight adults, at least 300 million of them obese.

● Obesity and being overweight pose a major risk for chronic diseases, including type 2 diabetes, cardiovascular disease, hypertension and stroke, and certain forms of cancer.

● The key causes are increased consumption of energy-dense foods high in saturated fats and sugars, and reduced physical activity.

1. In simple terms, what does each bulleted item mean? Make up your own sentence to state the main idea of each point. Use your own words.

2. What is the consequence of each bulleted fact? In other words, what result may occur in the future because of this fact?

3. How does each bulleted point relate to you? How does it relate to your family members or friends?

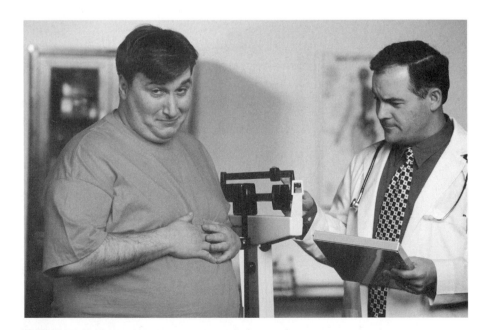

Reading Selection 1

OBESITY AND BEING OVERWEIGHT

FACTS:

- Globally, there are more than 1 billion overweight adults, at least 300 million of them obese.
- Obesity and being overweight pose a major risk for chronic diseases, including type 2 diabetes, cardiovascular disease, hypertension and stroke, and certain forms of cancer.
- The key causes are increased consumption of energy-dense foods high in saturated fats and sugars, and reduced physical activity.

1   Obesity has reached epidemic proportions globally, with more than one billion adults overweight—at least 300 million of them clinically obese—and is a major contributor to the global burden of chronic disease and disability. Often, coexisting in developing countries with under-nutrition, obesity is a complex condition, with serious social and psychological dimensions, affecting virtually all ages and socioeconomic groups.

2   Increased consumption of more energy-dense, nutrient-poor foods with high levels of sugar and saturated fats, combined with reduced physical activity, have led to obesity rates that have risen three-fold or more since 1980 in some areas of North America, the United Kingdom, Eastern Europe, the Middle East, the Pacific Islands, Australasia and China. The obesity epidemic is not restricted to industrialized societies; this increase is often faster in developing countries than in the developed world.

3   Obesity and being overweight pose a major risk for serious diet-related chronic diseases, including type 2 diabetes, cardiovascular disease, hypertension and stroke, and certain forms of cancer. The health consequences range from increased risk of premature death, to serious chronic conditions that reduce the overall quality of life. Of especial concern is the increasing incidence of child obesity.

Why Is This Happening?

4   The rising epidemic reflects the profound changes in society and in behavioral patterns of communities over recent decades. While genes are important in determining a person's susceptibility to weight gain, energy balance is determined by calorie intake and physical activity. Thus societal changes and worldwide nutrition transition are driving the obesity epidemic. Economic growth, modernization, urbanization and globalization of food markets are just some of the forces thought to underlie the epidemic.

5   As incomes rise and populations become more urban, diets high in complex carbohydrates give way to more varied diets with a higher proportion of fats, saturated fats and sugars. At the same time, large shifts towards less physically demanding work have been observed worldwide. Moves toward less physical activity are also found in the increasing use of automated transport, technology in the home, and more passive leisure pursuits.

How Do We Define Obesity and Being Overweight?

6   The prevalence of being overweight and obesity is commonly assessed by using body mass index (BMI), defined as the weight in kilograms divided by the square of the height in meters (kg/m^2). A BMI over 25 kg/m^2 is defined as overweight, and a BMI of over 30 kg/m^2 as obese. These markers provide common benchmarks for assessment, but the risks of disease in all populations can increase progressively from lower BMI levels.

7   Adult mean BMI levels of 22–23 kg/m^2 are found in Africa and Asia, while levels of 25–27 kg/m^2 are prevalent across North America, Europe, and in some Latin American, North African and Pacific Island countries. BMI increases amongst middle-aged elderly people, who are at the greatest risk of health complications. In countries undergoing nutrition transition, overnutrition often co-exists with undernutrition. People with a BMI below 18.5 kg/m^2 tend to be underweight.

8   The distribution of BMI is shifting upwards in many populations. And recent studies have shown the people who were undernourished in early life and then become obese in adulthood, tend to develop conditions such as high blood pressure, heart disease and diabetes at an earlier age and in more severe form than those who were never undernourished.

The Extent of the Problem

9   Currently more than 1 billion adults are overweight—and at least 300 million of them are clinically obese. Current obesity levels range from below 5% in China, Japan and certain African nations, to over 75% in urban Samoa. But even in relatively low prevalence countries like China, rates are almost 20% in some cities.

10   Childhood obesity is already epidemic in some areas and on the rise in others. An estimated 17.6 million children under five are estimated to be overweight worldwide. According to the U.S. Surgeon General, in the USA the number of overweight children has doubled and the number of overweight adolescents has trebled since 1980. The prevalence of obese children aged 6–11 years has more than doubled since the 1960s. Obesity prevalence in youths aged 12–17 has increased dramatically from 5% to 13% in boys and from 5% to 9% in girls between 1966–70 and 1988–91 in the USA. The problem is global and increasingly extends into the developing world; for example, in Thailand the prevalence of obesity in 5-to-12-year-old children rose from 12.2% to 15.6% in just two years.

11   Obesity accounts for 2–6% of total health care costs in several developed countries; some estimates put the figure as high as 7%. The true costs are undoubtedly much greater as not all obesity-related conditions are included in the calculations.

How Does Excess Body Fat Impact Health?

12   Being overweight and obesity lead to adverse metabolic effects on blood pressure, cholesterol, triglycerides and insulin resistance. Some confusion of the consequences of obesity arise because researchers have used different BMI cut-offs, and because the presence of many medical conditions involved in the development of obesity may confuse the effects of obesity itself.

13   The non-fatal, but debilitating health problems associated with obesity include respiratory difficulties, chronic musculoskeletal problems, skin problems and infertility. The more life-threatening problems fall into four main areas: cardiovascular disease problems; conditions associated with insulin resistance such as type 2 diabetes; certain types of cancers, especially the hormonally related and large-bowel cancers; and gallbladder disease.

14   The likelihood of developing type 2 diabetes and hypertension rises steeply with increasing body fatness. Confined to older adults for most of the 20th century, this disease now affects obese children even before puberty. Approximately 80% of people with diabetes are type 2, and of these, 90% are obese or overweight. And this is increasingly a developing world problem. In 1995, the Emerging Market Economics [1] had the highest number of diabetics. If current trends continue, India and the Middle Eastern crescent will have taken over by 2025. Large increases would also be observed in China, Latin America and the Caribbean, and the rest of Asia.

15   Raised BMI also increases the risks of cancer of the breast, colon, prostate, endometrium,[2] kidney and gallbladder. Chronic over-weight and obesity contribute significantly to osteoarthritis, a major cause of disability in adults. Although obesity should be considered a disease in its own right, it is also one of the key risk factors for other chronic diseases together with smoking, high blood pressure and high blood cholesterol. In the analyses carried out for *World Health Report 2002*, approximately 58% of diabetes and 21% of ischaemic[3] heart disease and 8–42% of certain cancers globally were attributable to a BMI above 21 kg/m².

What Can We Do about It?

16   Effective weight management for individuals and groups at risk of developing obesity involves a range of long-term strategies. These include prevention, weight maintenance, management of co-morbidities[4] and weight loss. They should be part of an integrated, multi-sectoral, population-based approach, which includes environmental support for healthy diets and regular physical activity. Key elements include:

- Creating supportive population-based environments through public policies that promote the availability and accessibility of a variety of low-fat, high-fiber foods, and that provide opportunities for physical activity.

1. Emerging Market Economies are developing countries with fast-growing economies. They are called "emerging" because they have begun to open up their markets to international business.
2. **en•do•me•tri•um** (ĕn′dō-mē′trē- əm) *n.* The glandular mucous membrane that lines the uterus, or womb.
3. **is•chae•mic** (ĭ-skē′mē- ə) *adj.* Relating to ischaemia (or ischemia), anemia in a given part of the body.
4. **mor•bid•i•ty** (môr-bĭd′ĭ-tē) *n.* The rate of incidence of a disease.

- Promoting healthy behaviors to encourage, motivate and enable individuals to lose weight by:

   eating more fruit and vegetables, as well as nuts and whole grains;
   engaging in daily moderate physical activity for at least 30 minutes;
   cutting the amount of fatty, sugary foods in the diet;
   moving from saturated animal-based fats to unsaturated vegetable-oil based fats.

- Mounting a clinical response to the existing burden of obesity and associated conditions through clinical programs and staff training to ensure effective support for those affected to lose weight or avoid further weight gain.

Source: *World Health Organization* Global Strategy on Diet, Physical Activity and Health. http://www.who.int/nut.

EXERCISE 7   **Answering prereading questions**

With your partner, reexamine the questions you wrote before reading. Did you find answers to the questions? If so, discuss the answers. If not, on the lines below, write the questions that you still have about this topic. Discuss the questions with your classmates.

_____

_____

_____

_____

_____

_____

_____

_____

_____

○ Assessing Your Learning

Demonstrating Comprehension

EXERCISE 8 **Checking comprehension of sentences**

Test your understanding of sentences from Reading Selection 1 by marking the following statements True or False, according to the reading. If you mark a statement false, rewrite it to make it true. Share your answers with your partner.

1. _____ Obesity rarely exists in populations that also have undernourished people.

2. _____ The increase in obesity is occurring faster in developed countries than in developing countries.

3. _____ Genes, the amount of calories taken in, and the level of activity can contribute to weight gain.

4. _____ Globally, there is an increase in physical labor.

5. _____ You can calculate overweight and obesity by using a mathematical formula that divides your weight by your height.

6. _____ If a person suffers from under-nutrition, and then becomes obese as an adult, he or she usually has less serious cases of hypertension, heart disease, and diabetes than another person who never experienced under-nutrition.

7. _____ Since 1980, the number of overweight children in the U.S. has trebled while the number of overweight adolescents has doubled.

8. _____ The heavier you are, the greater chance you have of getting type 2 diabetes and high blood pressure.

| **EXERCISE** **9** | **Outlining the major points** |

As you did in previous chapters, make a brief outline of the major points of Reading Selection 1. On separate paper, write your outline. Use the title and subheadings that mark the sections of the reading selection. Under each subheading, include at least one major supporting point per paragraph. Label these points A, B, C, and so on. The first one is partially done for you as an example. Write the points in brief phrases. Use your own words and words from the reading. Share your completed outlines with a partner.

I. Obesity and Being Overweight

   A. One billion overweight, 300 million obese worldwide

   B. Obesity coexisting with under-nutrition

   C. Obesity: a complex condition affecting all ages, socioeconomic groups

   D. Causes: _____

      _____

      _____

      _____

   E. Rates tripled since 1980 in _____

      _____

      _____

      _____

   F. Risks: _____

      _____

      _____

      _____

II. Why Is This Happening?

III. How Do We Define Obesity and Being Overweight?

IV. How Does Excess Body Fat Impact Health?

V. The Extent of the Problem

VI. What Can We Do about It?

Nouns and Noun Phrases in Informational Academic Texts

Many academic readings are considered informational texts because their main purpose is to inform. Typically, informational texts contain many nouns and long, complicated noun phrases. Being able to identify nouns and noun phrases can help you in three ways: (1) to improve your reading comprehension, (2) to identify key vocabulary terms that have to be memorized for tests, and (3) to write effectively about what you have read.

Study the bold-faced nouns and noun phrases in these sentences from Reading Selection 1:

1. **Obesity** has reached epidemic proportions globally . . .

    • Nouns are used as subjects or objects in a sentence. Sentence 1 has a single noun as the subject of the sentence.

2. **The rising epidemic** reflects the profound changes in society and in behavioral patterns of communities over recent decades.

    • *Noun phrase* is the name for the combination of a noun with other words. A noun phrase can have different structures. In sentence 2, the first phrase is article (*a, an, the*) + adjective + noun.

3. Obesity and being overweight pose **a major risk for serious diet-related chronic diseases . . .**

4. The health consequences range from increased risk of premature death, to **serious chronic conditions that reduce the overall quality of life.**

5. In **countries undergoing nutrition transition**, overnutrition co-exists with undernutrition.

    • A noun phrase can be long and complicated, with many words coming before or after the main noun. Sentence 3 shows an article + adjective + noun followed by a prepositional phrase (*for* + noun phrase). Sentence 4 shows adjectives + noun followed by a relative clause (*that* clause). Sentence 5 shows a noun followed by a reduced relative clause (*that* + *are* are omitted from the clause).

EXERCISE 10 Identifying noun phrases

Reread the sentences below from Reading Selection 1. Underline the nouns and noun phrases. Circle the main noun in each noun phrase. The first one is done as an example. Share your answers with a partner.

1. (Obesity) is a complex condition, with serious social and psychological (dimensions). . . .

2. Increased consumption of more energy-dense, nutrient-poor foods with high levels of sugar and saturated fats . . . has led to obesity rates that have risen three-fold since 1980 . . . .

3. Economic growth, modernization, urbanization and globalization of food markets are just some of the forces thought to underlie the epidemic.

4. Moves toward less physical activity are also found in the increasing use of automated transport, technology in the home, and more passive leisure pursuits.

5. The distribution of BMI is shifting upwards in many populations.

6. An estimated 17.6 million children under five are estimated to be overweight worldwide.

7. Approximately 80% of people with diabetes are type 2.

8. Effective weight management for individuals and groups at risk of developing obesity involves a range of long-term strategies.

EXERCISE 11 **Writing sentences with noun phrases**

On separate paper, use each noun phrase below to write a sentence about obesity and being overweight. Use the noun phrase as a subject or object in the sentence. Make sure the subject of the sentence agrees in number with the verb. Share your sentences with a partner.

1. a major cause
2. serious diseases
3. people in many countries
4. overweight children
5. the prevalence of obesity
6. weight management
7. daily physical activity
8. public policies

Examples

> **A major cause** of obesity is a lack of physical activity.
>
> The consumption of foods that are high in sugar and fat is **a major cause** of obesity.

○ Linking Concepts

EXERCISE 12 **Writing in your reading journal**

Choose one section from Reading Selection 1, "Obesity and Being Overweight." Write a one-page journal entry about one major point addressed in the section. Include your reactions to this point. Write your own sentence to express the point from the reading, or copy a sentence from the reading. If you copy a sentence, be sure to put it in quotations. In writing your reactions or opinions about this point, you may want to use these guiding questions:

- Were you surprised by this point?
- Does the point express a favorable or an unfavorable situation?
- If it is unfavorable, what can people do to solve the problem?
- What should governments do?

Reading Journal

_____

_____

_____

○ Learning Vocabulary

EXERCISE **13**   **Studying academic words**

Study the list of academic words found in Reading Selection 1. Put a check mark next to the words that are familiar to you. Create word study cards for unfamiliar words. Follow the guidelines suggested in Chapter 3.

1. ____ accessibility	17. ____ emerging	33. ____ pose
2. ____ adulthood	18. ____ enable	34. ____ promote
3. ____ analyses	19. ____ ensure	35. ____ proportions
4. ____ assessed	20. ____ environmental	36. ____ pursuits
5. ____ attributable	21. ____ estimated	37. ____ range
6. ____ automated	22. ____ factors	38. ____ restricted
7. ____ complex	23. ____ globalization	39. ____ shifting
8. ____ confined	24. ____ impact	40. ____ strategies
9. ____ consequences	25. ____ incidence	41. ____ transition
10. ____ consumption	26. ____ index	42. ____ transport
11. ____ contribute	27. ____ integrated	43. ____ trends
12. ____ decades	28. ____ involved	44. ____ undergoing
13. ____ dimensions	29. ____ maintenance	45. ____ underlie
14. ____ distribution	30. ____ motivate	46. ____ varied
15. ____ dramatically	31. ____ overall	47. ____ virtually
16. ____ elements	32. ____ passive	

EXERCISE 14 **Discussing questions with academic words**

Test your comprehension of some of the words listed above by discussing the questions that follow with a group of your classmates.

1. Does your school provide **accessibility** to students with physical handicaps? In what ways?

2. When you say that a problem is **attributable** to something, what do you mean?

3. If you break both of your legs, in what ways might you be **confined**?

4. When you speak about the **dimensions** of a room, what does that mean?

5. If a price rises **dramatically**, how much does it rise?

6. Is there a high **incidence** of crime in your neighborhood? Explain.

7. Is English **integrated** into your daily activities? Explain.

8. When someone angers you, do you react in a **passive** way? Explain.

9. If you **pose** a problem to your family members, what do you do to them?

10. What are your favorite free-time **pursuits**?

11. If your friend tells you he is in a **transition** period, what might he mean?

12. What values **underlie** a strong family?

13. If you do not study for an exam, what **consequences** might result?

14. What responsibilities do people face in **adulthood** that they don't have in **childhood**?

15. If someone is **emerging** from a building, is the person inside or outside the building? Explain.

EXERCISE 15 Choosing correct word forms

Complete the sentences below by circling the correct word forms. Then check your answers by finding the sentences in the reading.

1. Obesity has reached epidemic proportions (global / globally)....

2. Increased (consume / consumption) of more energy-dense, nutrient-poor foods with high levels of sugar and saturated fats, combined with reduced physical activity, have led to obesity rates....

3. The health (consequences / consequential) range from increased risk of premature death, to serious chronic conditions....

4. The rising epidemic reflects the profound changes in (social / society) and in behavioral patterns....

5. As incomes rise and populations become more urban, diets high in (complex / complexity) carbohydrates give way to more (varied / variety) diets with a higher proportion of fats, saturated fats and sugars.

6. These markers provide common benchmarks for (assess / assessment), but the risks of disease in all populations can increase progressively....

7. The (distribution / distribute) of BMI is shifting upwards in many populations.

8. ... [R]ecent studies have shown the people who were undernourished in early life and then become obese in (adult / adulthood), tend to develop conditions such as high blood pressure, heart disease, and diabetes at an earlier age....

9. The problem is global and increasingly (extension / extends) into the developing world....

10. The non-fatal (debilitating / debilitate) health problems associated with obesity include respiratory difficulties, chronic musculoskeletal problems, skin problems and infertility.

Reading Assignment 2

NEWS REPORTS FROM TWO COUNTRIES: "MORE MONEY, MORE OBESITY IN CHILDREN" AND "TACKLING ASIA'S GROWING WAISTLINE"

EXERCISE 16 Asking questions before reading

Work with a partner. Together, write questions about the text before you read. First, use the titles of the two news reports to give you ideas for questions. Then, read the first paragraph of each report, and write additional questions you may have about the topic. Finally, as you read, look for the answers to your questions.

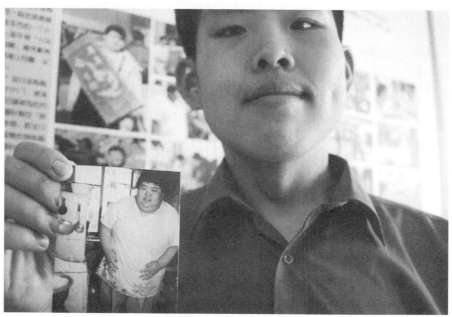

Meng Qinggang lost 176 pounds in 100 days.

Reading Selection 2

NEWS REPORT 1: MORE MONEY, MORE OBESITY IN CHILDREN

1   [SUNDAY, MAY 26, 2002] NEW DELHI: Affluence is now taking its toll on children's health, with a new study in Delhi indicating that every 15th school-going child in the high- or high-middle income group is obese.

2   The study conducted in a public school cautions that all these children are prone to hypertension, diabetes, coronary artery disease and overall morbidity and mortality during adult life.

3   "There is increasing evidence that children and adolescents of affluent families are overweight. It is possibly because of decreased physical activity, sedentary lifestyle, altered eating patterns with more fat content in the diet," Dr. Umesh Kapil, adjunct professor from the Department of Human Nutrition and Biostatistics at AIIMS,[1] who along with his team conducted the study, said.

4   "Only 19 percent of the school children were found to be engaged in outdoor activities in our study, while 90 percent of the obese children did not engage in any outdoor activity at all," Kapil said.

5   The research, involving 870 children, was carried out in a public school of Delhi catering to the affluent segment of the population. It reported an overall prevalence of obesity as 7.4 percent. An earlier study in 1990 had reported an almost similar prevalence of obesity, according to the paper published in the science journal *Indian Pediatrics*.

6   Kapil said prevalence of a disorder above five percent was a public health problem. These children would grow into adults and were likely to contribute to the ever increasing burden of non-communicable diseases, he said.

7   "Once obese, a child remains so in adulthood and even old age. Obesity also leads to hypertension, cardiovascular diseases, gall stones, osteoarthritis and diabetes," he said. Kapil said children from affluent sections were frequenting fast-food joints more often, were engaged in indoor activities like watching television and computer games and doing less physical activity. With affluence, there is a tendency to enhance consumption of costly fatty items and oil.

1. AIIMS = Abbreviation for All India Institute of Medical Sciences.

8   This led to a positive calorific[2] balance with children eating more calories than they are expending. "Forty to fifty years back, children used to engage in more outdoor activities," he said.

9   A large number of children in the study had a high calorific intake and visited fast-food joints. Besides, most of the children had to skip their morning breakfast as they had to leave for schools early. In the school, they would consume oily cafeteria stuff. He said 28 percent of the children visited fast-food joints once a week and 18 percent visited twice a week.

10   Only 19 percent of all of the children were engaged in outdoor activities—38 percent were entertained through TV, 21 percent through computers, 10 percent by music, and eight percent were engaged in reading.

11   The study also related obesity with nuclear families stating that 65 percent of the children in the study were from nuclear families. Kapil said in nuclear families there is no dearth of funds which might lead to children spending money on fatty food.

12   The phenomenon is prevalent in other parts of the world as well. During the past 20 years, the prevalence of obesity among children and adolescents has doubled in the U.S., the study said.

13   According to the statistics available with the U.S. National Center for Health, nearly 15 percent of adolescents are overweight (when ratio of weight and height is between 25 and 30) or obese (when this ratio is more than 30), it said.

14   The paper said the maximum prevalence of obesity was found during the pubertal period, between 10 and 12 years. This may be associated with the increase in fat tissues and overall weight gain during the pubertal growth spurt.

15   Kapil explained that one factor for this may be that children at this age start getting independent pocket money, which they might be spending on fatty eatables in school canteens.

16   He said the problem was that children were unaware of their nutritional needs, adding that adolescent education programs should be introduced in schools.

Source: *Times of India.* May 28, 2002.

---

2. **cal•o•rif•ic** (kăl′ ə-rĭf′ ĭk) *n.* Relating to or generating heat or calories

NEWS REPORT 2: TACKLING ASIA'S GROWING WAISTLINE

From Jaime FlorCruz
CNN Beijing Bureau Chief

1   Sunday, November 2, 2003 TIANJIN, China (CNN) — Acupuncture[1] needles get planted on the flabby frame of Cheng Jian, a 20-year-old student <u>undergoing</u> treatment to cure obesity.

2   "The discomfort," he says, "is nothing compared to the pain of being extremely obese."

3   "People talked behind my back because they hadn't seen a person as fat as I was," he tells CNN.

4   Cheng is one of the many Chinese and foreign patients who have checked into the Aimin Obesity Reduction Hospital to lose weight and gain self-esteem.

5   Twenty-five years of China's <u>economic</u> boom have brought the good life, sedentary lifestyles and fat-laden food—swelling people's waistlines.

6   "The number of obese youths grows 10 <u>percent</u> every year," says Aimin hospital director Shi Lidong. "It's partly because they are spoiled by doting parents and grandparents."

7   Aimin's doctors offer <u>unconventional</u> treatment. "Acupuncture mainly helps reduce appetite and improve metabolism. But our treatment is holistic."

8   In the <u>virtual</u> fat farm, patients are given meals with carefully counted calories. They are also counseled on how to change eating habits.

9   In between meals, they do <u>physical</u> exercises, like running and dance aerobics.

10   The fat farm's solution is basic: eat less, and exercise more. Here, the chubby <u>generation</u> learns how to burn calories and melt the fat away.

11   But some weight-watchers still get nightmares while trying to curb their cravings.

12   "A fellow patient dreamt of eating out with her parents, but they refused to give her food," says a camper, Wang Ping.

---

1. **ac•u•punc•ture** (ăk′yŏo-pŭngk′chər) *n.* The practice originating in traditional Chinese medicine in which thin needles are put into the body at specific points to relieve pain, treat a disease, or numb parts of the body during surgery.

13 "She shouted in her dream, 'why not let me eat!' We were all awakened by her screams."

14 Fat-farmers get emotional support and inspiration from graduates like Meng Qinggang, Aimin's most celebrated success story.

15 Meng weighed 215 kilograms (473 pounds) when he s̲o̲u̲g̲h̲t̲ Aimin's help three years ago.

16 "I used to eat five meals a day. I needed help to put on clothes or walk. I was close to dying," Meng tells CNN.

17 Meng then lost 80 kilos (176 pounds) in 100 days, and slimmed down even more. He now weighs 89 kilos (196 pounds).

18 "I can now drink beer and even eat fried, high-calorie food. It's okay as long as the amount is right," he says. "And I run regularly."

○ Assessing Your Learning

Demonstrating Comprehension

EXERCISE 17 **Expressing main ideas**

Write two sentences to express the main ideas of each news report. Begin each sentence with the name of the article (and author, if given), as in the example below.

1. ___The news report "More Money, More Obesity in Children"___
   ___states that . . .___

2. _____

   _____

STRATEGY

Use of Statistics to Support Statements

Academic readings that report on significant trends, results, or conclusions often use *statistics* as support. Statistics are "numerical data," or "the mathematics of the collection, organization, and interpretation of numerical data," according to the *American Heritage College Dictionary* (2002, p. 1351). Statistics can provide effective supporting evidence to prove that a statement is true or accurate.

Reading Selection 2 uses the pattern of statement + statistical support. Numerical data may be expressed in numbers, percentages, or words that indicate numbers, like *doubled, tripled,* and so on. To understand this pattern, study the example sentences from "More Money, More Obesity in Children" below.

> Statement
>
> In the school, they would consume oily cafeteria stuff. He said
>
> Statistic
>
> 28 percent of children visited fast-food joints once a week and
>
> Statistic
>
> 18 percent visited twice a week.

The first example sentence states that children ate oily food. The second sentence includes statistics that show a significant percentage of the children frequented fast-food restaurants. These numerical data serve as proof that the children consumed food that may not be healthy.

EXERCISE 18   **Analyzing statements and statistics**

Reread the statements from "More Money, More Obesity in Children" in the left-hand column of the chart. For each statement, find at least two sentences containing statistical support in the reading. Write the supporting sentences in the box next to the corresponding statement. One supporting sentence is provided as an example. Compare your answers with a partner's.

Statements	Statistical Supporting Sentences
"There is increasing evidence that children and adolescents of affluent families are overweight."	Affluence is now taking its toll of children's health, with a new study in Delhi indicating that every 15th school-going child in the high- or high-middle income group is obese.
"[Being overweight] is possibly because of decreased physical activity. . . ."	
"The phenomenon is prevalent in other parts of the world as well. . . ."	

Master Student Tip

Steps in the Scientific Method

The reading selections in Chapter 4 report the findings of research related to obesity and being overweight, a subject of study in nutrition and other health-related disciplines. Reading Selection 2 illustrates the *scientific method,* the steps that scientists use to find answers to questions. Scientific research generally includes the following steps.

- First, scientists make observations. They observe something significant or interesting that occurs around them.

- Second, they develop a hypothesis to explain the observations.

EXERCISE 19 Analyzing the steps in the scientific method

The chart below identifies statements from the two news reports in Reading Selection 2 that report steps in the scientific method. Read each statement in the left-hand column, and note the bold-faced step it represents in the right-hand column. With a group of your classmates, discuss why you think each statement represents this step.

Statement	Step in the Scientific Method
1. ["Being overweight] is possibly because of decreased physical activity, sedentary lifestyle, altered eating patterns with more fat content in the diet," Dr. Umesh Kapil, adjunct professor from the department of Human Nutrition and Biostatistics at AIIMS … said. ("More Money …" ¶ 3)	● Make observations. ✓ **Develop a hypothesis.** ● Test the hypothesis. ● Report the results or conclusions.
2. The research, involving 870 children, was carried out in a public school of Delhi catering to the affluent segment of the population. ("More Money …" ¶ 5)	● Make observations. ● Develop a hypothesis. ✓ **Test the hypothesis.** ● Report the results or conclusions.
3. [The study] reported an overall prevalence of obesity as 7.4 percent. ("More Money …" ¶ 5)	● Make observations. ● Develop a hypothesis. ● Test the hypothesis. ✓ **Report the results or conclusions.**
4. An earlier study in 1990 had reported an almost similar prevalence of obesity, according to the paper published in the science journal *Indian Pediatrics*. ("More Money …" ¶ 5)	● Make observations. ● Develop a hypothesis. ● Test the hypothesis. ✓ **Report the results or conclusions.**

- Third, they create a controlled situation in which to test the hypothesis. Then they test the hypothesis to see if it can explain their observations.
- After they complete the test, they report the results and make conclusions.

Statement	Step in the Scientific Method
5. Forty to fifty years back, children used to engage in more outdoor activities, [Dr. Umesh Kapil] said. ("More Money ..." ¶ 8)	✓ **Make observations.** • Develop a hypothesis. • Test the hypothesis. • Report the results or conclusions.
6. A large number of children in the study had high calorific intake and visited fast-food joints. ("More Money ..." ¶ 9)	✓ **Make observations.** • Develop a hypothesis. • Test the hypothesis. • Report the results or conclusions.
7. The study also related obesity with nuclear families stating that 65 percent of the children in the study were from nuclear families. ("More Money ..." ¶ 11)	• Make observations. • Develop a hypothesis. • Test the hypothesis. ✓ **Report the results or conclusions.**
8. He said the problem was that children were unaware of their nutritional needs, adding that adolescent education programs should be introduced in schools. ("More Money ..." ¶ 16)	• Make observations. • Develop a hypothesis. • Test the hypothesis. ✓ **Report the results or conclusions.**
9. Twenty-five years of China's economic boom have brought good life, sedentary lifestyles and fat-laden food—swelling people's waistlines. ("Tackling ..." ¶ 5)	✓ **Make observations.** • Develop a hypothesis. • Test the hypothesis. • Report the results or conclusions.
10. "The number of obese youths grows 10 percent every year," says Aimin hospital director Shi Lidong. ("Tackling ... ¶ 6)	✓ **Make observations.** • Develop a hypothesis. • Test the hypothesis. • Report the results or conclusions.

○ Questions for Discussion

EXERCISE 20 **Participating in group discussion**

Discuss the following questions with a group of your classmates.

1. The news report "More Money, More Obesity in Children" connects obesity with affluence. Do you think the connection between affluence and being overweight makes sense? Explain.
2. The report also connects obesity with nuclear families. Why do you think a child living in a nuclear family would be more likely to be overweight than a child in an extended family?
3. Do you think either or both of these factors in obesity (affluence and nuclear families) exist in countries other than India? Explain.
4. The news report "Tackling Asia's Growing Waistline" describes treatments for overweight patients. Which treatment described seems like an effective way to treat obesity and being overweight? Explain.
5. At the end of this report, Meng Qinggang, the Chinese man who lost more than 250 pounds, told the reporter he could drink beer and eat high-calorie food if "the amount is right" because he exercised regularly. What do you think of Meng's "formula" for maintaining his weight? Explain.

○ Linking Concepts

EXERCISE 21 **Writing in your reading journal**

Write a one-page reading journal entry to relate your personal reactions and connections to the young overweight people described in the news reports in Reading Selection 2. You may want to write answers to some of these questions in your journal entry:

- Do the eating habits of school-age children in India sound familiar?
- Do you share these eating habits?
- How do you think persons who are clinically obese feel?
- How do you think Meng feels now?
- Do you or does someone you know have an eating problem? If so, explain.

○ Learning Vocabulary

EXERCISE 22 **Studying academic words**

Study the list of academic words from Reading Selection 2. Put a check mark next to the words that are familiar to you. Make a word study card for each unfamiliar word.

1. _____ altered
2. _____ communicable
3. _____ conducted
4. _____ consume
5. _____ enhance
6. _____ evidence
7. _____ funds
8. _____ indicating
9. _____ items

10. _____ nuclear
11. _____ phenomenon
12. _____ published
13. _____ ratio
14. _____ sought
15. _____ statistics
16. _____ team
17. _____ unaware
18. _____ unconventional

The front of your vocabulary card
VOCABULARY WORD: **unconventional**
Part of Speech: adjective
Pronunciation and stress: ŭn-kən-ven′ shə-nəl

The back of the card

Word in use: Aimin's doctors offer unconventional treatment.
A definition: not adhering to convention; out of the ordinary.
Word family members:
    noun: un·con·ven·tion·al·i·ty
    adverb: un·con·ven·tion·al·ly
Collocation: He has some unconventional ideas about sports.

Reading Assignment 3

PICTURE THIS!—COMMUNICATING NUTRITION AROUND THE WORLD

○ Getting Ready to Read

Writers generally have an *audience*—the readership for a text—and a *purpose*—the reason or reasons for writing—in their minds. The audience may be *general* or *specific*, from a general audience of all people to specific readers of a particular age, gender, cultural background, or socioeconomic level. Academic texts may be geared toward readers with a particular academic background; for instance, a reading on nutrition may be written for an audience that is knowledgeable about science or medicine.

A writer may also have multiple purposes for writing. As mentioned earlier in the chapter, *informational* texts are written to provide information. In addition, *persuasive* texts generally aim to persuade readers to support a certain belief or to take certain action.

EXERCISE 23 Identifying audience and purpose in a reading

Read the first paragraph of Reading Selection 3, "Picture This!—Communicating Nutrition around the World." Notice the writer's use of you.

- Who is the writer's audience?
- Is the audience *general* or *specific*?
- What do you think the writer's purpose might be?
- Is the purpose to *inform* or to *persuade*?

As you read the entire selection, keep these questions in mind. You will delve into audience and purpose more deeply after you read.

A revision of the Food Guide Pyramid is scheduled for 2004.

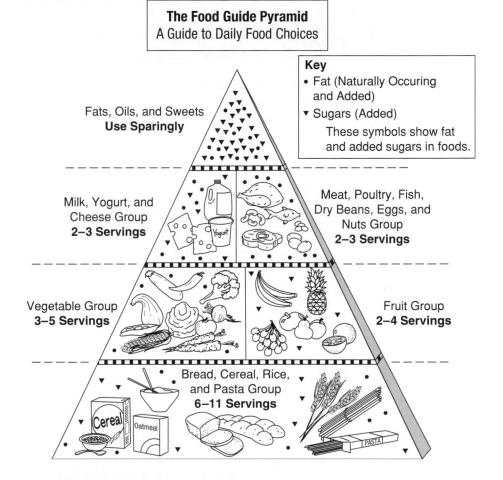

The Food Guide Pyramid
A Guide to Daily Food Choices

Key
- Fat (Naturally Occuring and Added)
- ▾ Sugars (Added)
  These symbols show fat and added sugars in foods.

Fats, Oils, and Sweets
Use Sparingly

Milk, Yogurt, and Cheese Group
2–3 Servings

Meat, Poultry, Fish, Dry Beans, Eggs, and Nuts Group
2–3 Servings

Vegetable Group
3–5 Servings

Fruit Group
2–4 Servings

Bread, Cereal, Rice, and Pasta Group
6–11 Servings

Reading Selection 3

PICTURE THIS!—COMMUNICATING NUTRITION AROUND THE WORLD

1   What picture comes to mind when you think of a healthful diet? The U.S. Departments of Agriculture (USDA) and Health and Human Services hope you think of their Food Guide Pyramid. Since 1992, the Pyramid has served as a visual adaptation of the U.S. Dietary Guidelines for Americans, the seven basic dietary recommendations to promote wellness and prevent chronic disease. Today, the Pyramid can be seen not only in nutrition education materials for children and adults, but also on grocery bags, food packages and in the media.

2   Food guides, such as the USDA's Food Guide Pyramid, are tools used to communicate complex scientific information in a consumer-friendly way. For the most part, government agencies use graphic depictions to communicate dietary guidance messages that provide population-wide recommendations for eating to promote health.

A Photographic History

3   Food guides are not new educational tools. The first United States food guide was developed in 1916 by the USDA and consisted of five food groups—milk and meat; cereals; vegetables and fruits; fats and fat foods; and sugars and sugar foods. By the 1940s, the food guide listed ten food groups, including water and eggs. Vegetables and fruits were split into three individual groups—leafy green and yellow vegetables; citrus, tomato and cabbage; and other vegetables and fruits. Ten food groups were difficult for consumers to remember, so these groups were trimmed to four food groups by the late 1950s.

4   Previous versions of the United States food guide were tools used to promote a diet containing essential vitamins and minerals. School children were often the educational target for the simple illustrations used to depict the optimal diet. One of the most familiar food guides of the past is the "Basic Four," containing four food groups—milk, fruit and vegetable, bread and cereal, and meat groups—which was used for nearly 25 years. The emphasis of the "Basic Four" food guide was to help Americans get a foundation diet, meaning, it was intended to meet only a portion of caloric and nutrient needs.

5   After the publication of the first Dietary Guidelines for Americans in 1980, work began on a new food guide graphic to reflect the latest science on diet and health. In addition to a review of existing research, government agencies conducted extensive quantitative and qualitative research with American consumers to ensure the resulting graphic communicated key dietary guideline concepts. The pyramid design proved most useful in graphically communicating the intended messages across various socioeconomic groups.

6   No single adaptation of the pyramid graphic can depict all of the eating practices of the diverse American populace. However, because of the simplicity and understandability of the pyramid shape, the U.S. Food Guide Pyramid can be translated to reflect the

customs of numerous ethnic and cultural groups within the United States. The pyramid concept has been adapted to Asian, Mexican, vegetarian and Mediterranean diets by various organizations. For instance, to better serve their state population, the Washington State Department of Health created materials using the pyramid shape to depict diets for Russians, Southeast Asians and Native Americans.

7   The pyramid concept has also been adapted to communicate other health-promoting activities. For example, a physical activity pyramid, developed by a private organization, promotes ways to stay active in everyday life, and a "life balance" pyramid by the same group offers ideas to build and maintain emotional well-being.

The Food Guide Pyramid of South Africa

Fats, Oils, and Sweets
Aim for Lower Intake

Milk, Yogurt, and Cheese Group
2–3 Servings

Meat, Poultry, Fish, Dry Beans, Eggs, and Nuts Group
2–3 Servings

Vegetable Group
3–5 Servings

Fruit Group
2–4 Servings

Bread, Cereal, Rice, and Pasta Group
6–11 Servings

Source: http://www.time-to-run.com/nutrition/pyramid.htm.

Pictures From Around the World

8   The use of the pyramid has been very successful in the United States. The pyramid shape appears to easily convey the concept of variety and the relative amounts to eat of the various food groups. However, because of cultural differences in communicating symbolism and other cultural norms, the pyramid is not necessarily the graphic of choice for food guides worldwide. No single graphic can portray the dietary guidelines of various countries around the world. Rainbows, circles, pyramids, and even a chalice[1] are used to represent the "optimal" diet. The different graphics used reflect cultural norms and symbols as well as the emphasis of the dietary guidelines of each country. In developed countries, food guides tend to promote a diet that prevents chronic disease. In developing countries, however, the goal of the food guide is to promote a diet that provides nutrients to safeguard against malnutrition.

9   Yet, despite the different pictorial representations, different countries communicate similar themes. Food guide graphics from countries as diverse as Italy and South Africa convey a common message—balance, variety and moderation in food choices. While the number of food groups displayed in the graphics varies from country to country, most guides attempt to illustrate the food groups' optimal proportion of the total diet, as does the U.S. Food Guide Pyramid. For instance, based on the Dietary Guidelines for Americans, grains should comprise the largest proportion of the diet. Therefore, grains are depicted at the base of the Pyramid—the largest part of the pyramid shape. Breads and grains, fruits, vegetables, dairy foods and meats are included in all the various guides.

---

1. **chal•ice** (chăl´ĭs) *n.* A cup or goblet.

The Balance of Good Health
The United Kingdom's Food Guide

10   The wheel or dinner plate design is a popular graphic that represents the total diet, with each section depicting a food group and its relative proportion to the total diet. This design is used in the United Kingdom, Germany and Norway, among other countries. Many of the food guide graphics used are unique to their respective countries. Japan depicts its "optimal" diet through the use of the numeral six as the basis of its food guide to remind consumers of the six food categories. The Japanese government has since developed new dietary guidelines. However, the same food guide is still used by many as a reference since a new food guide has not been developed.

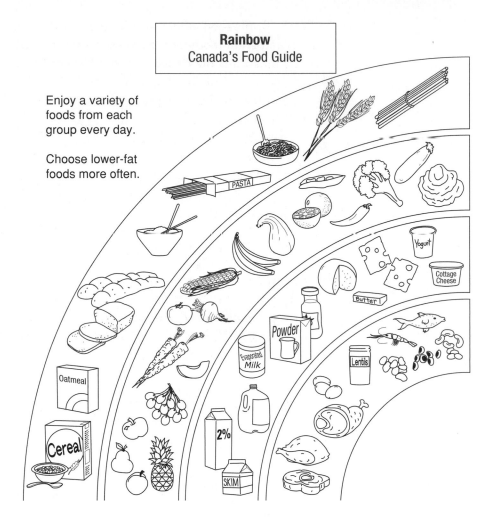

Rainbow
Canada's Food Guide

Enjoy a variety of
foods from each
group every day.

Choose lower-fat
foods more often.

11   Canada's Food Guide to Healthy Eating is a four-banded
rainbow, with each color representing one of its four food groups.
The rainbow shows that all food groups are important but different
amounts are needed from each group. The larger outer arcs of the
rainbow are the grain products and fruits and vegetables. According
to Canada's dietary guidelines, these foods should make up a larger
part of a healthy eating plan. Similarly, the smaller inner arcs make
up the milk products and meat and meat alternatives that should
make up a smaller amount of a healthy eating plan.

12   Many of the food guides around the world emphasize the bread, cereals and grain foods as the largest part of the diet. Israel's chalice graphic illustrates the importance of water for overall health by placing "water" at the top and largest section of the chalice. Israel has one of few food guides that characterize water as a principal part of the diet.

13   South Africa's food guide graphic contains the least number of food groups and organizes foods in a unique way—according to the foods' "function" in the body. Group 1 contains "Energy Food," and includes margarine, grains, porridge and maize. The second group is entitled "Body Building Food" and includes chicken, beans, milk and eggs. The third group is "Protective Food," to protect your body from illness and includes cabbage, carrots, pineapples and spinach.

A Picture Paints a Thousand Words

14   You've undoubtedly heard the phrase "a picture paints a thousand words" numerous times. Nutrition education has long proven this idiom to ring true through the use of food models and pictures to depict such things as portion sizes. Likewise, symbols such as a heart, checkmark or apple are often used on restaurant menus to denote choices that meet specific nutrition or health guidelines.

15   The primary role of food guides, whether in the United States or around the world, is to communicate an optimal diet for overall health of the population. Whether a star, a chalice, a square or a pyramid graphic is used, all are meant to improve quality of life and nutritional well-being in a simplified and understandable way.

Key Concepts for Dietary Patterns:

- Total diet, rather than nutrients or individual foods should be addressed.
- Dietary guidelines need to reflect food patterns rather than numeric nutrient goals.
- Various dietary patterns can be consistent with good health.

Food Insight, International Food Information Council newsletter, January/February 1999. Source of information: Food and Agriculture Organization of the United Nations and the World Health Organization.

○ Assessing Your Learning

Demonstrating Comprehension

EXERCISE 24   Outlining major points and support

Complete this outline with the major points and supporting ideas from Reading Selection 3, "Picture This!—Communicating Nutrition around the World." Write phrases to express the supporting ideas and major points. Compare your outline with a partner's.

Reading Selection 3: Picture This!—Communicating Nutrition around the World

I. U.S. Food Guide Pyramid

    A. The pyramid serves _____.

    B. You can see it in _____.

II. Food Guide definition: _____

    _____.

III. History of U.S. food guides

    A. 1916: _____

    B. 1940s: _____

    _____

    C. 1950s: _____

    D. "Basic Four": _____

    E. 1980: _____

    F. U.S. ethnic and cultural groups: _____

    IV. Pictures from around the world

        A. Different graphic shapes: _____

        B. Common messages:

            1. _____

            2. Grains: _____

        C. Wheel or dinner plate _____

            used in _____.

        D. Japan: _____.

        E. Canada: _____.

            1. Large outer arcs: _____.

            2. Smaller inner arcs: _____.

        F. Israel: _____.

        G. South Africa: _____.

            1. Group 1: _____.

            2. Group 2: _____.

            3. Group 3: _____.

  V. A picture paints 1,000 words

        A. Heart, check mark, or apple: _____.

        B. Primary role of food guides: _____.

  VI. Key concepts in eating patterns

        A. _____.

        B. _____.

        C. _____.

EXERCISE 25 **Identifying audience and purpose**

Identify the audiences and purposes of Reading Selection 3, "Picture This!—Communicating Nutrition around the World," by completing the sentences below. Circle the appropriate word or phrase to complete each sentence.

Audience

1. Selection 3 is probably written for readers who are (already very / not particularly) knowledgeable in nutrition.

2. The reading is directed at (men / women / both men and women) of (all / older / younger) ages.

Purpose

3. Because Selection 3 appeared in *Food Insight*, the newsletter of the International Food Information Council, the writer's main purpose is probably to (inform / persuade) readers about the different types of food guidelines in the world.

4. The writer may also have attempted to (inform / persuade) readers to eat healthy food.

STRATEGY

Drawing Plausible Inferences from Reading

Just as a scientist can make conclusions from research, a careful reader can draw *inferences* from reading. An *inference* is a logical conclusion you can make by using information given to you. In reading, a text may not state a conclusion directly, but it provides information that the reader can use to make a plausible, or likely, conclusion.

Reading Selection 2, "Tackling Asia's Growing Waistline," includes an example of information from which a reader can draw plausible inferences.

Information in Reading Selection 2:

"The number of obese youths grows 10 percent every year," says Aimin hospital director Shi Lidong. "It's partly because they are spoiled by doting parents and grandparents."

Plausible Inferences:

- Some Chinese parents and grandparents use food to spoil their children.
- Therefore, in some Chinese families, food must be a positive thing, a treat, or a reward to children.
- Also, the standard of living in China is probably high enough for families to provide children with excess food.

EXERCISE 26   **Drawing inferences from reading**

Reread the excerpts below from Reading Selections 2 and 3. You may want to reread the entire paragraphs from which the excerpts came. Then, read the two possible inferences you might draw from the information in the reading, and put a check mark next to the one you think is the most plausible. Share your answers in a group.

Reading Selection 3

1. Ten food groups were difficult for consumers to remember, so these groups were trimmed to four food groups [by the U.S. government] by the late 1950s. (¶ 3)

Plausible inference? (Check one.)

_____ The U.S. government thought people were having a hard time understanding so many food groups.

_____ There are really only four food groups.

2. In developed countries, food guides tend to promote a diet that prevents chronic disease. In developing countries, however, the goal of the food guide is to promote a diet that provides nutrients to safeguard against malnutrition. (¶ 8)

Plausible inference?

_____ People from developing countries don't have chronic disease.

_____ People from developing countries worry about malnutrition.

3. Israel's chalice graphic illustrates the importance of water for overall health by placing "water" at the top and largest section of the chalice. Israel has one of few food guides that characterize water as a principal part of the diet. (¶ 12)

   Plausible inference?

   _____   Water is in short supply in Israel.

   _____   Israel has a lot of water.

Reading Selection 2

4. Cheng is one of the many Chinese and foreign patients who have checked into the Aimin Obesity Reduction Hospital to lose weight and gain self-esteem. ("Tackling Asia's Growing Waistline," ¶ 4)

   Plausible inference?

   _____   Obese people have problems with their self-image.

   _____   In Chinese society, obesity is viewed as a positive characteristic.

5. Forty to fifty years back, children used to engage in more of outdoor activities," he said. ("More Money, More Obesity in Children," ¶ 8)

   Plausible inference?

   _____   Today's children have many more interesting indoor activities to do.

   _____   Children today get a lot of physical exercise.

6. Kapil explained that one factor may be that children at this age start getting independent pocket money, which they might be spending on fatty eatables in school canteens.

   Plausible inference?

   _____   The doctor has a negative attitude about children getting pocket money.

   _____   The doctor thinks children getting pocket money does not affect their eating.

○ Questions for Discussion

EXERCISE 27 **Participating in group discussion**

Discuss the following questions with a group of classmates.

1. Reading Selection 3 describes food guides as "tools used to communicate complex scientific information in a consumer-friendly way." They are also described as "understandable to most consumers." Do you find the food guides easy to understand? Explain.

2. Reread the specialized food guide pyramids presented at the beginning of this chapter, as well as the food guides included in Reading Selection 3. Which of these food guide illustrations best reflects your cultural background? Explain.

3. Which of the non-pyramid food guides described in Reading Selection 3 do you find the most effective? Explain.

4. If you were asked to revise the U.S. Food Guide Pyramid, how would you revise it? Would you change its shape? Its information?

5. What do you think are the three most important messages about eating that are relayed by the food guides in Selection 3? List them below:

_____

_____

_____

○ Learning Vocabulary

EXERCISE 28 **Studying academic words**

Study this list of academic words found in Reading Selection 3. Put a check mark next to the words that are familiar to you. Make word study cards of unfamiliar words so that you can study them.

1. _____ adaptation
2. _____ adapted
3. _____ alternatives
4. _____ categories
5. _____ components
6. _____ comprise
7. _____ concept
8. _____ consisted
9. _____ consistent
10. _____ consumer
11. _____ denote
12. _____ design
13. _____ despite
14. _____ displayed
15. _____ diverse
16. _____ ethnic
17. _____ evolution
18. _____ featured
19. _____ foundation
20. _____ function
21. _____ guideline

22. _____ highlight
23. _____ illustrations
24. _____ inappropriately
25. _____ insight
26. _____ instance
27. _____ issue
28. _____ likewise
29. _____ maintain
30. _____ media
31. _____ norms
32. _____ portion
33. _____ primary
34. _____ principal
35. _____ qualitative
36. _____ role
37. _____ symbolism
38. _____ symbols
39. _____ target
40. _____ themes
41. _____ unique
42. _____ versions

EXERCISE 29 Comprehending academic words

Test your comprehension of academic words by circling the best synonym for the bold-faced academic words in the sentences that follow. You may wish to use a dictionary to check your answers. Compare your answers with a partner's.

1. Food guide illustrations divide food into different **categories** (groups / individuals).

2. Food guides include **alternatives** (preferences / choices) such as rice and pasta in the bread group.

3. Illustrations of a bottle of milk and a piece of cheese **denote** (represent / suggest) foods in the dairy category.

4. On restaurant menus, the heart and the apple are two **symbols** (warnings / signs) for healthy foods.

5. The U.S. Food Guide Pyramid has been **adapted** (created / changed) to suit the dietary patterns of U.S. cultural and ethnic groups. There are specialized food guide pyramids for Latin Americans, Asian Americans, and other groups.

6. Israel's chalice is a **unique** (ordinary /special) design for a food guide illustration.

7. **Despite** the fact (Because of the fact / Even though) the food pyramid is popular, the U.S. Department of Agriculture may change the shape of its food guide.

8. In the U.S. food pyramid, the bottom layer is the **foundation** (top / base) of the pyramid.

9. China's pagoda food guide illustration **comprises** (includes / contrasts) "floors" of a building that indicate different food groups.

10. You can get an **insight** into (question of / understanding of) Chinese culture by studying the pagoda food guide.

◯ Linking Concepts

EXERCISE 30 **Synthesizing ideas from different sources**

Reflect on the major points in the chapter's readings by discussing the following questions with a group of your classmates. You may want to reread sections of the readings to help you answer the questions.

1. Which of the chapter reading selections more strongly expresses the problem of global obesity? Explain.

2. In Reading Selection 1, were you surprised by the list of countries in which obesity is increasing the most rapidly? If so, which countries were you surprised to see on the list?

3. In Reading Selection 2, which of the reasons given in the two news reports seemed the most plausible explanation for obesity? Did these reasons jibe with the causes for obesity presented in Reading Selection 1?

4. When you consider the causes for obesity presented in Selections 1 and 2, which of these causes do you think is the most difficult problem to overcome? Explain.

5. Do the food guides presented in Reading Selection 3 make it easier for people to manage their dietary patterns? If so, in what ways do the food guides help people eat more wisely?

◯ Assessing Your Learning at the End of a Chapter

Revisiting Objectives

Return to the first page of this chapter. Think about the chapter objectives. Put a check mark next to the ones you feel secure about. Review material in the chapter you still need to work on. When you are ready, answer the chapter review questions in Exercise 31.

◯ Practicing for a Chapter Test

EXERCISE 31   Reviewing comprehension

Check your comprehension of main concepts, or ideas, in this chapter by answering the following questions. First, write notes to answer the questions <u>without</u> looking back at the readings. Then, use the readings to check your answers and revise them, if necessary. Write your final answers in <u>complete</u> sentences on separate paper.

1. In Reading Selection 1, how many people did the World Health Organization report are overweight worldwide? How many are obese?
2. Name <u>four</u> major health risks posed by obesity and being overweight.
3. Name <u>four</u> major reasons for the global increase in obesity.
4. How does a health professional commonly assess whether a person is overweight or obese?
5. What are <u>three</u> less serious health effects of obesity and overweight?
6. What are <u>three</u> main strategies for effective weight management, according to Reading Selection 1?
7. In Reading Selection 2, what main groups of children in India are becoming more overweight?
8. What are <u>two</u> main causes that researchers found for the rise in child obesity in India?
9. In the CNN report from China, what treatments were being used to overcome obesity?
10. What reason did the CNN report give for increased obesity among young people in China?
11. According to Reading Selection 3, what is the overall purpose of a food guide?
12. In the history of U.S. food guides, what was the "Basic Four"?
13. According to food guides around the world, which type of food should make up the largest proportion of the diet?
14. Name <u>five</u> countries and the shapes of their food guides.
15. How is Israel's food guide unique?
16. How is South Africa's food guide unique?
17. Name <u>one</u> key concept for dietary patterns that Reading Selection 3 lists.

EXERCISE 32 **Reviewing academic vocabulary**

The reading selections in Chapter 4 presented many academic words with different forms, or endings. Review some of the academic words you studied in Chapter 4 by completing the sentences with the correct form of the academic word. Check your answers by finding the sentences in the readings.

1. consumption   consumers

   a. Increased _____ of more energy-dense, nutrient-poor foods . . . [has] led to obesity. . . . (*Selection 1*)

   b. Ten food groups were difficult for _____ to remember, so these groups were trimmed to four food groups by the late 1950s. (*Selection 3*)

2. adult   adulthood

   a. _____ mean BMI levels of 22–23 kg/m² are found in Africa and Asia, while levels of 25–27 kg/m² are prevalent across North America, Europe, and in some Latin American, North African and Pacific Island countries. (*Selection 1*)

   b. And recent studies have shown the people who were undernourished in early life and then become obese in _____, tend to develop conditions such as high blood pressure, heart disease and diabetes at an earlier age and in more severe form than those who were never undernourished. (*Selection 1*)

3. assessed   assessment

   a. The prevalence of being overweight and obesity is commonly _____ by using body mass index (BMI), defined as the weight in kilograms divided by the square of the height in meters (kg/m²). (*Selection 1*)

   b. These markers provide common benchmarks for _____, but the risks of disease in all populations can increase progressively from lower BMI levels. (*Selection 1*)

4. maintenance   maintain

   a. These include prevention, weight _____,
      management of co-morbidities and weight loss. (*Selection 1*)

   b. For example, a physical activity pyramid, developed by a private
      organization, promotes ways to stay active in everyday life,
      and a "life balance" pyramid by the same group offers ideas to
      build and _____ emotional well-being.
      (*Selection 3*)

5. symbolism   symbols

   a. However, because of cultural differences in communicating
      _____ and other cultural norms, the
      pyramid is not necessarily the graphic of choice for food guides
      worldwide. (*Selection 3*)

   b. Likewise, _____ such as a heart, check
      mark or apple are often used on restaurant menus to denote
      choices that meet specific nutrition or health guidelines.
      (*Selection 3*)

EXERCISE 33   **Reviewing more academic vocabulary**

*Study the sentences in which the bold-faced academic words appear. Put a
check mark above the academic words you think you know well. Circle the
academic words you need to study. Create word study cards for unfamiliar
words. Include on each card a brief definition, the part of speech, and the
sentence in which the word is used.*

1. Obesity has reached epidemic **proportions globally**.

2. Societal changes and worldwide nutrition **transition** are driving the
   obesity epidemic.

3. **Economic** growth, modernization, urbanization and **globalization** of
   food markets are just some of the forces thought to **underlie** the
   epidemic.

4. Moves toward less **physical** activity are also found in the increasing use of **automated transport**, **technology** in the home, and more **passive** leisure **pursuits**.

5. In 1995, the **Emerging** Market **Economies** had the highest number of diabetics.

6. **Creating** supportive population-based **environments** through public **policies** that **promote** the **availability** and **accessibility** of a **variety** of low-fat, high-fiber foods, and that provide opportunities for **physical** activity.

7. According to the **statistics** available with the U.S. National Center for Health, nearly 15 **percent** of adolescents are overweight (when **ratio** of weight and height is between 25 and 30) or obese (when this **ratio** is more than 30), it said.

8. Since 1992, the Pyramid has served as a **visual adaptation** of the U.S. Dietary **Guidelines** for Americans, the seven basic dietary recommendations to **promote** wellness and prevent chronic disease.

9. The **emphasis** of the "Basic Four" food guide was to help Americans get a **foundation** diet, meaning, it was intended to meet only a **portion** of caloric and nutrient needs.

WEB POWER

Visit http://esl.college.hmco.com/students to view more readings about global obesity, plus exercises that will help you study the selections and the academic words in this chapter.

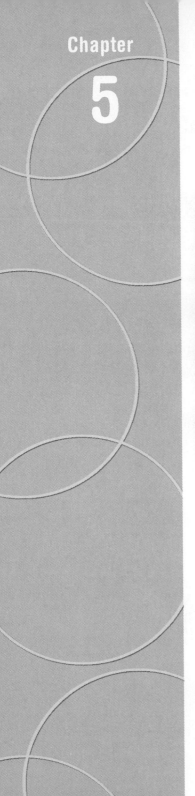

Chapter

5

The Thread of Life

ACADEMIC FOCUS: GENETICS

Academic Reading Objectives

After completing this chapter, you should be able to:

✓ Check here as you master each objective

1. Use visual aids in texts to improve reading comprehension ☐
2. Refine paraphrasing skills for use in academic tasks ☐
3. Identify and understand citations in academic texts ☐
4. Identify and understand metaphors in scientific readings ☐

Genetics Objectives

1. Transfer insights gained from reading about genetics to your own genetic makeup ☐
2. Develop a perspective through exploration of research in genetics ☐
3. Use a timeline to better understand historical advances in science ☐

Getting Ready to Read

EXERCISE 1 Participating in group discussion

Study the photographs below. Work with a partner to make notes about similarities and differences between the living things in each pair of photographs. If there is only one photograph, find the similarities and differences between the living things in the photograph. Discuss your answers in a group.

Pair A

Photograph 1

Photograph 2

Similarities: _____

Differences: _____

Photograph B

Photograph 3

Similarities: _____

Differences: _____

Pair C

Photograph 4

Photograph 5

Similarities: _____

Differences: _____

Pair D

Photograph 6

Photograph 7

Similarities: _____

Differences: _____

○ Focusing on Genetics

Chapter 5 explores the academic field of *genetics*, which is an important aspect of biology. College students encounter genetics in courses ranging from biology, anatomy, physiology, chemistry, and psychology to child development. Read the definition of genetics in the box below.

What Is Genetics?

1. The branch of biology that deals with heredity, especially the mechanisms of hereditary transmission and the variation of inherited characteristics among similar or related organisms.
2. The genetic constitution of an individual, group, or class.

Next, study the illustration and read the short text that follows, "Principles of Genetics and Heredity."

Levels for Examining Heredity

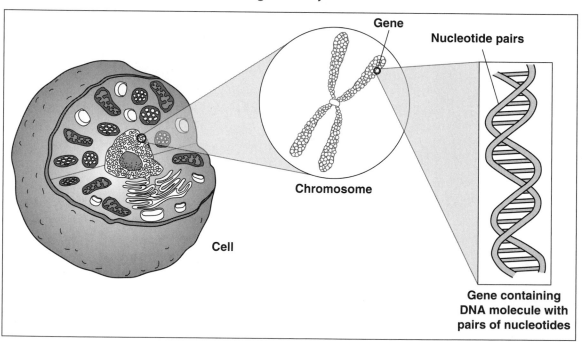

Gene

Nucleotide pairs

Chromosome

Cell

Gene containing
DNA molecule with
pairs of nucleotides

Principles of Genetics and Heredity

The structures and principles of heredity must be examined at several levels, including (1) the individual, (2) the cells making up the body of that individual, (3) the chromosomes located within the nucleus of those cells, (4) the genes comprising segments of each chromosome, and (5) the nucleotide pairs that form the biochemical building blocks for the genes.

EXERCISE 2 Discussing genetics

Discuss the questions that follow with a group of your classmates.

1. The photographs in "Getting Ready to Read," on pages 190–191, represent *individuals* that are studied by geneticists. In the short text on genetics, above, what does the term *individual* refer to?
2. Look at the drawing on page 192, and discuss the labeled parts. Do you understand the concepts that are illustrated? Explain what you know about these components.
3. Next, match each part of the drawing on page 192 with a sentence in the short reading above. Does the drawing help you understand the text more easily? If not, which parts are unclear? Discuss these in your group and with your entire class.
4. The drawing and text above describe the ways scientists examine heredity. In what ways do you think the study of genetics and heredity is more challenging at the cell level and smaller?
5. What are some ways that scientists are using their knowledge of genetics and heredity to change humans, other animals, and plants today? How might scientists be able to change humans, animals, or plants in the future?

EXERCISE 3 Learning key terms in genetics

Study the list of key terms in genetics, which includes some terms you discussed in Exercise 2. Put a check mark next to the words you know. Use a dictionary to find definitions of unfamiliar words. Make a word study card for each unfamiliar word.

_____ heredity _____ organisms _____ ancestry _____ species

_____ evolved _____ molecules _____ genes _____ genome

_____ chromosomes _____ nucleus _____ nucleotides _____ DNA

EXERCISE 4 **Using key terms in genetics**

Test your knowledge of the key terms you learned in Exercise 3 on page 193 by placing the words in the appropriate sentences below. These sentences are from readings on genetics. The first one is completed as an example. Try to complete the items you feel confident about first, and then eliminate the words as you use them in order to finish this exercise. Refer to your definitions from Exercise 3 to help you.

1. Gregor Mendel, an Austrian monk, theorized that hereditary characteristics are determined by pairs of particles called *factors* (later termed genes, the specialized sequences of __molecules__ that form the genotype).

2. Mendel also outlined the basic principle by which _____ are transferred from one generation to another.

3. At about the same time Mendel's research was published, biologists discovered _____, long, threadlike cellular structures found in the nucleus of nearly every cell in the body.

4. Researchers have completed a map of the entire human _____, the set of genes and sequencing of complex molecules that make up the genetic information contained in all forty-six chromosomes.

5. The genes, in turn, are made up of various arrangements of four different chemical building blocks called _____ that contain one of four different nitrogen-based molecules (*adenine, thymine, cytosine,* or *guanine*).

6. The nucleotides link together in one of only two kinds of pairings to
    form the rungs of a remarkably long, spiral, ladderlike structure called
    _____, or deoxyribonucleic acid.

7. I don't know when I first became aware of science's efforts to weave all
    the world's _____ into a great family tree, systematically
    relating one thing to another by way of likeness.

8. When I was twelve or thirteen, my father taught me the Latin
    binominals for common _____ of birds: *Dendroica
    pinus, Dendroica discolor, Sitta carolinensis, Sitta pusilla.*

9. Charles Darwin gave ground for the view that the likenesses Linnaeus
    observed were quite literally *family* likenesses, that individual species
    were netted together by threads of _____.

10. All modern species diverged from a set of ancestors which themselves
    had _____ from still fewer ancestors, going back to the
    beginning of life.

Sources: Bukatko, D., & Daehler, M. W. (2001). *Child Development: A Thematic Approach* and Ackerman, J. (2001). *Chance in the House of Fate: A Natural History of Heredity,* both published by Houghton Mifflin Company.

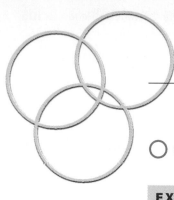

Reading Assignment 1

GENETICS AND HEREDITY

○ **Getting Ready to Read**

EXERCISE 5 Previewing the text

Reading Selection 1, "Genetics and Heredity," is from a textbook on child development. Before you read, preview the text by answering the questions below. Share your answers with your classmates.

1. In your own words, what does the title of the reading mean? What does the title tell you about the content of the reading?

2. Look at the subheadings in the reading: "Principles of Hereditary Transmission" and "The Building Blocks of Heredity."
   a. What does each subheading mean?
   b. What areas of genetics do you think the first section of the reading will cover?
   c. What might the second section cover?

3. This selection also contains a figure on page 202. Study the drawings in the figure, and scan the captions above and below the drawings (numbered 1, 2, etc.).
   a. Which areas of genetics presented in the figure have you previously studied?
   b. Which areas are unfamiliar or unclear to you?

4. Notice that key terms in genetics are printed in **bold** type in the reading.
   a. Scan the selection to find key terms.
   b. In your notebook, list the key terms. You will study them after you read.

EXERCISE 6 **Reading the text introduction**

As you observed in previous chapters, reading selections sometimes begin with an introductory passage. Reading Selection 1, "Genetics and Heredity," has a two-paragraph introduction, printed on pages 198–199 in italicized type. Read the introduction, and then answer the questions below. Discuss your answers in a group.

1. From the introduction, what topic or topics can you infer that the reading will cover?

   _____

   _____

   _____

2. Why would geneticists be interested in the twins Jasmine and Alyssa?

   _____

   _____

   _____

3. How are these twin sisters similar? How are they different?

   _____

   _____

   _____

4. The introduction closes with a question: *Why were they similar in so many ways but at the same time clearly different?* Write your ideas about the question.

   _____

   _____

   _____

5. Why do you think the textbook writer began the reading with this introduction?

   _____

   _____

   _____

Reading Selection 1

GENETICS AND HEREDITY

1   *"Make a wish before you blow out the candles!" But before Sheila could finish speaking, all twelve candles had been extinguished. It had been a great birthday party for the two five-year-olds and their guests. Fortunately, enough candles had been found to signal each year of growth and to continue the custom of adding "one to grow on."*

2   *When Sheila first learned that she would become a mother, she had not realized just how much work it would be to rear a child, even though her husband had been an enormous help. Then again, she had not planned on having identical twins! Thus, for this party (as for just about everything else) there were two cakes to be decorated, two presents to be wrapped, two sets of friends to invite to the festivities. Jasmine and Alyssa seemed to bask in the attention they were receiving on their special day. Their excited voices sounded so much alike, indistinguishable by others, including their parents, unless the listener could see which of the twins was speaking (and could remember what each was wearing for the day). The twins enjoyed many of the same games and activities; they displayed the same impatience when others couldn't tell whether they were speaking with Jasmine or Alyssa. But there were differences, too. Jasmine was more*

impulsive, willing to try new things, likely to jump into the fray of things without a second thought, and less sensitive to the concerns of others. Alyssa was more cautious and careful and seemed to become upset easily, but she was also more willing to help her friends. And although they shared many friends, each twin had preferences for certain playmates. For their mother, it was a puzzle: Why were they similar in so many ways but at the same time clearly different?

Principles of Hereditary Transmission

3   Whether we have freckles, blonde hair, or a certain type of personality can be influenced by genetic factors, but none of these characteristics is bestowed[1] on us at conception any more directly than our ultimate height is. We must make a distinction, then, between what is supplied as our genetic makeup and the kinds of individuals we eventually become. That difference serves as the basis for distinguishing between **genotype**, a person's constant, inherited genetic endowment, and **phenotype**, an individual's observable, measurable features, characteristics, and behaviors. A given phenotype is the product of complex interactions involving the genotype and the many events that comprise an individual's *experience*.

4   Modern theories of the genotype can be traced to a series of experiments reported in 1866 by Gregor Mendel, an Austrian monk. From his observations of the characteristics of successive generations of peas, Mendel theorized that hereditary characteristics are determined by pairs of particles called *factors* (later termed genes, the specialized sequences of molecules that form the genotype). He also proposed that the information provided by the two members of a pair of genes is not always identical. These different forms of a gene are today known as **alleles**. The terms *gene* and *allele* are often used interchangeably, but an allele refers to the specific variation (and sometimes many possible variations exist) found in a particular gene.

---

1. **be•stowed** (bǐ stō´d) *tr.v.* gave or presented as a gift or an honor.

5   Mendel also outlined the basic principle by which genes are transferred from one generation to another. He concluded that offspring randomly receive one member of every pair of genes from the mother and one from the father. This is possible because the parents' **gametes**, or sex cells (egg and sperm), carry only one member of each pair of genes. Thus, when egg and sperm combined during fertilization, a new pair of genes, one member of the pair inherited from each parent, is reestablished in the offspring. That individual, in turn, may transmit either member of this new pair to subsequent children. In this way, a given genotype can be passed on from one generation to the next.

6   At about the same time Mendel's research was published, biologists discovered **chromosomes**, long, threadlike structures in the nucleus of nearly every cell in the body. In the early 1900s, several researchers independently hypothesized that genes are located on chromosomes. Yet another major breakthrough occurred in 1953 when James Watson and Frances Crick deciphered[2] the structure of chromosomes and, in so doing, proposed a powerfully elegant way by which genes are duplicated during cell division. By 1956, researchers had documented the existence of forty-six chromosomes in normal human body cells. [Researchers have completed a map of] the entire **human genome**, the set of genes and sequencing of complex molecules that make up the genetic information contained in all forty-six chromosomes (Collins et al., 1998[3]; Guyer & Collins, 1993[4]).

The Building Blocks of Heredity

7   How could hereditary factors play a part in the similarities displayed by Jasmine and Alyssa, or in a child's remarkable mathematical ability or yet another's mental retardation? To understand the genotype and its effects on appearance, behavior, personality, or intellectual ability, we must consider genetic mechanisms at many different levels.

---

2. **de•ci•phered** (dĭ sī′fərd) *tr.v.* read or interpreted something hard to understand; changed from a code to ordinary language.
3. Collins, F. S., Patrinos, A., Jordan, E., Chakravarti, A., Gesteland, R., Walters, L., & the Members of the DOE and NIH Planning Groups. (1998). New goals for the U.S. Human Genome Project: 1998–2003. *Science, 282,* 682–689.
4. Guyer, M. S., & Collins, F. S. (1993). The Human Genome Project and the future of medicine. *American Journal of Disease in Children, 147,* 1145–1152.

8   To begin with, every living organism is composed of cells—in
the case of mature humans, trillions of cells. As Figure 3.1 indicates
on page 202, within the nucleus of nearly all cells are the
chromosomes that carry genetic information critical to their
functioning. Genes, regions within the strands of chromosomes,
determine the production of enzymes and specific proteins in the
cell. The genes, in turn, are made up of various arrangements of four
different chemical building blocks called nucleotides that contain
one of four nitrogen-based molecules (*adenine, thymine, cytosine,* or
guanine). The nucleotides link together in one of only two kinds of
pairings to form the rungs of a remarkably long, spiral, ladderlike
structure called DNA or deoxyribonucleic acid (see Figure 3.1). An
average of about a thousand nucleotide pairs make up each gene,
although some genes have substantially more pairings (National
Research Council, 1998).[5] Specific genes differ from one another in
number and sequence of nucleotide pairings and in their location on
the chemical spiral staircases, or chains of DNA that we call the
chromosomes.

9   Just as Mendel had theorized, hereditary attributes are, in most
cases, influenced by pairs of genes or, more specifically, the two
allelic[6] forms of the pair. One member of the pair is located on a
chromosome inherited from the mother, the other on a
chromosome inherited from the father. These two chromosomes are
called *homologous* (similar). Human beings have twenty-three pairs,
or a total of forty-six chromosomes.

10   Hereditary contributions to development can be observed at
many levels. Figure 3.1 depicts five major levels. Nearly every cell
in the human body carries the genetic blueprint for development in
the chromosomes. Specific regions on each chromosome, the genes,
regulate protein and enzyme production and can be further
examined in terms of the nucleotides, chemical molecules that are
the building blocks for the genes. Each of these different levels of
the individual's biological makeup can offer insights into the
mechanisms by which the genotype affects the phenotype, the
observable expression of traits and behaviors.

5. National Research Council, Committee on Mapping and Sequencing the Human
   Genome. (1998). *Mapping and sequencing the human genome.* Washington, DC:
   National Academy Press.
6. **al•le•lic** (ă lē′lĭc) *adj.* Relating to alleles, or pairs of genes that occupy a specific
   position on a specific chromosome.

Figure 3.1 The Building Blocks of Heredity

1. The **human body** has about 10 trillion cells. Proteins determine the structure and function of each cell.

2. Most **cells** contain a nucleus. Located within the nucleus are forty-six chromosomes that carry the instructions that signal the cell to manufacture various proteins.

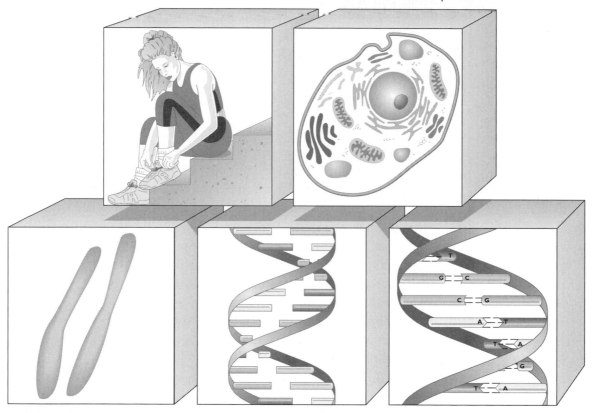

3. A **chromosome** is a long thin strand of DNA organized as a coiled double helix. A full set of forty-six chromosomes in humans is believed to contain somewhere between 26,000 and 38,000 genes, far fewer than had been believed before the human genome was mapped.

4. A **gene** is made up of thousands of nucleotide pairs. Each gene typically has information designed to specify the production of one or more particular proteins.

5. **Nucleotides**, composed of four different kinds of chemical building blocks—adenine (A), thymine (T), cytosine (C), and guanine (G)—are the smallest genetic unit and are paired in specific combinations. Nearly 3 billion pairs of nucleotides make up the total complement of DNA in humans.

Source: Bukatko, D., & Daehler, M.W. (1986). *Child Development: A Thematic Approach* (4th ed.). Boston: Houghton Mifflin Company, p. 68.[7]

7. Isensee, W. (1986, September 3). *The Chronicle of Higher Education, 33.*

○ Assessing Your Learning

Demonstrating Comprehension

EXERCISE **7** **Outlining major points**

Fill in the major points in the outline of Selection 1. Use words from the reading or your own words to fill in the missing information. Compare your outline with a partner's.

I. Principles of Hereditary Transmission

    A. ___Genotype___ means the genetic factors a person is born with.

    B. Phenotype is _____

    _____.

    C. Gregor Mendel studied _____.

        1. His theory: _____

        _____. These characteristics were

        later termed _____.

        2. Alleles are _____.

        3. Mendel: The basic principle for gene transfer from

        generation to generation is that _____

        _____.

    D. Biologists discovered _____, which are

    _____.

        1. Early 1900s: _____

        2. 1953: _____

        3. 1956: _____

        4. Researchers have completed a map of the _____,

        which is _____.

II. Building Blocks of Heredity

    A. Genetic mechanisms

        1. Every living thing is made of _____.

        2. Chromosomes are located _____.

        3. Genes are located _____.

        4. Genes contain four chemical building blocks, or _____

        _____.

            a. Each nucleotide has one of four _____:

            adenine, _____,

            _____, or _____.

            b. _____ connect to form a long,

            ladderlike structure called _____, or

            _____.

    B. Each human has _____ pairs, or a total

    of _____ chromosomes. One member

    of the pair of genes on a chromosome comes from the

    _____, and the other from the

    _____.

STRATEGY

Visual Aids in a Textbook

In academic reading, thinking through illustrations can help clarify difficult concepts. Textbooks like *Child Development: A Thematic Approach* use visual aids such as drawings, charts, and graphs to aid students' comprehension of textual information.

EXERCISE 8 **Using visual aids in a textbook**

With a group of your classmates, study Figure 3.1 on page 202. Examine each cubic drawing in the illustration, and read the caption under it. Discuss the following questions.

1. What does drawing 1 show? What does its caption mean? Which paragraphs from Reading Selection 1 tell about the same information as the drawing and caption?
2. What does drawing 2 show? What does its caption mean? Which paragraphs tell the same information? Does the picture help you better understand the text? If so, in what way?
3. Drawing 3 shows a chromosome. Why does the drawing show two objects? Which paragraphs give the same information as the caption? Which is easier to understand—the paragraph(s) from the reading or the caption? Why?
4. Drawings 4 and 5 are similar. What do both drawings depict? Read the captions of drawings 4 and 5. Which paragraph(s) have the same information as each drawing?
5. In general, do the drawings help you understand the reading selection? Which drawing(s) is most helpful?
6. Which parts of the illustration and the corresponding text do you still have trouble understanding?

 STRATEGY

Refining Paraphrasing Skills

To *paraphrase* means to restate a text or passage in another form or other words, often to clarify meaning. As you learned in Chapter 3, paraphrasing is a useful skill that may be applied to academic tasks.

Refining your paraphrasing skills can aid you in performing many essential academic tasks. In the following pages, you will:

- **Check your comprehension by identifying paraphrases** made from difficult sentences.
- **Clarify your understanding by writing your own paraphrases** of difficult sentences or passages.

- **Include your paraphrased sentences in a summary** of a reading, as you did in Chapter 3.

To refine your paraphrasing skills, follow these steps:

- **First, divide a complicated sentence into logical parts.** Look up unfamiliar words in a dictionary. You may want to underline sections and separate them by spaces, as in the example below.

Whether we have freckles, blonde hair, or a certain type of personality can be influenced by genetic factors, but none of these characteristics is bestowed on us at conception any more directly than our ultimate height is.

- **Next, paraphrase, or rewrite, the sentence section by section.** Follow these guidelines:

- **In general, try to use simpler vocabulary.**

1. Use synonyms whenever possible, as you learned in Chapter 3.
2. Don't change technological or scientific words, names of geographical places, parts of government, fields of study, or other types of specific or technical words.

- **In general, make the grammar simpler.**

1. Change word forms such as a *noun* form to an *adjective* form.
2. Make verbs simpler—for example, *is done* to *do*.
3. Change transition words and sentence connectors such as *on the other hand* to *but*.
4. You may reorder sections of the sentence to simplify the grammar.

Here is a possible paraphrase for the example sentence above. Notice how the paraphrase writer followed the guidelines above:

ORIGINAL

Whether we have freckles, blonde hair, or a certain type of personality can be influenced by genetic factors, but none of these characteristics is bestowed on us at conception any more directly than our ultimate height is.

PARAPHRASE

Our skin, hair, personality, and height are all affected by genetic factors.

EXERCISE 9 **Analyzing paraphrases**

In the box below, read each original sentence from Reading Selection 1, "Genetics and Heredity." Sections of each sentence have been underlined to show which groups of words go together logically. Next, read the paraphrase of each sentence. Identify each section of the paraphrase that matches the ideas in a section of the original sentence. Underline the sections. Draw a line to connect the matching sections. Above each paraphrased sentence, make notes about the kinds of changes made from the original sentence to the paraphrase. Consult the above guidelines for paraphrasing. Discuss your answers in a group. The first one is done for you as an example.

Original	Paraphrase
1. We must make a distinction, then, between what is supplied as our genetic makeup and the kinds of individuals we eventually become.	*Synonyms: "make a distinction" = understand the difference* We must understand the difference *Synonym: "makeup" = characteristics* between our genetic characteristics. *Synonyms: "individuals" = person: "eventually" = later* the person we later become
2. That difference serves as the basis for distinguishing between genotype, a person's constant, inherited genetic endowment, and phenotype, an individual's observable, measurable features, characteristics, and behaviors.	2. Genotype means what we get from our genes, and phenotype refers to the characteristics and behavior we display.
3. A given phenotype is the product of complex interactions involving the genotype and the many events that comprise an individual's experience.	3. A person's phenotype comes from both her or his genes and experience.

EXERCISE 10 Identifying paraphrases

Study each original sentence from Reading Selection 1, in the left-hand column below. Reread the paragraph of the reading in which each sentence appears. Then, choose a sentence on the right that best paraphrases each original sentence. Write the appropriate letter next to each original sentence. Check your answers in your group, and discuss the differences between the original sentences and their paraphrases.

Original	Paraphrase
_____ 1. From his observations of the characteristics of successive generations of peas, Mendel theorized that hereditary characteristics are determined by pairs of particles called *factors* (later termed genes, the specialized sequences of molecules that form the genotype). (¶ 4)	A. During fertilization, a new offspring receives one gene each from each of its parents, so its genetic makeup is different from its parents'.
_____ 2. He [Mendel] concluded that offspring randomly receive one member of every pair of genes from the mother and one from the father. (¶ 5)	B. Researchers have made a "map" of all the chromosomes that humans have.
_____ 3. Thus, when egg and sperm combined during fertilization, a new pair of genes, one member of the pair inherited from each parent, is reestablished in the offspring. (¶ 5)	C. Mendel's research proved that a living thing gets one gene each from each of its parents.
_____ 4. That individual, in turn, may transmit either member of this new pair to subsequent children. (¶ 5)	D. Then, when the offspring has its own offspring, it will transmit one of its genes to the new offspring.

Original	Paraphrase
_____ 5. [Researchers have completed a map of] the entire human genome, the set of genes and sequencing of complex molecules that make up the genetic information contained in all forty-six chromosomes. (¶ 6)	E. Genes (which are parts of a chromosome) control the amount of protein and enzymes a living thing produces. Genes, in turn, are made up of chemicals.
_____ 6. Specific genes differ from one another in number and sequence of nucleotide pairings and in their location on the chemical spiral staircases, or chains of DNA that we call the chromosomes. (¶ 8)	F Mendel called genes "factors." From his study of peas, he discovered that hereditary traits (the "factors") are passed from generation to generation.
_____ 7. Specific regions on each chromosome, the genes, regulate protein and enzyme production and can be further examined in in terms of the nucleotides, chemical molecules thatare the building blocks for the genes. (Figure 3.1)	G. Every level of a person's genetic makeup gives us more information about the effects inherited genes have on a person's phenotype, or behavior.
_____ 8. Each of these different levels of theindividual's biological makeup can offer insights intothe mechanisms by which the genotype affects thethe phenotype, the observable expression of traits and behaviors. (Figure 3.1)	H. Each gene is different because it has a different pair of nucleotides in a different order on the DNA "ladder."

STRATEGY

Citations in Academic Texts

Scientific readings commonly contain citations, or references to authoritative sources that help support ideas mentioned in the text. As you learned in Chapter 2, citations are indicators of research, so they strengthen a reading by providing evidence that the information presented has been confirmed by an authority or by research.

In Reading Selection 1, the citations in parentheses in the body of the text identify an author and the date of her or his publication. Footnotes at the bottom of the reading pages further identify the sources. Here are some common characteristics of citations:

- The citation begins with the author (last name, first initial or name) of the source material.
- The year of publication is usually included.
- The title of an article is printed in regular type. The title of a book, magazine, journal (a scholarly magazine), or newspaper is printed in italic type or underlined. The citation may also include page numbers of the periodical in which a source article appeared.
- The place and publisher of books is included.

EXERCISE 11   **Reading citations in a text**

Scan Reading Selection 1 to find the four footnotes that contain citations to the sources of ideas presented in the reading. Write the appropriate footnote number next to the correct descriptions in the chart.

Footnote Number	Description
_____	This footnote cites an article from *Science* magazine about the Human Genome Project.
_____	This footnote tells where the textbook writer got the information from the illustration on page 202. The information came from an article in a newspaper, *The Chronicle of Higher Education*.
_____	This footnote indicates the information came from a book about the Human Genome Project, published by National Academy Press.
_____	This footnote comes from an article in the *American Journal of Disease in Children*. The article connects the Human Genome Project with medicine.

○ Questions for Discussion

EXERCISE 12 **Participating in group discussion**

The terms genotype *and* phenotype *may seem difficult to grasp, but if you read further and discuss the terms, you can gain a basic understanding of these concepts. Discuss the following questions with a group of your classmates.*

1. Read the short definitions below. What do you think are the differences between these two words?

   gen-o-type, *n.* Total genetic endowment inherited by an individual
   phe-no-type, *n.* Observable and measurable characteristics and traits of an individual

Definitions of *genotype* and *phenotype* from Bukatko, D., & Daehler, M. W. (2001). *Child Development: A Thematic Approach.* Boston: Houghton Mifflin Company, p. 66.

2. Next, look over the following questions to guide your reading focus. Then read the three paragraphs about genotype and phenotype below the questions that further clarify the two terms. Be prepared to discuss answers to the questions after you read.

   A. How does the text define *genotype*?
   B. How does a person's genotype affect her or his *phenotype*?
   C. What is a *dominant* allele?
   D. What is a *recessive* allele?
   E. What blood type will a child have when one parent has Type A blood and the other has Type O? Why?
   F. So, if we use the letter A to stand for Type A blood and O to stand for Type O blood, which letter or letters best represent the offspring's *genotype*? Which letter or letters best represent the offspring's *phenotype*?

   How does the genotype affect the phenotype? That is, how does the underlying genetic blueprint promote the appearance of blue eyes, baldness, and dark skin or such complex traits as shyness, schizophrenia, and intelligent problem solving? The answer begins with the alleles, the specific form a particular gene may take.

We have already learned that each of us typically inherits two genes that code a particular enzyme or protein in the cell, one from our mother and the other from our father. These may be identical—that is, have the same allelic form—or they may differ. When both have the same allelic form, a person's genotype is said to be **homozygous**[1] for whatever characteristic that gene affects. For example, three different alleles exist for the gene that governs blood type: A, B, and O. When both inherited alleles are A, both B, or both O, a person has a homozygous genotype for blood type. But if an individual inherits two different alleles of the gene for blood type, let's say A and B, that person's genotype is **heterozygous;**[2] he or she has Type AB blood.

The consequences of a homozygous genotype are usually straightforward: the child's phenotype will be influenced by whatever characteristics are specified by that particular allelic form. But the effects of a heterozygous genotype depends on how the alleles influence each other. When a child's phenotype shows the effects of only one of the two allelic forms, the one whose characteristics are observed is **dominant;**[3] the allelic form whose influence is not evident in the phenotype is **recessive.**[4] For example, a person who inherits both an A and an O allele for blood type will still be classified as having Type A; the allele for Type A is dominant and the allele for Type O recessive.

Source: Bukatko, D., & Daehler, M. W. (2001). *Child Development: A Thematic Approach.* Boston: Houghton Mifflin Company, pp. 71–72.

1. **ho•mo•zy•gous** (hō′mō-zī′gəs) *adj.* Having a genotype in which two alleles of a gene are different. The effects on a trait will depend on how the two alleles interact.
2. **het•er•o•zy•gous** (hĕt′ər-ə-zī′gəs) *adj.* Having a genotype in which two alleles of a gene are different. The effects on a trait will depend on how the two alleles interact.
3. **dom•i•nant al•lele** (dŏm′ə-nənt) *n.* Allele whose characteristics are reflected in the phenotype even when part of a heterozygous genotype. Its genetic characteristics tend to mask the characteristics of other alleles.
4. **re•ces•sive al•lele** (rĭ-sĕs′ĭv) *n.* Allele whose characteristics do not tend to be expressed when part of a heterozygous genotype. Its genetic characteristics tend to be masked by other alleles.

STRATEGY

Transferring Insights from Reading to Your Own Life

You don't need to treat reading about an intriguing academic subject such as genetics like just another reading assignment. Apply the information and insights you gain from academic reading to your own life. In the case of the Chapter 5 theme, you can understand more about your genetic makeup when you transfer the information in the reading selections to your own life. At the same time, you will gain a better understanding of the concepts in your reading.

EXERCISE 13 Transferring insights to your own life

Read the list of dominant and recessive traits below. Think about your own physical characteristics and those of your parents and siblings. In the chart, write S next to each trait you have.

If you don't have a large family, think about another family you know well as you read the list of traits. In the chart, write O next to each trait that one offspring in the family has.

Then, answer the questions that follow.

Alleles of Genes That Display a Dominant and Recessive Pattern of Phenotypic Expression

Dominant traits	Mother, father, or self?	Recessive traits	Mother, father, or self?
Brown eyes		Gray, green, blue, hazel eyes	
Curly hair		Straight hair	
Normal amount of hair		Baldness	
Dark hair		Light or blond hair	

Alleles of Genes That Display a Dominant and Recessive Pattern of Phenotypic Expression

Dominant traits	Mother, father, or self?	Recessive traits	Mother, father, or self?
Nonred hair (blond, brunette)		Red hair	
Thick lips		Thin lips	
Roman nose		Straight nose	
Earlobe free		Earlobe attached	
Cheek dimples		No dimples	
Second toe longer than big toe		Big toe longer than second toe	
Farsightedness		Normal vision	

Source: Bukatko, D., & Daehler, M. W. (2001). *Child Development: A Thematic Approach*. Boston: Houghton Mifflin Company, p. 73.

Answer the following questions.

1. Think of a set of parents (your own or another set). Which of the dominant traits above does each parent have? Write *M* next to traits the mother has, and *F* next to the traits the father has. (Skip those traits for which you have no information.)

2. Which of these characteristics have been passed down to the parents' offspring (you, or someone else you know)? Were the same characteristics passed down to all the offspring? If not, explain where the differences appeared. (Skip those traits for which you have no information.)

How can you explain the differences in each pair of traits passed down from parents to offspring?

○ Reading Journal

Reread the introductory passage of Reading Selection 1. The mother of the twins asks this question: "Why were they similar in so many ways but at the same time clearly different?" Use the knowledge you have gained from the reading and the postreading exercises to write a one-page journal entry to answer this question. In your answer, discuss each twin's genotype and phenotype. Support your ideas with examples of siblings you know who have similarities and differences.

○ Learning Vocabulary

EXERCISE 14 **Reviewing academic vocabulary**

Study the list of academic vocabulary items in Reading Selection 1. Put a check mark next to the words you already know. Create word study cards for words that are unfamiliar to you. Follow the guidelines suggested in Chapter 3. Write the word, its pronunciation, its part of speech, its definition, and a sentence using the word on the card. Copy a sentence from the reading passage in which the word appears, or write your own sentence using the word.

| _____ conception | _____ constant | _____ complex |
| _____ comprise | _____ concluded | _____ displayed |

Front of the card
VOCABULARY WORD: conception
Part of Speech: noun
Pronunciation and stress: ken-səp´-shən

Back of the card

Word in use: . . . None of these characteristics is bestowed on us at
conception.

A definition: fertilization; the entity formed by the union of the male
sperm and female ovum; the ability to form or
understand mental concepts; something conceived in
the mind

Word family
members: conceptional, *adj*; conceptive, *adj*; conceptively, *adv*

Collocation: The parents were uncertain about the date of the
conception of their child.

EXERCISE 15   **Understanding key terms in genetics**

*Reread the key terms you studied in Exercise 3 (p. 193). Read the sentences
in which each key term is used correctly.*

*Next, test your understanding of additional key terms in genetics that
appear in Reading Selection 1. Use the terms in the list below to complete
the sentences in the two paragraphs that follow.*

genotype	phenotype	genetic makeup	offspring
alleles	gametes	recessive	traits

"THE FATHER OF GENETICS"

Gregor Mendel was an Austrian monk who studied how

(1) _____ are passed from parents to their

(2) _____. For fourteen years, Mendel observed pea

plants, and then concluded that offspring plants contained factors, or

genes, for tallness or seed color and size. According to Mendel, each

characteristic is determined by a single pair of genes, and each form

of the gene, called an (3) _____, is either dominant or

(4) _____.

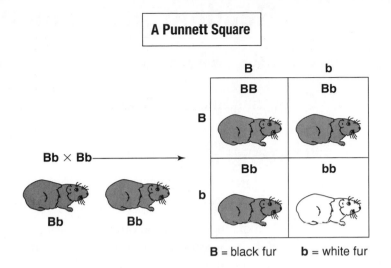

B = black fur   b = white fur

"PUNNETT SQUARES"

British geneticist Reginald C. Punnett created a chart called a Punnett Square to show the possible gene combinations between two organisms. The squares shown here represent the first (F_1) and second (F_2) generation of offspring from two parent guinea pigs, one with black hair and one with white hair. The squares confirm Mendel's findings: that from the parents' (**5**) _____, or sex cells, offspring receive one member of every pair of genes from the mother and one from the father. The squares also clarify the terms *genotype* and *phenotype*. Notice that each of the F_1 guinea pigs carries genes for hair color from both parents: Bb. However, their physical appearance, or (**6**) _____, looks the same as a pure black-haired guinea pig (BB). Each F_1 offspring still carries the white hair gene; therefore, Bb represents the offspring's (**7**) _____. The *genotype* is the organism's actual (**8**) _____, which includes the observable *phenotype.*

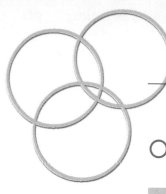

Reading Assignment 2

THE REAL EVE

○ **Getting Ready to Read**

EXERCISE 16 Previewing the text

As you did in Chapter 2, preview Reading Selection 2, "The Real Eve," by reading the first paragraph. Then, answer the questions that follow.

1. The question "How did our species arise and spread around the globe to become the most dominant creature on the planet?" is raised in this paragraph. In your own words, what does the question mean?
2. What did genetic research uncover two decades ago?
3. What details about this event are still unclear?

EXERCISE 17 Understanding key terms in science

Reading Selection 2 contains key terms in the scientific fields of genetics, archaeology, and geology. In the list below are some terms you will find in the reading. Use each term to complete one of the sentences below, taken from the selection.

fossils	conception	interbreeding
mitochondria	DNA	mutations

1. Based on analysis of thousands of _____ samples from people worldwide, Richards' research reveals a detailed map of the human family tree and its various branches.

2. During _____, half the mother's DNA and half the father's DNA merge to create a unique suite of genes that goes into creating a human being.

3. Part of every cell in the human body, _____ produce the energy needed by all living creatures and, remarkably, possess their own DNA that is completely independent of the principal cellular DNA residing in the nucleus.

4. That's because like all DNA, mtDNA is subject to random _____ over the eons. And because these mutations are passed intact to the next generations, they in effect become "tracers" of family branches.

5. While the two species of humans shared the continent for more than 10,000 years, recent studies of DNA drawn from Neanderthal _____ reveal that there was no _____ between the two populations that left a trace in the modern world.

Reading Selection 2

THE REAL EVE

By William F. Allman

1 The greatest journey ever undertaken left behind a trail of unanswered questions: How did our species arise and spread around the globe to become the most dominant creature on the planet? Part of the answer came two decades ago, when scientists stunned the world with the finding, based on genetic research, that all humans alive today can claim as a common ancestor a woman who lived in Africa some 150,000 years ago—dubbed,[1] inevitably, "Eve." But while the notion of an African origin of the human family has grown to be accepted by most scientists, the details of how Eve's ancestors swept out of Africa to populate the rest of the world have remained murky.[2]

1. **dubbed** (dŭbd) *tr.v.* Gave a humorous name or nickname to.
2. **murk•y** (mûr′kē) *adj.* Unclear, cloudy.

2   Now a team of scientists claim that, based on research on the ancient climate, findings in archaeology and a new, clearer genetic picture of how the human family tree has branched over the eons,[3] the ancient itinerary of the human diaspora[4] can finally be pieced together. It is an epic story of escape from starvation, glaciers and volcanoes, and braving shark-infested waters in flimsy rafts. And like any good tale, it has a surprise ending: Contrary to established thinking, it appears that our human ancestors took a more southerly route out of Africa, traveling east across the Red Sea into what is now Yemen, and then through India and all the way to the far reaches of Australia, before they swung up into Europe. "There was only one migration out of Africa," says Stephen Oppenheimer of Oxford University, who is a leading proponent of this new synthesis of our species' incredible journey. "They couldn't go north—that was blocked by a desert—so they had to go south."

3   A crucial cornerstone of Oppenheimer's piecing together of the human itinerary is the recent finding by Huddersfield University geneticist Martin Richards and his colleagues that the world's entire population can be traced back to a family tree that has its roots in Africa and a single branch leading out of the continent and into the rest of the world. Based on analysis of thousands of DNA samples from people worldwide, Richards' research reveals a detailed map of the human family tree and its various branches.

Digging Through Genes

4   Richards' research extended the work of scientists over the past two decades who have been reconstructing human origins by studying snippets[5] of DNA from tiny cellular structures called mitochondria. Part of every cell in the human body, mitochondria produce the energy needed by all living creatures and, remarkably, possess their own DNA that is completely independent of the principal cellular DNA residing in the nucleus. Known as mitochondrial DNA—or mtDNA—this genetic material has a property that makes it a unique tool for studying human origins: During conception, half the mother's DNA and half the father's DNA merge to create a unique suite of genes that goes into creating a human being. But mtDNA does not undergo this genetic reshuffling;

---

3. **e•on** (ē′ŏn) *n.* Extremely long period of time; division of geologic time.
4. **di•as•po•ra** (dī-ăs′pər-ə) *n.* A dispersion of a people from their homeland.
5. **snip•pet** (snĭp′ĭt) *n.* Bit, scrap, or morsel.

rather, the mitochondria—along with their mtDNA—in a sperm cell wither and die, while the mitochondria present in the egg cell live on intact from generation to generation. Thus everyone carries with them a more-or-less exact copy of the mtDNA from their mother, and their mother's mother, and her mother, and her mother, and so on back through countless generations.

5   The term "more or less exact" is the key to scientists solving the mystery of human origins. That's because like all DNA, mtDNA is subject to random mutations over the eons. And because these mutations are passed intact to the next generations, they in effect become "tracers" of family branches. If two strands of mtDNA from two different people reveal the same mutation, these people must share the same ancient great-great-great-grandmother from whence this mutation arose. Working from the a̲s̲s̲u̲m̲p̲t̲i̲o̲n̲ that genetic mutations occur more or less regularly over time, scientists can compare two samples of mtDNA, noting where they have shared mutations and where they do not share mutations, and resolve the time in prehistory when the peoples' ancestral populations diverged. Using this technique, researcher Rebecca Cann and her c̲o̲l̲l̲e̲a̲g̲u̲e̲s̲ showed that all humans can be traced back to an ancient mitochondrial "Eve" who lived in Africa perhaps 150,000 years ago.

6   This "Eve" was by no means the source of all the genes in the world's living population. After all, each person is a reshuffled combination of 30,000 genes from many different ancestors stretching back generations. But each person's mtDNA is a copy from only one direct line of ancestors: their mother's mother's mother's mother, etc. In the same way, the mtDNA from Eve merely acts as a tracer that links all present-day humans to a single population of ancient humans, estimated at 10,000 people or so, who lived in Africa several hundred thousand years ago.

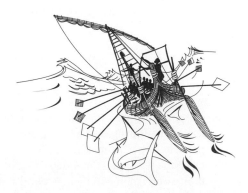

The Climate Connection

7   While Richards' genetic research suggests that only one branch of ancient humans migrated out of Africa to give rise to modern populations, research on ancient climate changes helps pinpoint the time when this migration must have occurred, argues Oppenheimer. Some 80,000 years ago, the world's climate began to cool into a period of glaciation.[6] The polar ice caps reached far down into Europe, lowering sea levels and turning much of Africa into arid desert. This climatic shift occurred roughly at the time when the genetic evidence suggests that the tree of human life sprouted a branch that crossed onto the Arabian Peninsula toward India and Southeast Asia. Indeed, notes Oppenheimer, human-made tools dating back nearly 75,000 years have been found as far east as Malaysia. From there, our human ancestors pushed across shark-infested waters to Australia, where they left behind stone artifacts dating back 60,000 years. There were no doubt other human migrations out of Africa before this time. For example, ancient human remains dating from 100,000 to 120,000 years ago have been unearthed in what is now Israel. However, these populations, like others, perished[7] without leaving their genetic imprint on present-day humans. By the time the climatic changes gave rise to the exodus[8] some 80,000 years ago, the migration pathway out of Africa through the Near East was blocked by the Sahara desert, says Oppenheimer, and so the only way out was southward.

8   It was only after the climate shifted again some 50,000 years ago, creating strong monsoons[9] that turned what was once desert into the lush growth of the so-called "Fertile Crescent" stretching from the Arabian Gulf to Turkey, that humans had the pathway to begin the push into what is now modern-day Europe. The land at that time was populated by another kind of human—Neanderthals—who had reached there hundreds of thousands of years before.

---

6. **gla•ci•a•tion** (glā´cē ā´shŭn) *n.* Condition of being covered with a huge mass of ice slowly flowing over a land mass.
7. **per•ished** (pĕr´ĭshd) *v.* Died.
8. **ex•o•dus** (ĕk´sə-dəs) *n.* A departure of a large number of people.
9. **mon•soon** (mŏn-sōōn´) *n.* A Wind system that influences large climatic regions and reverse direction seasonally; the rains that accompany these winds.

9   While the two species of humans shared the continent for more than 10,000 years, recent studies of DNA drawn from Neanderthal fossils reveal that there was no interbreeding between the two populations that left a trace in the modern world. Indeed, nearly all Europeans—and by extension, many Americans—can trace their ancestors to only four mtDNA lines, which appeared between 10,000 and 50,000 years ago and originated from South Asia.

The Incredible Journey

10   The final stage in the human odyssey[10] was again triggered[11] by climate change: The genetic evidence suggests that as the seas retreated during the buildup of the polar ice caps 20,000 to 25,000 years ago, humans crossed over the bridge of land—now underwater—that connects what is now Siberia and Alaska, says Cambridge University's Peter Forster. The distinctive markers in the strands of mtDNA they brought with them are still found in Siberia and Asia today. These ancient humans spread throughout all of the Americas, surviving the intense glaciation that followed, and leaving stone tools dating back 16,000 years at a site in present-day Pennsylvania. The peopling of the planet was complete.

11   Despite the sweeping saga of migration and branching of the human family tree over the past 7,000 generations since "Eve," perhaps the most startling result of the new picture of human evolution is how very closely related are all humans. In fact, the research reveals that there is less genetic variation among Earth's entire population of humans than there is in a typical troop of our closest relative, the chimpanzee. In the quest[12] to find ancient family ties, one need look only to one's neighbor—or to the far end of the globe. "We are all born with an extraordinary interest in where we came from, and who our relatives are," says Oppenheimer. "This really brings home that we are just one big, very close family."

Source: Article "Eve Explained: How Ancient Humans Spread Across the Earth" at Discovery Channel website
http://dsc.discovery.com/convergence/realeve/feature/feature.html.

10. **od•ys•sey** (ŏd´ĭ-sē) *n.* A long adventurous voyage or trip.
11. **trig•gered** (trĭg´ərd) *tr.v.* Set off; initiated.
12. **quest** (kwĕst) *n.* A search.

○ Assessing Your Learning

Demonstrating Comprehension

EXERCISE 18 Writing a main idea sentence

Write a sentence that summarizes the main idea of Reading Selection 2.
You may want to begin your sentence like this:

The main point of Selection 2, "The Real Eve," is _____

_____

_____

_____

_____

_____

_____

_____

Compare your sentence with those of your classmates.

EXERCISE 19 Outlining the reading selection

The headings in the reading selection help you identify its main sections.
On separate paper, use the information below to make a brief outline of the
reading. Under Roman numeral I, copy the main idea sentence you wrote
in Exercise 18. Then, copy one sentence each from paragraphs 2 and 3 that
states the major point of each paragraph. Under numerals II–IV, copy one
major point sentence per paragraph. Add one sentence at the end of section
IV that you think concludes the reading. Look back at the reading to find
the one sentence that states the major point of each paragraph in the
section. Part of numeral I in the outline is filled in as an example. Share
your outlines with a group of your classmates.

I. Introduction and Main Idea

    A. [Main idea]

    B. Now a team of scientists claim that, based on research on the ancient climate, findings in archaeology and a new, clearer genetic picture of how the human family tree has branched over the eons, the ancient itinerary of the human diaspora can finally be pieced together.

    C. A crucial cornerstone of Oppenheimer's piecing together of the human itinerary is the recent finding by Huddersfield University geneticist Martin Richards and his colleagues that the world's entire population can be traced back to a family tree that has its roots in Africa and a single branch leading out of the continent and into the rest of the world.

II. Digging Through Genes

    A.

    B.

    C.

    D.

III. The Climate Connection

    A.

    B.

    C.

IV. The Incredible Journey

    A.

    B.

    C. Conclusion

EXERCISE 20 Identifying paraphrases

Study each original sentence from Selection 2, in the left-hand column of the chart below. Reread the paragraph of the reading in which each sentence appears. Then, choose one of the two sentences on the right that better paraphrases each original sentence. Put a check mark next to the more accurate paraphrase. Check your answers in your group, and discuss the differences between the original sentences and their paraphrases.

Original	Paraphrase (Check one in each box.)
1. . . . two decades ago, . . . scientists stunned the world with the finding, based on genetic research, that all humans alive today can claim as a common ancestor a woman who lived in Africa some 150,000 years ago—dubbed, inevitably, "Eve." (¶ 1)	☐ Today's genetic researchers have discovered that all people have a common ancestor: an African woman who lived 150,000 years ago. ☐ Twenty years ago, genetic researchers discovered that all people descend from an African woman who lived 150,000 years ago.
2. But while the notion of an African origin of the human family has grown to be accepted by most scientists, the details of how Eve's ancestors swept out of Africa to populate the rest of the world have remained murky. (¶ 1)	☐ Most scientists accept that humans originated in Africa, but they don't know exactly how the original humans left Africa. ☐ Most scientists recognize that humans originated in Africa, and they are clear about how our ancient ancestors left Africa to populate the world.

Original	Paraphrase (Check one in each box.)
3. Now a team of scientists claim that, based on research on the ancient climate, findings in archaeology and a new, clearer genetic picture of how the human family tree has branched over the eons, the ancient itinerary of the human diaspora can finally be pieced together. (¶ 2)	☐ Due to new research, scientists now know more about ancient climate and archaeology. ☐ Due to new research in ancient climate, archaeology, and the history of human genetics, the route that the ancient humans took can be reconstructed.
4. Contrary to established thinking, it appears that our human ancestors took a more southerly route out of Africa, traveling east across the Red Sea into what is now Yemen, and then through India and all the way to the far reaches of Australia, before they swung up into Europe. (¶ 2)	☐ Ancient humans first traveled south as they left Africa and eventually moved into the Middle East, India, Australia, and Europe, as people believed. ☐ Ancient humans first traveled south as they left Africa and eventually moved into the Middle East, India, Australia, and Europe, unlike popular beliefs.
5. A crucial cornerstone of Oppenheimer's piecing together of the human itinerary is the recent finding by Huddersfield University geneticist Martin Richards and his colleagues that the world's entire population can be traced back to a family tree that has its roots in Africa and a single branch leading out of the continent and into the rest of the world. (¶ 3)	☐ An important piece in Oppenheimer's reconstruction of the route of ancient humans is research that finds a single movement of people from Africa to the rest of the world. ☐ An important piece in Oppenheimer's reconstruction of the route of ancient humans is research that finds that ancient trees in Africa were transplanted to other parts of the world.

EXERCISE 21   Paraphrasing major point sentences

Study the changes made in original sentence #3 from Exercise 20 and the simplified paraphrases (see below). Corresponding sections of the original sentences and the paraphrases are numbered and underlined. Did you select the more accurate paraphrase in Exercise 20?

Now that you have completed your outline of Selection 2, paraphrase each original sentence you copied and put into your outline. Follow the guidelines for paraphrasing on pages 204–206. On separate paper, rewrite the outline, replacing the original sentences with your paraphrased sentences.

---

3. Now a team of scientists claim that, (1) <u>based on research on the ancient climate, findings in archaeology and a new, clearer genetic picture of how the human family tree has branched over the eons,</u> (2) <u>the ancient itinerary of the human diaspora can finally be pieced together.</u> (¶ 2)

☐ (1) <u>As a result of new research, scientists now know more about ancient climate and archaeology.</u>

☐ (1) <u>As a result of new research in ancient climate, archaeology, and history of human genetics,</u> (2) <u>the route that the ancient humans took can be reconstructed.</u>

EXERCISE 22   Writing a brief summary

Use your outline to write a brief summary of Reading Selection 2, "The Real Eve." To show the order of ideas from one section to the next, you may want to add chronological organizers like first, next, in the third part of the reading, in conclusion, *and so on. Compare your summary with a partner's.*

> Reading Selection 2, "The Real Eve" by William F. Allman, explains how ancient humans spread cross the Earth. More importantly, the article suggests that based on genetic research, all humans alive today . . .

○ Questions for Discussion

EXERCISE 23   **Developing a perspective through research**

Selection 2, "The Real Eve," presents an explanation related to the origin of humans. This explanation is based on scientific research in genetics, archaeology, and related scientific fields. As you think about the information presented in the reading, try to "step outside" the realm of your previous beliefs and knowledge and consider the information from the perspective of a geneticist or archaeologist. Discuss the following questions with a group of classmates.

1. What is your overall reaction to the scientific research findings presented in Reading Selection 2, "The Real Eve"? Do you believe them? Explain.

     _____

2. The reading states that "all humans alive today can claim as a common ancestor a woman who lived in Africa some 150,000 years ago." Explain what that statement means to you.

     _____

3. What other knowledge or beliefs do you bring to the discussion of human origins? Does the reading selection confirm or contradict this information or belief system? Explain.

     _____

4. Has reading "The Real Eve" changed your perspective in any way? If so, explain.

     _____

5. How do you think scientists balance the findings of scientific research with their own beliefs about human origins?

     _____

○ Reading Journal

Write a one-page journal entry in answer to one or more of the discussion questions in Exercise 23. Include information from Reading Selection 2, "The Real Eve," and your own personal knowledge and beliefs in your journal entry.

◯ **Learning Vocabulary**

EXERCISE 24 **Reviewing academic vocabulary**

Study the list of the academic vocabulary items in Reading Selection 2. Put a check mark next to the words you already know. Create word study cards for words that are unfamiliar to you. Follow the guidelines suggested in Chapter 3. Write the word, its pronunciation, its part of speech, its definition, and a sentence using the word on the card. Copy a sentence from the reading passage in which the word appears, or write your own sentence using the word.

_____ decades	_____ contrary	_____ crucial
_____ colleagues	_____ analysis	_____ conception
_____ create		

EXERCISE 25 **Studying key terms in science disciplines**

Study the following charts listing science key terms found in Reading Selection 2. For each unfamiliar word, make a word study card. Work with a partner to test each other on words and definitions, using your word cards.

1. Key Term	**species**
Definition	*n.* A fundamental category of related organisms capable of interbreeding.
Word in Use	"How did our **species** arise and spread around the globe to become the dominant creature on the planet?" (¶ 1)

2. Key Term	**ancestor**
Definition	*n.* A person from whom one is descended.
Word in Use	"... [A]ll humans alive today can claim as a common **ancestor** a woman who lived in Africa some 150,000 years ago...." (¶ 1)

3. Key Term	**archaeology**
Definition	*n.* The study of past human life and culture.
Word in Use	"Now a team of scientists claim that, based on research on the ancient climate, findings in **archaeology** and a new, clearer picture of how the human family tree has branched over the eons, the ancient history of the human diaspora can finally be pieced together." (¶ 2)

4. Key Term	**mitochondria**
Definition	*n.pl.* Parts of a cell containing important genetic material.
Word in Use	"... scientists over the past two decades ... have been reconstructing human origins by studying snippets of DNA from tiny cellular structures called **mitochondria**." (¶ 4)

5. Key Term	**mutations**
Definition	*n.pl.* Alterations or changes, as in nature, form, or quality.
Word in Use	"... [L]ike all DNA, mtDNA is subject to random **mutations** over the eons." (¶ 5)

6. Key Term	**migrate**
Definition	*i.v.* To move from one country or region and settle in another.
Word in Use	"While Richards' genetic research suggests that only one branch of ancient humans migrated out of Africa...." (¶ 7)

7. Key Term	**artifacts**
Definition	*n.pl.* Objects produced or shaped by human craft, especially tools, weapons.
Word in Use	"From there, our human ancestors pushed across shark-infested waters to Australia, where they left behind stone artifacts dating back 60,000 years." (¶ 7)

8. Key Term	**Neanderthal**
Definition	*n.pl.* An extinct human species.
Word in Use	"The land at that time was populated by another kind of human—**Neanderthals**—who had reached there hundreds of thousands of years before." (¶ 8)

Your Word Study Card
Key Term
Definition
Word in Use

Reading Assignment 3

○ **Getting Ready to Read**

EXERCISE 26 Previewing the text

In Reading Selection 3, "The Great Family Tree," you will gain further information about genetics. As you did in Chapter 2, preview the text by reading the first two paragraphs of the selection. Then answer the following questions. Discuss your answers in a group.

1. How does the writer define "a great family tree" in paragraph 1?

   _____

   _____

2. What plant families (having common characteristics) does the writer describe?

   _____

   _____

3. What do the first two paragraphs say about the writer's childhood interests?

   _____

   _____

4. In paragraph 2, what words does the writer use to describe the sounds of birds?

   _____

   _____

5. What does the writer say about family ties among wrens?

   _____

   _____

S T R A T E G Y

Understanding Metaphors in Readings

Academic readings commonly rely on *metaphors* to explain key concepts. A *metaphor* is a figure of speech in which a word or phrase that usually describes one thing is used in place of another to suggest a likeness between them. Understanding metaphors will aid in your general reading comprehension as well as your comprehension of key concepts in difficult academic disciplines like genetics.

Study this sentence from Selection 1, "Genetics and Heredity," that uses a metaphor to help students understand the concept of *chromosomes*:

> . . . biologists discovered **chromosomes**, long threadlike structures in the nucleus of every cell in the body.

Here, *chromosomes* are described as *threads*. The metaphor is used to help students visualize a chromosome by comparing it to an everyday item: thread.

EXERCISE 27 Understanding metaphors

As you read Reading Selection 3, consider the metaphor presented in the title: "The Great Family Tree." Before you read, discuss the following questions with a group of your classmates. After you read, be prepared to discuss additional metaphors found in the reading.

1. The title of the reading is "The Great Family Tree." Here, a *tree* serves as a metaphor for a family with its members. How does the common item, the *tree*, help you understand connections between living things? Explain how the parts of the tree represent the parts of a family.
2. Have you ever seen or made a *family tree* for your family? How does such a drawing look? What makes it comparable to a tree?

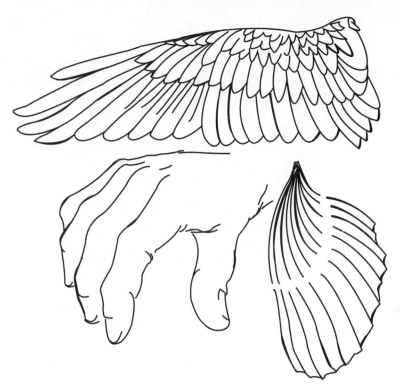

British scientist Richard Owen (1848) found homologies in diverse organisms.

Reading Selection 3

THE GREAT FAMILY TREE

By Jennifer Ackerman

1   I don't know when I first became <u>aware</u> of science's efforts to
weave all the world's organisms into a great family tree,
systematically relating one thing to another by way of likeness. I do
remember learning from my older sister the neat trick of spotting
families of flowers through common characteristics. The crucifers—
cabbage, turnip, radish—have a slender seedpod and four petals[1]
that form a cross. A violet you can tell by its five petals and by its
pistil,[2] shaped like a short beak. Through the mint family, Labiatae,
run two flaring lips, square stems, and a <u>distinctive</u> aroma.

1. **pe•tal** (pĕt′l) *n.* An often brightly colored part of a flower.
2. **pis•til** (pĭs′tĭl) *n.* The female, ovule-bearing organ of a flower.

2   When I was twelve or thirteen, my father taught me the Latin binomials[3] for common species of birds: *Dendroica pinus, Dencroica discolor, Sitta carolinensis, Sitta pusilla.* We rose early in the morning to watch birds together, moving quietly in late starlight. Small sounds would hatch[4] from the foliage,[5] not just the normal morning short calls, the hoots, squawks, jargles, whistles, and rasps, but clear strands of real music that seemed to be sung for joy. If luck was with us, we would be jogged awake by the thin fluting notes of a goldfinch or the chromatic[6] cry of a whitethroat. (Later I would learn the surprising fact that stripe-backed wrens so systematically pass their vocalization down from father to son and from mother to daughter, like a beloved heirloom,[7] that their songs are a highly reliable way of determining family ties.)

3   Most bird families were a joy to learn: the three little titmice, Paridae; three nuthatches, Sittadae; six swallows, Hirundinidae; seven woodpeckers, Picidae. I loved finding that I could join two birds and see in them one nature; then three birds; then twelve, the faint tracings of individual species converging into major family paths. I remember how the discovery that the natural world had been classified and given two-part scientific names—names that were, in fact, a way of weaving creatures together by natural principles of likeness—shot through me like a bolt of happiness.

4   In the eighteenth century Linnaeus arranged living things in a pattern based on these principles (and freely admitted to being the one chosen to do so, the one whom "God has suffered . . . to peep[8] into his secret cabinet"). I grew to love the Linnaean system, the great animal and botanical[9] divisions, the tidy nests within nests, all the shreds of creation revealed and broken down into pieces, then stitched back together in a great familial tree.

Swedish botanist and physician Carolus Linnaeus

3. **bi•no•mi•al** (bī-nō′mē-əl) *n.* Two-word scientific name of organisms.
4. **hatch** (hăch) *v.* To emerge from or break out, as of from an egg.
5. **fo•li•age** (fō′lē-ĭj) *n.* A cluster of leaves.
6. **chro•mat•ic** (krō-măt′ĭk) *adj.* Relating to chords or harmonies based on nonharmonic tones.
7. **heir•loom** (âr′lo͞om′) *n.* A valued possession passed down in a family through succeeding generations.
8. **peep** (pēp) *v.* To sneak a quick glance or look.
9. **bo•tan•i•cal** (bə-tăn′ĭ-kəl) *adj.* Relating to plants or plant life; relating to the science of botany.

English naturalist
Charles Darwin

5   Charles Darwin gave ground for the view that the likenesses Linnaeus observed were quite literally *family* likenesses, that individual species were netted together by threads of ancestry. As he wrote in *Origin of Species*: "All living things have much in common, in their chemical composition, their germinal[10] vesicles,[11] their cellular structure, and their laws of growth and reproduction." In the book's only illustration, Darwin showed variants within a species as branches of a tree. He later explained that the "limbs divided into great branches . . . were themselves once, when the tree was small, budding twigs." All modern species diverged from a set of ancestors, which themselves had evolved from still fewer ancestors, going back to the beginning of life. The relations among all could be represented as a single great dendritic[12] tree.

What Is Man? Sketch by English poet William Blake, 1793

10. **ger•mi•nal** (jûr´mə-nəl) *adj*. Relating to a germ cell; occurring in the earliest stages of development.
11. **ves•i•cle** (vĕs´ĭ-kəl) *n*. Small bladderlike cell or cavity.
12. **den•drit•ic** (dĕn-drĭt´ĭk) *adj*. Resembling a dendrite, a branched extension of a nerve cell.

6 Darwin himself was heir to assorted intuitions[13] on the kinship of living things. In 1793 William Blake wrote:

> Am not I
> A fly like thee?
> Or art not thou
> A man like me?

A drawing made by Blake the same year shows a caterpillar on a leaf arched over a lower leaf, on which reclines a second simple, cocoonlike[14] form, this one with the face of a baby. The drawing is titled *What Is Man?*

7 John Clare called flies "the small or dwarfish portion of our own family." That was in 1837, just before the English nature poet was declared insane and committed to an asylum.[15]

8 "It seems that Nature has taken pleasure in varying the same mechanism in an infinity of different ways," wrote the eighteenth-century French philosopher Denis Diderot. "She abandons one type of product only after having multiplied individuals in all possible modes."

9 Diderot's contemporary, the naturalist Georges Louis Leclerc, Comte de Buffon, came close to anticipating Darwin. He wrote, "It may be assumed that all animals arise from a single form of life which in the course of time produced the rest by process of perfection and degeneration." A single plan of organization could be traced back from man through fish, said Buffon in his encyclopedic *Histoire naturelle*.

---

13. **in•tu•i•tions** (ĭn´tōō-ĭsh´ənz) *n.* Acts of knowing or sensing without the use of rational processes; perceptive insights.

14. **co•coon•like** (kə-kōōn´ lĭk) *adj.* Resembling a cocoon, a protective case of silk spun by moths and some other insects.

15. **a•sy•lum** (ə-sī´ləm) *n.* An institution for the care of people who require organized supervision or assistance, especially those with physical or mental impairments.

10   Richard Owen, a quick-witted and prescient[16] British anatomist,[17] made detailed observations of the unities underlying life's wild range of differences. The wing of the bird, fin of the fish, hand of man, he wrote in 1848, were all built according to a single design. These "homologies"[18] were of far greater importance in the scheme of God's grand plan than the minor adaptations that distinguished the organ of one creature from that of the next.

11   The mind must embrace the whole and deduce a general type from it, wrote Goethe. The German polymath,[19] whose interest in unity grew out of the terrible divisions of his age, possessed the rare ability to leap from science to poetry and back, and—when he was not writing literature—did important work in anatomy, botany, and geology, coined the term "morphology,"[20] and even managed to discover a new bone in the human upper jaw. Goethe wrote that all individual organisms have universal tendencies, to transform themselves, to expand and contract, to divide and unite, to arise and vanish, and he claimed to have traced "the manifold[21] specific phenomena in the magnificent garden of the universe back to one simple general principle."

12   After Darwin, natural historians saw the reconstruction of life's tree as their most important task, scrutinizing the details of shape in adult animals and embryos,[22] the number of rays in a fin, of rows of scales, to deduce the degree of relation. From these, they drew up careful family descriptions, leaving little doubt that fish, amphibians, reptiles, birds, and mammals all descended from a common ancestor. But it would take another century, and a bevy[23]

16. **pre•scient** (prĕsh´ənt) *adj.* Relating to knowledge of actions or events before they occur.
17. **a•nat•o•mist** (ə-năt´ə-mĭst) *n.* An expert in or a student of anatomy, the science of the shape and structure of organisms.
18. **ho•mol•o•gies** (hə-mŏl´ə-jēz) *n.* Body parts similar in structure and evolutionary origin although not necessarily in function.
19. **pol•y•math** (pŏl´ē-măth´) *n.* A person of great or varied learning.
20. **mor•phol•o•gy** (môr-fŏl´ə-jē) *n.* The form and structure of an organism or one of its parts without considering the function.
21. **man•i•fold** (măn´ə-fōld´) *adj.* Many and varied.
22. **em•bry•os** (ĕm´brē-ōz´) *n.* Organisms in early stages of development, before they have reached recognizable forms.
23. **bev•y** (bĕv´ē) *n.* A group.

of bright, restless scientists with minds full of physics and with pluck on their side, to unmask the molecular likeness at the heart of life. Strung through all organisms was a single genetic thread made of the same molecular stitches. The difference between a bacterium and a bullfrog lay largely in the order and the sequence of those stitches as well as their total number.

13   So it was true. The whole code of nature could be written on a thumbnail. Compound it how you will, salamander, German philosopher, algal mat,[24] gingko tree, it is but one stuff, the eye of the needle through which all life passes. "Nature uses only the longest threads to weave her patterns," wrote the late physicist Richard Feynman, "so each small piece of her fabric reveals the organization of the entire tapestry."

14   The findings of the last few decades have made this fact more urgent. Among the genes for tune deafness and hairy palms in McKusick's masterly catalogue are genes for the making of cytochrome C, crystallin, ubiquitin, Hox proteins,[25] and other useful molecules, found not just in members of the human family but in nearly all organisms: worm, ladybird, siskin.[26] When scientists learned to read genes and compare them in separate organisms, their really big shock came on finding the easy way genes from vastly different creatures fell into families, with sequences of stitches so similar that they had to be of common ancestry. These small shared sequences were like family earmarks as distinctive as the square stem of the mint family.

24. **al•gal mat** (ăl′gəl măt) *n.* A thickly tangled mass of organisms that can make their own food and that range in size from a single cell to giant seaweed.
25. **Hox pro•teins** (hôx prō′tēnz) *n.* Groups of complex organic molecules that are fundamental components of living cells
26. **sis•kin** (sĭs′kĭn) *n.* Any of several small finches, a type of bird, found in North America.

15   If a gene has endured almost intact for millions of years in so
diverse a panoply[27] of creatures, it likely serves a vital purpose;
disable that gene, and the consequences may be catastrophic.
Scientists recently scratched around in the yeast genome[28] for
sequences like those in certain human genes that, when mutated,
are known to cause disease. They found that one in four of these
human genes matched a yeast gene, including one involved in
cystic fibrosis.[29] And listen to this, William Blake and John Clare:
of the 289 known human "disease" genes, 177 have direct
counterparts in the fruit fly. (This is good news for research on
disease. When scientists find a gene in a worm or a fly that matches
a human gene, they can study that gene and its functions more
easily in the simpler organism than they can in humans, whose
genomes are much more complicated.)

16   Accepted wisdom had it that genes were unique and
idiosyncratic, peculiar to particular species. But now it seems that
many are close relatives in one degree or another, belonging to one
of a few thousand families. Genes shared by the widest range of
organisms are probably modern versions of life's oldest genes.
Suddenly it's possible for scientists to draw up life's evolutionary
tree, to sort out the relations among modern creatures and their
distant ancestors, not on the loose basis of appearance—the shapes
of leaves and fins, the color of feathers, which are often deceptive—
but with tight molecular precision. By drawing the family trees of
genes in modern forms of life and running them backward to the
genes at the root of the tree, they may even define the nature of the
universal ancestor from which all life sprang.

Source: Ackerman, J. (2001). *Chance in the House of Fate: A Natural History of
Heredity.* New York: Mariner Books, pp. 9–13.

27. **pan•o•ply** (păn´ə-plē) *n.* A splendid or striking array, or display.
28. **ge•nome** (jē´nōm´) *n.* The total genetic content of an organism.
29. **cys•tic fi•bro•sis** (sĭs´tĭk fī-brō´sĭs) *n.* A hereditary disease of certain glands
    and in which thick mucus is produced that obstructs breathing.

◯ Assessing Your Learning

Demonstrating Comprehension

EXERCISE 28 Writing a general conclusion from research

As you studied in Chapter 4, scientists use the scientific method *to conduct research. The final step in the scientific method is to make a conclusion based on the results of the research. What general conclusion have scientists reached after years of scientific research? Write one sentence in your own words to express the conclusion reported in Selection 3. Keep in mind the title of the reading: "The Great Family Tree." Share your sentence with your classmates.*

_____

_____

_____

_____

EXERCISE 29 Scanning for information

The statements below summarize important discoveries in genetic history, which are described in Reading Selection 3. Match the information with a paragraph or paragraphs in the reading. Put the paragraph number or numbers in the blank. Compare your answers with a partner's.

1. _____ A scientist found that certain genes appeared in humans as well as nearly all other organisms.

2. _____ Two poets believed that humans and insects were similar.

3. _____ A famous scientist's studies led him to theorize that all modern species could be represented as one great family tree.

4. _____ Physicists uncovered the molecular similarity at the center of all living things.

5. _____ A pre-Darwin scientist stated that all animals come from a single life form.

6. _____ A writer and scientist theorized that all living things share such universal tendencies as changing themselves and becoming larger and smaller.

7. _____ Scientists now believe that genes shared by a variety of living things are likely similar to life's oldest genes.

8. _____ Later, scientists discovered that very different living things possessed similar genetic sequences.

9. _____ Scientists found that humans share genetic characteristics with flies and yeast.

10. _____ Scientists showed that all animals came from a common ancestor.

11. _____ A scientist grouped animals and plants into divisions.

12. _____ Another scientist saw "homologies," or similarities, in many animals.

S T R A T E G Y

Text Organization: Timelines

Reading Selection 3 presents a history of ideas and observations that scientists have made over time about genetics. One way to better understand the major points of the reading and connect the ideas together is to construct a *timeline* of the scientists and their ideas. A timeline is a schedule of key events within a certain historical time period.

Here is a timeline of some events described in Reading Selection 2, "The Real Eve."

"The Real Eve": From Africa to North America

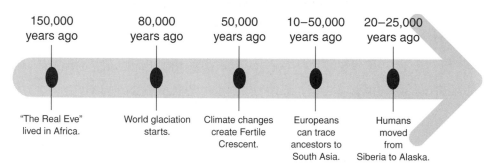

150,000 years ago	80,000 years ago	50,000 years ago	10–50,000 years ago	20–25,000 years ago
"The Real Eve" lived in Africa.	World glaciation starts.	Climate changes create Fertile Crescent.	Europeans can trace ancestors to South Asia.	Humans moved from Siberia to Alaska.

Early Human Events as Described in "The Real Eve"

EXERCISE 30 **Constructing a timeline**

On separate paper, construct a timeline similar to the one printed below. Label the time with dates and names of famous scientists who contributed to advances in genetics. Under the name of each scientist, write a sentence to express his main contribution to genetics. Use information from Exercise 29, in which you scanned Reading Selection 3 to locate important historical events in the history of genetics. Share your timelines with a group of your classmates.

Historical Advances in Genetics

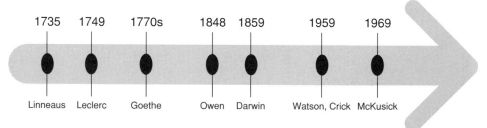

1735	1749	1770s	1848	1859	1959	1969
Linneaus	Leclerc	Goethe	Owen	Darwin	Watson, Crick	McKusick

EXERCISE 31 **Analyzing audience and purpose**

Selection 3, "The Great Family Tree," is an excerpt from Chance in the House of Fate: A Natural History of Heredity, *by science writer Jennifer Ackerman. To better understand the reading, reread the passage below to analyze the writer's audience and purpose. Complete the sentences following the passage by circling the phrase that best identifies the writer's audience and purpose. Refer to the explanation of audience and purpose on page 168 of Chapter 4. Discuss your answers with a group of your classmates.*

Richard Owen, a quick-witted and prescient British anatomist, made detailed observations of the unities underlying life's wild range of differences. The wing of the bird, fin of the fish, hand of man, he wrote in 1848, were all built according to a single design. These "homologies" were of far greater importance in the scheme of God's grand plan than the minor adaptations that distinguished the organ of one creature from that of the next.

The mind must embrace the whole and deduce a general type from it, wrote Goethe. The German polymath, whose interest in unity grew out of the terrible divisions of his age, possessed the rare ability to leap from science to poetry and back, and—when he was not writing literature—did important work in anatomy, botany, and geology, coined the term "morphology," and even managed to discover a new bone in the human upper jaw. Goethe wrote that all individual organisms have universal tendencies, to transform themselves, to expand and contract, to divide and unite, to arise and vanish, and he claimed to have traced "the manifold specific phenomena in the magnificent garden of the universe back to one simple general principle."

Audience

The author is writing to an audience that is (underline{uneducated / educated}). Furthermore, Ackerman is likely to consider that her audience has (underline{absolutely no / some / a great deal of}) knowledge of science. The text is probably written for (underline{men / women / either men or women}).

Purpose

Ackerman's main purpose in writing is (underline{to persuade / to inform}). She may also want to (underline{increase / decrease}) readers' interest in heredity and genetics. In addition, she might want to persuade readers to (underline{take up a career in science / pay more attention to the living world around them}).

EXERCISE 32 **Explaining metaphors in scientific writing**

Reading Selection 3, "The Great Family Tree," contains several metaphors that help readers better understand or visualize scientific concepts. Read each sentence below, from the reading. In each sentence, the writer compares a scientific concept to something else. The metaphors are underlined. On the blank lines, explain the metaphoric comparison; in other words, explain the two things that are being compared. Then, briefly state why you think the writer used this metaphor. Discuss your answers with a group of your classmates. The first one is done as an example.

1. "The cruc<u>ifers</u>—cabbage, turnip, radish—have a slender seedpod <u>and four petals that form a cross</u>." (¶ 1)

   Metaphor: The parts of the plant are compared to a cross. That's why these plants are called "crucifers." The metaphor makes it easy to visualize the plant.

2. "I remember how the discovery that the natural world had been classified and given two-part scientific names—names that were, in fact, a way of <u>weaving creatures together</u> by natural principles of likeness—shot through me <u>like a bolt</u> of happiness." (¶ 3)

   Metaphor 1:

   _____

   _____

   _____

   _____

   Metaphor 2:

   _____

   _____

   _____

   _____

3. "In the eighteenth century Linnaeus arranged living things in a pattern based on these principles (and freely admitted to being the one chosen to do so, the one whom "God has suffered . . . to peep into his secret cabinet"). (¶ 4)

Metaphor 1:

_____

_____

_____

4. "I grew to love the Linnaean system, the great animal and botanical divisions, the tidy nests within nests, all the shreds of creation revealed and broken down into pieces . . . then stitched back together in a great familial tree." (¶ 4)

Metaphor 1:

_____

_____

_____

Metaphor 2:

_____

_____

_____

5. In the book's only illustration, Darwin showed variants within a species as branches of a tree. He later explained that "limbs divided into great branches . . . were themselves, when the tree was small, budding twigs." (¶ 5)

Metaphor 1:

_____

_____

_____

6. Strung through all the organisms was a single genetic <u>thread</u> made of the same molecular <u>stitches</u>. The difference between a bacterium and a bullfrog lay largely in the order and the sequence of those <u>stitches</u> as well as their total number. (¶ 12)

Metaphor 1:

_____

_____

_____

7. "Nature uses only the longest <u>threads to weave her patterns,</u>" wrote the late physicist Richard Feynman, so <u>each small piece of her fabric reveals the organization of the entire tapestry.</u>" (¶ 13)

Metaphor 1:

_____

_____

_____

○ Questions for Discussion

EXERCISE 33 **Participating in group discussion**

Discuss the following questions with a group of your classmates.

1. In Exercise 28 on page 242, you wrote a sentence to state the general conclusion that scientists have reached after years of scientific research. What is that conclusion? What is your reaction to the findings?

2. The reading states that in the early nineteenth century, British scientist Richard Owen observed that the wing of a bird, fin of a fish, and human hand were all built from a single design. Do you find this idea logical? Explain.

3. In Selection 3, the writer states one scientist found that humans share hundreds of "disease" genes with fruit flies. What do you think is the implication of this information? In other words, in which ways might scientists use this information in their future work?

○ Learning Vocabulary

EXERCISE 34 Studying academic vocabulary

The following is a list of some academic vocabulary in Selection 3. Study the list. Put a check mark next to the words you already know.

_____ reliable

_____ composition

_____ mechanism

_____ contemporary

_____ adaptations

_____ phenomena

_____ reveals

_____ diverse

_____ versions

_____ principles

_____ illustration

_____ philosopher

_____ anticipating

_____ transform

_____ task

_____ decades

_____ functions

_____ evolutionary

_____ creation

_____ variants

_____ abandons

_____ underlying

_____ expand

_____ reconstruction

_____ sequences

_____ unique

_____ precision

_____ revealed

_____ committed

_____ modes

_____ minor

_____ contract, *v.*

_____ compound

_____ distinctive

_____ range

EXERCISE 35 **Using academic vocabulary**

Check your knowledge of some of the words on the list with the multiple-choice test below. Circle the most appropriate answer.

1. If a scientist asked you, "What is the **composition** of this **chemical compound**?", he or she would be asking
   a. what the chemical compound was made of.
   b. where the chemical compound came from.
   c. how the chemicals joined together.

2. To say there are many **modes** of scientific **research** means that there is a **range** of
   a. reasons for scientific research.
   b. ways that scientists conduct research.
   c. effects of scientific research.

3. Reading Selection 3 **revealed** that ___ were **contemporary** scientists who both attempted to **reconstruct** the **evolutionary sequence** that led to present-day humans.
   a. Owen and Darwin
   b. Linnaeus and McKusick
   c. Leclerc and Feynman

4. Scientists find that species of plants and animals may be **distinctive** but that they share **similar sequences** of genes. This means
   a. animals are unique, yet they have genes in the same order.
   b. animals are unique, yet they share the same types of genes.

5. Scientists' conclusion is that **underlying** the **diversity** of all organisms is a number of shared genes, probably modern **versions** of life's oldest genes. This means
   a. organisms may look different, but they are similar in that they share genes that are similar to the most modern genes.
   b. organisms may look different, but they are similar in that they share genes that are similar to the oldest genes.

EXERCISE 36 Studying academic vocabulary

Make a word study card for each unfamiliar word. As the guidelines suggest in Chapter 3, write the word, its pronunciation, its part of speech, its definition, and a sentence using the word on the card. Copy a sentence from the reading selection in which the word appears, or write your own sentence using the word.

○ Assessing Your Learning at the End of a Chapter

Revisiting Objectives

Return to the first page of this chapter. Think about the chapter objectives. Put a check mark next to the ones you feel secure about. Review material in the chapter you still need to work on. When you are ready, answer the chapter review questions below.

○ Practicing for a Chapter Test

EXERCISE 37 Reviewing comprehension

Check your comprehension of main concepts, or ideas, in this chapter by answering the following questions. First, write notes to answer the questions without looking back at the readings. Then, use the readings to check your answers and revise them, if necessary. Write your final answers in complete sentences on separate paper.

1. What is genetics?
2. What are the five levels on which scientists must examine heredity?
3. What is the difference between these two terms: *genotype* and *phenotype*?
4. What is the general conclusion of scientific research related to "The Real Eve"?
5. According to Reading Selection 2, what was the itinerary that Eve's ancestors took from Africa?
6. What are mitochondria?
7. How do mitochondria relate to "The Real Eve"?

8. According to Reading Selection 2, how closely related are all humans?
9. What is the general conclusion of scientific research related to Reading Selection 3, "The Great Family Tree"?
10. What information do scientists use as evidence that all human organisms are related?

○ Linking Concepts

EXERCISE 38 **Linking ideas from chapter readings**

The following questions are about learning and reading and about the scientific topic of genetics and heredity. You can respond to these questions in three possible ways.

1. Write responses in your reading journal.
2. Discuss these questions in groups and as a whole class.
3. Provide short written answers to share with your classmates and/or your instructor.

Your instructor will provide specific instructions on how to respond to the questions.

Reflections on Learning

1. Chapter 5 presented a conceptually challenging topic: genetics. How would you rate your overall comprehension of the reading selections? Explain.
2. Did visual aids like graphics, drawings, and photographs help you understand the topic? If so, explain.
3. Did you find the vocabulary in the chapter challenging? If so, name some academic words and key terms you learned.

Reflections on Genetics

1. Did you learn anything about your own genetic makeup after completing the chapter? If so, explain what you learned.
2. Did the readings raise questions in your mind about the connections among humans? If so, explain.
3. Did the chapter make you think differently about the connections among all living things? If so, explain.

EXERCISE 39 Reviewing academic vocabulary

Here are some academic words you studied in Chapter 5. In the chart, check the box that describes your knowledge of each word. Review the words that are less familiar to you.

For each word you checked the box "I can use it in a sentence," write a sentence to use the word. Compare your sentences with those from a group of your classmates. Discuss the words you are less familiar with. Write less familiar words, sentences, and other standard information about the words on word study cards.

Academic word	I think I know what this word means.	I know this word.	I know this word so well that I can use it in a sentence.
factors, *n.pl.*			
conception, *n.*			
complex, *adj.*			
comprise, *v.*			
attributes, *n.pl.*			
crucial, *adj.*			
assumption, *n.*			
principles, *n.pl.*			
structure, *n.*			
variants, *n.pl.*			
mechanism, *n.*			

Academic word	I think I know what this word means.	I know this word.	I know this word so well that I can use it in a sentence.
committed, *v.*			
adaptations, *n.pl.*			
deduce, *v.*			
phenomena, *n.pl.*			
sequence, *n.*			
precision, *n.*			

WEB POWER

Go to http://esl.college.hmco.com/students to view more readings about genetics and heredity, plus exercises that will help you study the chapter selections and academic words.

A New Century

ACADEMIC FOCUS: HISTORY

Academic Reading Objectives

After completing this chapter,
you should be able to:

✓ Check here as you
master each objective.

1. Distinguish among statements of fact, explanation,
   and commentary ☐
2. Identify topics and themes from titles ☐
3. Locate statements that support themes in passages ☐
4. Analyze how facts and examples are used to support
   and explain ☐
5. Notice parallel development patterns in writing about
   events in a chronology ☐
6. Use graphs and photographs to aid understanding ☐

History Objectives

1. Compare political, economic, and cultural factors across
   twentieth-century American history ☐
2. Develop a perspective on gains and challenges
   surrounding civil rights issues in the United States ☐
3. Identify key elements of American society at the end of
   the twentieth century ☐

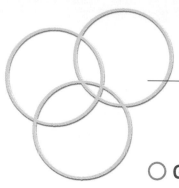

Reading Assignment 1

THE AMERICAN PEOPLE FACE A NEW CENTURY (PART I)

○ Getting Ready to Read

EXERCISE 1 Discussing in a small group

Look at the opening photograph in this chapter, and then discuss the following questions with your classmates in a small group. These questions are designed to start you thinking about America at the beginning of a new century. There may be more than one answer to each question. Assign one member of your group to lead the discussion and another to report back to the whole class.

1. What do you see immediately when you look at this photograph?
2. What are the students doing? Write down a list of verbs or verb phrases.
3. Where do you think this photograph was taken?
4. When do you think it was taken?
5. What students do you see in this picture? How do you describe them?
6. How might this photograph be different from an adult classroom scene in another country?
7. This is a picture of an ESL classroom in the United States. The title of the selection you will read for this chapter is "The American People Face a New Century." How is this photograph an illustration for that title?

○ Focusing on History

History is an academic subject that includes the study of events from the past. We learn what happened at a certain time, to certain people, in specific places. A study of history, however, requires that students investigate the cultural, political, and economic contexts in which events occur. Consequently, history is made up of stories about people who were instrumental to events or who were affected by events as they unfolded.

History can thus be defined as "a chronological record of events . . . often including an explanation of or commentary on those events" (*American Heritage College Dictionary*, 2002, p. 657). It is the job of historians to recall historical events, suggest explanations for their occurrence, and offer commentary on the significance of the events.

EXERCISE 2   **Matching events, explanation, and commentary**

The left column below contains five sentences from the history selections you will read in this chapter. Draw a line to match each sentence with the correct term in the right column. The first one has been done for you.

Reading selection sentences	What is it?
1. "The United States by the late 1990s was home to more than 31 million Hispanics."	**A.** Historical fact
2. "Median household income declined somewhat in the early 1990s but rebounded by 1998 to about $39,000."	**B.** Commentary on recent history and the future
3. "The twenty-first century began much like the twentieth, with American society continuing to be rejuvenated by fresh waves of immigrants, full of energy and ambition."	**C.** Fact about the cultural makeup of America
4. "On September 11, 2001, . . . suicidal terrorists slammed two hijacked airliners . . . into the twin towers of New York City's World Trade Center."	**D.** Explanation of American social history with commentary
5. "The terrorist threat reminded Americans of the urgency of resolving the ethnic and cultural conflicts that continued to plague the planet after the Cold War's end."	**E.** Economic fact used to describe a short period of history

When authors write about history, they include facts, explanations, and commentary. When you read the chapter selections, think about the purpose of each section. Understanding an author's use of facts, explanations, and commentary will make you a better reader of historical texts.

STRATEGY

Chapter Themes

Most titles indicate the chapter topic (subject matter). An example is "America in World War II." Other titles reveal the chapter theme. **A theme is the main idea that the author emphasizes and repeats in a chapter.** A theme also is what the author thinks students should remember and what would probably be included in a test. When the theme is in the title, it helps the reader understand what the author believes is important in an upcoming chapter.

EXERCISE 3   **Using topics and themes**

This exercise includes two chapter titles from the history textbook An American Pageant. *Each chapter title contains a theme. Study the titles listed and put a check mark next to the items you think would be addressed in the chapter.*

Chapter title: "Industry Comes of Age"

The topic is "Industry." "Comes of Age" is the theme. "Comes of Age" is an idiom meaning "to grow up and become an adult." What does the chapter theme tell you about industry? Check the questions you think might be answered in this chapter.

____ When did industry grow up?

____ When was industry a child?

____ How did industry grow up?

____ What made industry grow up?

____ What are examples of growing up?

____ What is the significance of growing up?

Chapter title: "The Resurgence of Conservatism"

"Conservatism" is the topic. "Resurgence" is the theme. Resurgence *means to come back and to increase in strength.* The *American Heritage College Dictionary (2002, p. 305) defines conservatism as "The inclination [or tendency], especially in politics, to maintain the existing or traditional order." Check the questions you think might be answered in this chapter.*

____   When did conservatism resurge?

____   Why did it experience resurgence?

____   What happened to nonconservatism?

____   What does it mean for politics?

____   What are examples of resurgence?

____   Who led the resurgence of conservatism?

◯ Reading for a Purpose

Sometimes when reading, our eyes want to skip over titles and jump ahead to a passage. It is important to slow down and think about titles because writers are careful and precise about the meaning-rich words they include in titles.

David M. Kennedy, the author of the history book *The American Pageant,* uses very few words in his chapter titles. Many titles are only three words long, and the longest is just seven words. With so few words, an author must make them count in order to give the reader an indication of the upcoming chapter's content and theme. The title of Reading Selection 1 comes from the chapter "The American People Face a New Century" in Kennedy's book. It is an unusual title because it is a grammatically complete sentence with a subject, verb, and object. Each part of this title is rich with meanings.

Master Student Tip

Understanding Dates

The twentieth century was from 1901 to 2000. The twenty-first century is from 2001 to 2100.

EXERCISE 4   Understanding the title

Discuss these questions about the title "The American People Face a New Century."

1. The subject of the title is "The American People." When the author uses this phrase, which people is he referring to? Where do they come from? What qualities do they have?

2. The verb of the title is "Face." What does it mean to face something? Who is facing whom or what? How would the meaning of the title be changed if the author had used the verb *approach* rather than the verb *face*?

3. The object of the title is "a New Century." It tells us what the American people will face. How would the meaning of the title be changed if the author had used "the Twenty-first Century" rather than "a New Century?"

4. Can you think of any new discoveries, products, or challenges of the twenty-first century? How have they influenced us positively or negatively?

EXERCISE 5   Expanding the title

Remember, titles say a lot in just a few words. For Exercise 4, you discussed details of the three parts (the subject, verb, and object) of a title. Now put those details into sentences and write a short paragraph expanding the title. Imagine what the author might have been thinking when he chose those seven words. Write on separate paper. An example paragraph has been started for you. You can continue with that paragraph or start a new one of your own.

"The American People Face a New Century"
by David M. Kennedy

The people of America are made up of the people....

In addition to writing meaningful titles, authors often use introductory quotations to lead readers to the chapter theme. Kennedy begins this selection with a quotation from Abraham Lincoln immediately below the title. Lincoln was the President of the United States during the Civil War period of U.S. history. In 1862, when the United States was in the middle of that war, Lincoln made this statement:

As our case is new, so we must think anew and act anew. We must disenthrall ourselves, and then we shall save our country.

EXERCISE 6 **Understanding the introductory quote**

Consider why Kennedy used Lincoln's statement to introduce this chapter and how Lincoln's words reflect the chapter title. Check the statements below that indicate the connection you think the author saw between Lincoln's words and our current world.

____   Our world in the twenty-first century is exactly like Lincoln's world in the nineteenth century.

____   Americans have a new situation in the world, as did Lincoln during his time.

____   Americans must think and act just as Lincoln did.

____   Americans must think and act in a new way.

____   Americans must separate themselves from the past to save the country.

____   Americans must make the future just like the past.

What do you think Lincoln's words mean as the American people face the twenty-first century?

◯ Reading the Selection

The reading selections for this chapter are excerpted from David M. Kennedy's textbook *The American Pageant* (12th ed., 2002, Boston: Houghton Mifflin).

Reading Selection 1

THE AMERICAN PEOPLE FACE A NEW CENTURY (PART 1)

As our case is new, so we must think anew and act anew. We must disenthrall ourselves, and then we shall save our country.
—*Abraham Lincoln, 1862*

1 More than two hundred years old as the twenty first century began, the United States was both an old and a new nation. It boasted one of the longest uninterrupted <u>traditions</u> of democratic government of any country on earth. Indeed, it had pioneered the

techniques of mass democracy and was, in that sense, the oldest modern polity.[1] As one of the earliest countries to industrialize, America had also dwelt in the modern economic era longer than most nations.

2   But the Republic was in many ways still youthful as well. Innovation, entrepreneurship, and risk taking—all characteristics of youth—were honored national values. The twenty-first century began much like the twentieth, with American society continuing to be rejuvenated[2] by fresh waves of immigrants, full of energy and ambition. The U.S. economy, despite problems, was generating new jobs at a rate of some 2 million per year. American inventions, especially computer and communications technologies, were transforming the face of global society. The world seemed to worship the icons of American culture—downing soft drinks and donning blue jeans, watching Hollywood films, listening to rock or country and western music, even adopting indigenous American sports like baseball and basketball. In the realm of consumerism, American products appear to have Coca-Colonized the globe.

3   The history of American society also seemed to have increased global significance as the third millennium of the Christian era opened. Americans were a pluralistic people who had struggled for centuries to provide opportunity and to achieve tolerance and justice for many different religious, ethnic, and racial groups. Their historical experience could offer valuable lessons to the rapidly internationalizing planetary society that was emerging at the end of the twenty-first century.

4   In politics, economics, and culture, the great social experiment of American democracy was far from completed as the United States faced its future. Much history remained to be made as the country entered its third century of nationhood. But men and women make history only within the framework bequeathed to them by earlier generations. For better or worse, they march forward along time's path bearing the burdens of the past. Knowing when they have come to a truly new turn in the road, when they can lay part of their burden down and when they cannot, or should not—all this constitutes the sort of wisdom that only historical study can engender.

1. **pol•i•ty** (pŏl´ĭ-tē) *n.* An organized society, such as a nation, having a specific form of government.
2. **re•ju•ve•nat•ed** (rĭ-jōō´və-nāt´) *v.* Restored to an original or new condition; made young again.

Economic Revolutions

5   When the twentieth century opened, United States Steel Corporation was the flagship[3] business of America's booming industrial revolution. U.S. Steel was a typical "heavy industry," cranking out the ingots and girders and sheet metal that built the nation's basic physical infrastructure. A generation later, General Motors, annually producing millions of automobiles, became the characteristic American corporation, signaling the historic shift to a mass consumer economy that began in the 1920s and flowered fully in the 1950s. Following World War II, the rise of International Business Machines (IBM) symbolized[4] yet another momentous transformation, to the fast-paced "information age," when the storing, organizing, and processing of data became an industry in its own right.

6   The pace of the information age soon accelerated. By century's end, the rapid emergence of Microsoft Corporation and the phenomenal[5] growth of the Internet heralded an explosive communications revolution. Americans now rocketed down the "information superhighway" toward the uncharted terrain of an electronic global village, where traditional geographic, social, and political boundaries could be vaulted with the tap of a keypad.

7   The communications revolution was full of both promise and peril. In the blink of an eye, ordinary citizens could gain access to information once available only to privileged elites with vast libraries or expert staffs at their disposal. Businesspeople instantaneously girdled[6] the planet with transactions of prodigious scope and serpentine complexity. Japanese bankers might sell wheat contracts in Chicago and simultaneously direct the profits to buying oil shipments from the Persian Gulf offered by a broker in Amsterdam. By the late 1990s, a "dot-com" explosion of new commercial ventures quickly expanded the market (and the stock-market stakes) for entrepreneurs leading the way in making the Internet a twenty-first-century electronic mall, library, and entertainment center rolled into one.

3. **flag•ship** (flăg′shĭp′) *n.* The chief business in a related group or industrial sector.
4. **sym•bol•ized** (sĭm′bə-līz′) *v.* Served as a symbol of; represented.
5. **phe•nom•e•nal** (fĭ-nŏm′ə-nəl) *adj.* Extraordinary; outstanding.
6. **gir•dled** (gûr′dl) *tr.v.* Encircled with as if with a belt.

8   But the very speed and efficiency of the new communications tools threatened to wipe out entire occupational categories. Postal delivery people, travel agents, store clerks, bank tellers, stockbrokers, and all kinds of other workers whose business it was to mediate between product and client, might find themselves rendered obsolete[7] in the era of the Internet. And as the computer makes possible "classrooms without walls," where students can pursue learning largely on their own, even teachers, whose job is essentially to mediate between students and various bodies of knowledge, might well end up as road kill on the information superhighway.

9   Increasingly, scientific research was the engine that drove the economy, and new scientific knowledge posed new social and moral dilemmas.[8] When scientists first unlocked the secrets of molecular genetic structure in the 1950s, the road lay open to breeding new strains of high-yield, pest and weather resistant crops; to curing hereditary disease; and also, unfortunately, to unleashing genetic mutations that might threaten the fragile ecological balance of the wondrous biosphere in which humankind was delicately suspended. As technical mastery of biological and medical techniques advanced, unprecedented ethical questions clamored for resolution. Should the human gene pool itself be "engineered"? What principles should govern the allocation of human organs for lifesaving transplants, or of scarce dialysis machines, or of artificial hearts? Was it wise in the first place to spend money on such costly devices rather than devote society's resources to improved sanitation, maternal and infant care, nutritional and health education? Who was the rightful parent of a child born to a "surrogate mother" or conceived by artificial insemination? How, if at all, should society regulate[9] the increasingly lengthy and often painful process of dying? What rules should guide efforts to clone human beings, or should such efforts even be attempted?

7. **ob•so•lete** (ŏb´sə-lēt´) *adj.* Outmoded in design, style, or construction.
8. **di•lem•mas** (dĭ-lĕm´ə) *n.* Problems that seem to defy a satisfactory solution; difficult to solve.
9. **reg•u•late** (rĕg´yə-lāt´) *v.* To control or direct according to rule, principle, or law.

Affluence and Inequality

10   Americans were still an affluent[10] people at the beginning of the twenty-first century. Median household income declined somewhat in the early 1990s but rebounded by 1998 to about $39,000. Yet even those Americans with incomes below the government's official poverty level (defined in 1998 as $16,600 for a family of four) enjoyed a standard of living higher than that of two-thirds of the rest of human kind.

Two Nations?

While decaying neighborhoods and the sad legions of the homeless blighted American urban life in the closing decades of the twentieth century, affluent Americans took refuge in gated communities like this one in the Brentwood section of Los Angeles.

11   Americans were no longer the world's wealthiest people in the 1990s, as they had been in the quarter century after World War II. Citizens of several other countries enjoyed higher average per capita incomes, and many nations boasted more equitable distributions of wealth. In an unsettling reversal of long-term trends in American

10. **af•flu•ent** (ăf´lōo-ənt) *adj.* Generously supplied with money, property, or possessions; prosperous or rich.

society, during the last two decades of the twentieth century, the rich
got much richer, while the poor got an ever-shrinking share of the pie.
The richest 20 percent of Americans in the 1990s raked in nearly half
the nation's income, whereas the poorest 20 percent received less
than 4 percent. The gap between rich and poor began to widen in the
1980s and widened further in the following decade. That trend was
evident in many industrial societies, but it was most pronounced in
the United States. Between 1968 and 1998, the share of the nation's
income that flowed to the top 20 percent of its households swelled
from 40 percent to more than 49 percent. Even more striking, in the
same period the top 5 percent of income earners saw their share of
the national income grow from about 15 percent to more than
20 percent. The Welfare Reform Bill of 1996,[11] restricting access to
social services and requiring able-bodied welfare recipients to find
work, weakened the financial footing of many impoverished families
still further.

Widening Income Inequality

Share of aggregate income	1980	1990	1999
Lowest fifth	4.3	3.9	3.6
Second fifth	10.3	9.6	8.9
Middle fifth	16.9	15.9	14.9
Fourth fifth	24.9	24.0	23.2
Highest fifth	43.7	46.6	49.4
Top 5%	15.8	18.6	21.5

During the last two decades of the twentieth century, the top fifth of the country's households made
significant gains in income, while everyone else lost ground. (Source: U.S. Census)

11. **The Welfare Reform Bill of 1996** Welfare is financial or other aid provided
especially by the government to people in need. In 1996, the U. S. government
dramatically changed its welfare system, which meant fewer people qualified to
receive financial assistance. It also meant they were frequently given incentives
to go to work.

12   Widening inequality[12] could be measured in other ways as well: chief executives in the 1970s typically earned forty-one times the income of the average worker in their corporations; by the 1990s they earned 225 times as much. At the same time, some 34 million people, 12.7 percent of all Americans (10.5 percent of whites, 26.1 percent of African-Americans, and 25.6 percent of Latinos), remained mired in poverty, a depressing indictment of the inequities afflicting an affluent and allegedly egalitarian republic.

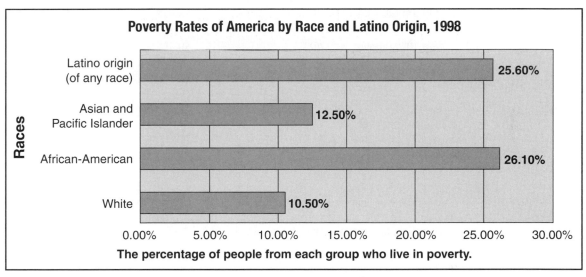

(Source: U.S. Bureau of the Census, March Current Population Survey)

13   What caused the widening income gap? Some critics pointed to the tax and fiscal policies of the Reagan and Bush years, which favored the wealthy and penalized the poor. But deeper-running historical currents probably played a more powerful role, as suggested by the similar experiences of other industrialized societies. Among the most conspicuous causes were intensifying[13] global economic competition; the shrinkage in high paying manufacturing jobs for semiskilled and unskilled workers; the greater economic rewards commanded by educated workers in high-tech industries; the decline of unions; the growth of part-time and temporary work; the rising tide of relatively low skill immigrants; and the increasing tendency of educated men and women to marry one another and both work, creating households with very high incomes.

12. **in·e·qual·i·ty** (ĭn´ĭ-kwŏl´ĭ-tē) *n*. Lack of equality, as of opportunity, treatment, or status.
13. **in·ten·si·fy·ing** (ĭn-tĕn´sə-fī´) *tr.v.* Increasing or making more intense.

Who Pays Federal Income Taxes?
(share of U.S. income tax, by income percentile)

Income Group (base income shown as of 1998)	1994	1998
Top 1% (above $269,496)	28.7%	34.8%
Top 5% (above $114,729)	47.4%	53.8%
Top 10% (above $83,220)	59.1%	65.0%
Top 25% (above $50,607)	79.5%	82.7%
Top 50% (above $25,491)	95.2%	95.8%
Bottom 50% (below $25,491)	4.8%	4.2%

Because the United States has long had a "progressive" income tax system, in which tax obligations are distributed according to ability to pay, widening income inequality was reflected in a redistribution[14] of tax burdens. In the booming 1990s, the rich did indeed get richer, but they also paid an increasing fraction of the total federal tax take. (Source: *Internal Revenue Service* data, Tax Foundation.)

Source: Kennedy, D. M. (2002). *The American Pageant* (12th ed.). Boston: Houghton Mifflin, pp. 1014–1018.

14. **re•dis•tri•bu•tion** (rē′dĭs-trə-byōō′shən) *n.* The act of distributing, especially wealth, more equally. To change who pays taxes; in the United States, as a person's income increases, that person pays more in taxes.

○ **Assessing Your Learning**

Demonstrating Comprehension

EXERCISE 7 **Checking comprehension**

Reading Selection 1 is the introductory part for "The American People Face a New Century" chapter. It gives the information and the orientation readers need to begin the chapter. Fill in the boxes below with short notes from the passage to show what you think the author wants readers to know about the listed chapter aspects. The first one is done for you as an example.

Theme	What does the author want you to know about America? Look for key points.
1. America as an established country (¶ 1)	America is old & new. Longest uninterrupted democracy...Early to industrialize. A modern country for a long time....
2. American values (¶ 2)	
3. America's economy and culture (¶ 2)	
4. America as a country that includes people from many places (¶ 3)	
5. New challenges in America's future (¶ 4)	
6. How history is made (¶ 4)	

○ **Focusing on History**

There is truly an element of "story" in history because we are reading about events that occurred in the lives of people who lived in the past. Passages written about history generally follow narrative patterns of development and reflect chronological order. Often, however, there are no longer living witnesses to the events. Consequently, historians need to seek information from many sources and many perspectives in order to reconstruct historical facts with candor as they write.

The author of the textbook you are studying in this chapter wants to draw the reader's attention to parallels in historical events. To do so, the author, David Kennedy, uses writing style elements that include repeating patterns. In the reading section titled "Economic Revolutions" (¶ 5–9), Kennedy introduces the idea that America has experienced several economic revolutions in the past 100 years. He tells us about each important revolution following a similar pattern. He describes successive economic revolutions in chronological order. He uses a pattern of providing similar details about each time period so that readers can compare the economic revolutions.

Compare the following outline of "Economic Revolutions" (¶ 5–9) with actual text to better understand how the author uses a repeating pattern to make the meaning of the words clearer.

1. Early 1900's
   a. New economic event
   b. Details
2. 1920's–1940's
   a. New economic event
   b. Details
3. 1940's–1970's
   a. New economic event
   b. Details
4. 1970's–1990's
   a. New economic event
   b. Details

EXERCISE 8 Seeing the pattern

Complete the table below with historical details about "Economic Revolutions"
(¶ 5–9). Pay attention to the pattern that develops. Follow the example from
the first column.

Time period	The 1900s—at the turn of the century.	The 1920s–early 40s	The late 1940s–1970s	The 1980s and 1990s—at the end of the century
Main industry	Heavy industry			
A leading company	United States Steel Corporation			
The product	Ingots, girders, sheet metal			
The importance of the revolution	It built the physical infrastructure of the nation.			

EXERCISE **9** **Discussing patterns**

In this chapter's section titled "Getting Ready to Read," you learned about the differences between **facts,** **explanations,** *and* **commentary.** *Keep those words in mind as you work on these questions. Work individually and then share your answers with a partner. The first one has been done for you.*

1. Was the product of the 1900s small and personal or big and general?

   The product of the 1900s was big and general. It was industrial and not made for individuals.

2. How has the product changed over the twentieth century?

   _____

   _____

3. Why does the author call each economic change "revolution"?

   _____

   _____

4. A pattern means that some parts are repeated several times. After you filled in some answers for the chart above, did you see a pattern in the author's writing? If you answered no, go back to find a pattern and discuss it with your classmates. If you answered yes, then did seeing the pattern in the author's writing help you understand this section of the textbook?

   _____

   _____

5. The first sentence of paragraph 9 in the section "Economic Revolutions" states, "Increasingly, scientific research was the engine that drove the economy, and new scientific knowledge posed new social and moral dilemmas." Read the entire paragraph, and then use your understanding of the paragraph to complete the following sentences:

   a. Scientific research led to revolutions in the economy by

      _____

   b. An example of a social/moral problem brought about by increasing scientific knowledge is

      _____

6. In writing about the economy, the author uses facts, explanations, and commentary. All these elements are needed in history, but which element gives you the most understanding of this historical period? Why?

   _____

   _____

7. When you take a test on this section of the book, what will your instructor expect you to remember as important? Why? What are the key points of the section?

   _____

   _____

EXERCISE 10 **Understanding a comparison**

Put a check mark next to the sentence that best restates the author's meaning for the following sentence:

"Citizens of several other countries enjoyed higher average per capita* incomes, and many nations boasted more equitable distribution* of wealth* [than America]." (¶ 11)

> *per capita—Per unit of population.
> *distribution—The act of dividing and giving out portions of something, such as money, to people or a nation.
> *wealth—The money or capital a person or country owns.

——— America leads the world in distributing wealth to its citizens.

——— Many countries do a better job of distributing wealth than America.

——— America is among the worst countries in distributing wealth to its citizens.

Here the author compares America with other countries. In the next exercise, the author supports another comparison with facts.

EXERCISE 11 Supporting a comparison

Draw lines to match the following words with their definitions.

1. supporting evidence	A position an author takes based on knowledge and evidence.
2. a statement	Information such as facts that can be proved.

Examine how the author supports a statement with facts.

The statement or position the author takes	**"Americans were still an affluent people at the beginning of the twenty-first century."** This is a statement. The author as a historian must provide evidence to support this statement. Evidence is usually a factual statement that we know is true and that supports an author's position.
The supporting evidence	**"Median household income declined somewhat in the early 1990s but rebounded by 1998 to about $39,000."** This factual evidence can be proved and directly supports the earlier statement.

EXERCISE 12 Locating support for a comparison

In comparing the rich and the not-so-rich, the author makes the following statement:

> In an unsettling reversal of long-term trends in American society, during the last two decades of the twentieth century, the rich got much richer, while the poor got an ever-shrinking share of the pie.

In this exercise, back up this statement with supporting facts from the chapter. The first two examples of evidence are provided, and the next three are started. Complete those three and find two more. Finally, indicate if the evidence supports the idea that the rich get richer or the poor get poorer by checking the boxes in the columns to the right.

The evidence	Supports the idea that "the rich got much richer."	Supports the idea that "the poor got an ever-shrinking share of the pie."
1. "The richest 20 percent of Americans in the 1990s raked in nearly half the nation's income." (¶ 11)	✓	
2. ". . . whereas the poorest 20 percent received less than 4 percent."		
3. "Between 1968 and 1998, the share of the nation's income that flowed to the top 20 percent of its households swelled from . . ."		
4. "Even more striking, in the same period the top 5 percent of income earners saw . . ."		
5. "The Welfare Reform Bill of 1996, . . ."		
6.		
7.		

EXERCISE 13   Understanding graphics

The author includes two tables and two photographs in the chapter section titled "Affluence and Inequality" (¶ 10–13). These are included to support the chapter themes. One key theme of this chapter is that the gap in the distribution of wealth in the United States has been widening. Explain how the graphic elements support each of these two statements about this theme.

1. "Citizens of several other countries enjoyed higher average per capita incomes and many nations boasted more equitable distributions of wealth." (Compare with these photos from this chapter.)

2. "In an unsettling reversal of long-term trends in American society, during the last two decades of the twentieth century, the rich got much richer, while the poor got an ever-shrinking share of the pie." (Compare with this chart from this chapter.)

Share of aggregate income	1980	1990	1999
Lowest fifth	4.3	3.9	3.6
Second fifth	10.3	9.6	8.9
Middle fifth	16.9	15.9	14.9
Fourth fifth	24.9	24.0	23.2
Highest fifth	43.7	46.6	49.4
Top 5%	15.8	18.6	21.5

During the last two decades of the twentieth century, the top fifth of the country's households made significant gains in income, while everyone else lost ground. (Source: U.S. Census)

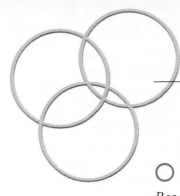

Reading Assignment 2

THE AMERICAN PEOPLE FACE A NEW CENTURY (PART 2)

◯ Reading the Selection

Read this selection two times before you begin the postreading exercises. First, read to find the main idea. Try to read fairly quickly without stopping. Concentrate on the main themes: ethnic pride and minority America.

Next, read the passage a second time, even more quickly, scanning only for new vocabulary. Pay special attention to the AWL words with dotted underlines. Mark the words in the passage that you want to learn more about. Try to learn something about the words from the context. You can also use structure and word-part clues to help.

Reading Selection 2

THE AMERICAN PEOPLE FACE A NEW CENTURY (PART 2)

Ethnic Pride

1   Thanks both to continued immigration and to their own high birthrate, Hispanic-Americans were becoming an increasingly important minority. The United States by the late 1990s was home to more than 31 million Hispanics. They included some 21 million Chicanos, or Mexican-Americans, mostly in the Southwest, as well as 3 million Puerto Ricans, chiefly in the Northeast, and more than 1 million Cubans in Florida (where it was jokingly said that Miami had become the most "Anglo" city in Latin America).

2   Flexing their political muscles, Latinos elected mayors of Miami, Denver, and San Antonio. After years of struggle, the United Farm Workers Organizing Committee (UFWOC), headed by the soft-spoken and charismatic Caesar Chavez, succeeded[1] in improving work conditions for the mostly Chicano "stoop laborers" who followed the cycle of planting and harvesting across the American West.

---

1. **suc·ceed·ed** (sək-sēd´) *intr.v.* Accomplished something desired or intended.

Hispanic influence[2] seemed likely to grow, as suggested by the increasing presence of Spanish-language ballots and television broadcasts. Hispanic-Americans, newly confident and organized, were destined[3] to become the nation's largest ethnic minority, out-numbering even African-Americans, in the early twenty-first century. Indeed, by the first decade of the new century, the Chicano population of America's [most populous] state, California, equaled the Anglo population, making the state a patchwork of minorities with no single ethnic majority.

3   Asian-Americans also made great strides. By the 1980s they were America's fastest-growing minority. Their numbers nearly doubled in that decade alone, thanks to heavy immigration, and continued to swell[4] in the 1990s. Once feared and hated as the "yellow peril" and relegated to the most menial[5] and degrading jobs, citizens of Asian ancestry were now counted among the most prosperous and successful of Americans—a "model minority." The typical Asian-American household enjoyed an income nearly 20 percent greater than that of the typical white household. In 1996 the voters of Washington elected the first Asian-American to serve as governor of a mainland American state.

4   Indians, the original Americans, shared in the general awakening of ethnic and cultural pride. The 2000 census counted some 2.4 million Native Americans, half of whom had left their reservations to live in cities. Meanwhile, unemployment and alcoholism had blighted reservation life. Many tribes tried to take advantage of their special legal status as independent nations by opening bingo halls and gambling casinos for white patrons on reservation lands, but the cycle of discrimination and poverty proved hard to break.

2. **in•flu•ence** (ĭn´flōō-ə ns) *n.* The power to affect persons, things, or courses of events based on prestige, wealth, ability, or position.
3. **des•tined** (dĕs´tĭn) *v.* Determined beforehand; meant to be.
4. **swell** (swĕl) *v.* To grow or increase.
5. **me•ni•al** (mē´nē-ə l) *adj.* Relating to basic, often dirty or difficult physical work. Sometimes done by a servant or person in an entry-level job.

Minority America

5   Racial and ethnic tensions also exacerbated[6] the problems of American cities. These stresses were especially evident in Los Angeles, which, like New York a century earlier, was a magnet for minorities, especially immigrants from Asia and Latin America. When in 1992 a mostly white jury exonerated[7] white Los Angeles police officers who had been videotaped ferociously beating a black suspect, the minority neighborhoods of South Central Los Angeles erupted in rage. Arson and looting laid waste entire city blocks, and scores of people were killed. In a sobering demonstration of the complexity of modem American racial rivalries, many black rioters vented their anger at the white police and the judicial system by attacking Asian shopkeepers, who in turn formed armed patrols to protect their property.

6   The Los Angeles riots vividly testified to black skepticism about the American system of justice. Just three years later, again in Los Angeles, the gaudy televised spectacle of former football star 0. J. Simpson's murder trial fed white disillusionment with the state of race relations. After months of testimony that seemed to point to Simpson's guilt, the jury acquitted[8] him, presumably because certain Los Angeles police officers involved in the case had been shown to harbor racist sentiments. In a later civil trial, another jury unanimously found Simpson liable for the "wrongful deaths" of his former wife and another victim. The reaction to the Simpson verdicts revealed the yawning chasm that separated white and black America, as most whites continued to believe Simpson guilty, while a majority of African-Americans told pollsters that the original not-guilty verdict was justified. African-American charges that they had been unlawfully kept from the polls during the 2000 presidential election in Florida convinced many blacks that they were still facing a Jim Crow South[9] of black disenfranchisement.

6. **ex•ac•er•bat•ed** (ĭg-zăs´ər-bāt´) *v.* Increased or made something stronger. If continued, it may lead to a violent or bitter result.
7. **ex•on•er•at•ed** (ĭg-zŏn´ə-rāt´) *tr.v.* Freed from blame.
8. **ac•quit•ted** (ə-kwĭt´) *tr.v.* Freed or cleared from a charge or accusation.
9. **Jim Crow South** The Civil War (1860–1865) was followed by Reconstruction, a period when the southern states were controlled by the federal government before being readmitted to the Union. From the end of Reconstruction to the beginning of the twentieth century, the South experienced the Jim Crow period, in which there was the systematic practice of discriminating against and segregating black people.

7   American cities have always held an astonishing variety of ethnic and racial groups, but in the late twentieth century, minorities made up a majority of the population of many American cities, as whites fled to the suburbs. More than three-quarters of African-Americans lived in cities by the 1990s, whereas only about one-quarter of whites did. The most desperate black ghettos, housing a hapless "underclass" in the inner core of the old industrial cities, were especially problematic. Successful blacks who had benefited from the civil rights revolution of the 1950s and 1960s followed whites to the suburbs, leaving a residue of the poorest poor in the old ghettos. Without a middle class to sustain community institutions like schools and small businesses, the inner cities, plagued[10] by unemployment and drug addiction, seemed bereft of leadership, cohesion, resources, and hope.

8   The friendless underclass, heavily composed of blacks and other minorities, represented a sorry and dangerous social failure that eluded any known remedy. But other segments of the African-American community had clearly prospered in the wake of the civil rights gains of the 1950s and 1960s, though they still had a long hill to climb before reaching full equality. By the 1990s about 40 percent of blacks were counted in the middle class (defined as enjoying family income greater than $25,000 per year). The number of black elected officials had risen above the seven thousand mark, including more than a thousand in the Old South, some two dozen members of Congress, and the mayors of several large cities. Voting tallies demonstrated that successful black politicians were moving beyond isolated racial constituencies and into the political mainstream by appealing to a wide variety of voters. In 1989 Virginians, only 15 percent of whom were black, chose L. Douglas Wilder as the first African-American elected to serve as a state governor. In 1994 voters in Illinois made Carol Moseley-Braun the first African-American woman elected to the U.S. Senate.

---

10. **plagued** (plāg) *tr.v.* Affected by negative factors that may cause a bad situation to become worse.

9   Single women headed over half of black families, almost three times the rate for whites. Many of those African-American women, husbandless and jobless, necessarily depended on welfare to feed their children. As social scientists increasingly emphasized the importance of the home environment for success in school, it became clear that many fatherless, impoverished African-American children seemed consigned[11] to suffer from educational handicaps that were difficult to overcome. Black youths in the 1990s still had about one year less schooling than whites of the same age and were less than half as likely to earn college degrees. As the American economy became ever more driven by new applications of computers and biotechnology, these disadvantages were bound to widen the racial gap of employment opportunity. The political assault against affirmative action in California and elsewhere only compounded the obstacles to advanced training for many young African-Americans.

Source: Kennedy, D. M. (2002). *The American Pageant* (12th ed.). Boston: Houghton Mifflin, pp. 1024–1025.

11. **con•signed** (kən-sīn´) *v.* Given permanently to a lasting condition; controlled by circumstances or one's situation in life.

○ **Assessing Your Learning**

Learning Vocabulary

EXERCISE 14 **Studying academic vocabulary**

Study the academic words in the box below. Review how they are used in Reading Selection 2. If necessary, look up the words in a dictionary. Then use some of these words and phrases to complete the sentences that follow. Check off the words or phrases as you use them.

☐ minority	☐ income
☐ constituencies	☐ compounded cycle of discrimination
☐ evident	
☐ convinced	☐ reaction
☐ ethnic minority	☐ benefited
☐ welfare	☐ legal status
☐ demonstration	☐ revealed
☐ suburbs	☐ civil rights revolution
☐ environment	☐ sustain community institutions
☐ complexity	
☐ whereas	☐ ethnic tensions
☐ decade	☐ justified
☐ economy	☐ stresses
☐ presumably	☐ resources
☐ core	

1. Immigrants must be careful to keep their visas current in order to maintain their _____ _____.

2. After World War II, many middle-class Americans moved out of the city into the _____.

3. Personal _____ is usually the amount of money a

   person earns.

4. In history, there has been an unfortunate _____

   _____ _____ _____ where

   people have suffered because of their race, ethnicity, religion, or origin.

5. In the 1960s, Martin Luther King Jr. helped lead the _____

   _____ _____ movement, which changed

   America forever.

6. One benefit of having a middle class is that it had _____

   institutions, such as schools and small businesses, which strengthen

   communities.

7. Over the past 50 years, the social _____ concerning race

   and discrimination has improved, but many things still need to

   change.

8. The years 1960 to 1970 were a _____ of major social

   change in America.

9. Voters of different political _____ must work together to

   gain any real power.

10. Minorities who make gains over time have _____ from

    their efforts.

○ Focusing on History

Throughout its history, the United States has dealt with issues of civil rights. The textbook we are studying, *The American Pageant*, identifies both gains that bring greater equality to all Americans and continued challenges for America.

EXERCISE 15 Recognizing implications

Study the following quotes related to civil rights issues selected from Reading Selection 2. Indicate if the quote identifies a gain, a continued challenge, or both. Explain your responses in the spaces provided. Discuss your answers with your classmates. The first one has been done for you as an example. Paragraph locations are also provided in the parentheses for reference.

Civil rights issues	It's an example of a . . .	
Quotes from Reading Selection 2	gain.	continued challenge.
1. "Thanks both to continued immigration and to their own high birthrate, Hispanic-Americans were becoming an increasingly important minority." (¶ 1)	✓	✓

Explanation:

It's a gain because they are more important. It's a challenge too because population relationships will change, and some people might not be happy about that.

2. "Asian-Americans also made great strides . . . Once feared and hated as the 'yellow peril' and relegated to the most menial and degrading jobs, citizens of Asian ancestry were now counted among the most prosperous and successful of Americans, a 'model minority.'" (¶ 3)		

Explanation:

_____

_____

3. "Indians, the original Americans, shared in the general awakening of ethnic and cultural pride." (¶ 4)		

Explanation:

_____

_____

Civil rights issues (cont.)	It's an example of a . . .	
Quotes from Reading Selection 2	**gain.**	**continued challenge.**
4. "Racial and ethnic tensions also exacerbated the problems of American cities." (¶ 5)		
Explanation:		
_____ _____ _____		
5. "The Los Angeles riots vividly testified to black skepticism about the American system of justice." (¶ 6)		
Explanation:		
_____ _____ _____		
6. "American cities have always held an astonishing variety of ethnic and racial groups, but in the late twentieth century, minorities made up a majority of the population of many American cities, as whites fled to the suburbs." (¶ 7)		
Explanation:		
_____ _____ _____		

Civil rights issues (cont.)	It's an example of a . . .	
Quotes from Reading Selection 2	gain.	continued challenge.
7. "But other segments of the African-American community had clearly prospered in the wake of the civil rights gains of the 1950s and 1960s, though they still had a long hill to climb before reaching full equality." (¶ 8)		

Explanation:

_____

_____

_____

8. "Find another quote that speaks of an example of a gain. Place it here and explain it."

_____

_____

Explanation:

_____

_____

_____

9. Find one last new quote with an example of a continued challenge. Place it here and explain it too.

_____

_____

Explanation:

_____

_____

Reading Assignment 3

**LIVING IN A DANGEROUS WORLD—
AMERICA AND THE WORLD AFTER
SEPTEMBER 11TH, 2001**

○ Getting Ready to Read

EXERCISE 16 Previewing and recognizing related topics

In preparing for the next reading selection, preview the title, subtitle, the first sentence of each paragraph and the entire last paragraph. To help guide your previewing, these sections have been shaded.

After you preview by skimming for the main ideas, check the topics listed below that you believe the author will discuss directly in the selection. Be ready to support your choices in a class discussion.

_____ The events of September 11, 2001

_____ The impact of 9/11 events on the American mind

_____ The impact of 9/11 events for Europe

_____ President Bush's response to 9/11

_____ The war on Afghanistan

_____ The military power of America

_____ The UN inspectors in Iraq

_____ The activities of Islamic terrorists around the world

_____ The impact of 9/11 on the world economy

_____ The impact of 9/11 on civil rights and immigrant rights

_____ The connection between America's cultural conflicts and 9/11

_____ The history of terrorism

_____ America's role in the world

Reading Selection 3

LIVING IN A DANGEROUS WORLD—AMERICA AND THE WORLD AFTER SEPTEMBER 11TH, 2001

1   On September 11, 2001, America's good luck apparently ran out. Out of a crystal-clear sky, suicidal terrorists slammed two hijacked airliners, loaded with passengers and jet fuel, into the twin towers of New York City's World Trade Center. They flew a third plane into the military nerve-center of the Pentagon, near Washington, D.C., killing 189 people. Heroic passengers forced another hijacked aircraft to crash in rural Pennsylvania, killing all 44 aboard but depriving the terrorists of a fourth weapon of mass destruction. As the two giant New York skyscrapers thunderously collapsed, some three thousand innocent victims perished, including peoples of many races and faiths from more than sixty countries, as well as hundreds of New York's police—and fire—department rescue workers. A stunned nation blossomed with flags, as grieving and outraged Americans struggled to express their sorrow and solidarity[1] in the face of catastrophic[2] terrorism.

2   The murderous events of that late-summer morning reanimated American patriotism. They also dramatically ended an historical era. For nearly two centuries, the United States had been spared from foreign attack against its homeland. All but unique among modern peoples, that degree of national security had undergirded[3] the values of openness and individual freedom that defined the distinctive character of American society. Now American security and American liberty alike were imperiled.[4]

---

1. **sol•i•dar•i•ty** (sŏl´ĭ-dăr´i-tē) *n.* A union of interests, purposes, or sympathies among members of a group.
2. **cat•a•stroph•ic** (kăt´ə-strŏf´ĭk) *adj.* Involving a great and/or sudden negative situation.
3. **un•der•gird•ed** (ŭn´der-gûrd´) *tr.v.* Supported or strengthened from beneath.
4. **im•per•iled** (ĭm-pĕr´ əl) *tr.v.* Out into a dangerous situation; facing the possibility of being wiped out or eliminated.

3   President Bush responded with a sober but stirring address to Congress nine days later. His solemn demeanor and the gravity of the situation helped to dissipate[5] the cloud of illegitimacy that had shadowed his presidency since the disputed election of 2000. Warning that the struggle against terrorism would be long and messy, he pledged "we will not tire, we will not falter, and we will not fail" until "we bring our enemies to justice, or bring justice to our enemies." While emphasizing his respect for the Islamic religion and Muslim peoples, he identified the principal enemy as Osama bin Laden, head of a shadowy terrorist network known as Al Qaeda ("the base" in Arabic). A wealthy extremist exiled from his native Saudi Arabia, bin Laden was associated with earlier attacks on American embassies in East Africa and on a U.S. Naval vessel in Yemen. He had taken refuge in land-locked Afghanistan, ruled by Islamic fundamentalists called the Taliban. (Ironically, the United States had indirectly helped bring the Taliban to power, when it supported religious rebels resisting the Soviet invasion of Afghanistan in the 1980s.) Bin Laden was known to harbor bitter resentments toward the United States for its economic embargo against Saddam Hussein's Iraq, its military presence on the sacred soil of the Arabian peninsula, and its support for Israel's hostility to Palestinian nationalism.[6] Bin Laden also fed on world-wide resentment[7] of America's enormous economic, military, and cultural power. Ironically, America's most conspicuous[8] strengths had made it a conspicuous target.

5. **dis•si•pate** (dĭs´ə-pāt´) *v.* Drive away; cause to no longer exist.
6. **na•tion•al•ism** (năsh´ə-na-lĭz´əm) *n.* Devotion to the interests or culture of one's nation.
7. **re•sent•ment** (rĭ-zĕnt´mənt) *n.* Ill will felt as a result of a real or imagined grievance.
8. **con•spic•u•ous** (kən-spĭk´yoo-əs) *adj.* Easy to notice; obvious.

The American Prospect in the Age of Terrorism

4   When the Taliban refused to hand over bin Laden, Bush ordered a massive military campaign against Afghanistan. Within three months, American and Afghani rebel forces had overthrown the Taliban and were poised to flush bin Laden out of the fortified[9] underground sanctuary where he was believed to have holed up.

5   The campaign in Afghanistan impressively demonstrated the wallop and sophistication of American air power and "smart," precision-guided munitions. But it remained an open question whether in the longer run America's high-tech arsenal would prove effective against foes so elusive, zealous, and determined—foes who sought not simply to destroy the United States but to demoralize it, perhaps to corrupt its very soul. Behind bin Laden lurked[10] countless terrorist "cells" in several dozen countries, some of them possibly in possession of biochemical or even nuclear weapons. Some alarmed critics even warned that the events of September 11 heralded the onset of a protracted[11] clash of civilizations, pitting millions of Muslims desperate to defend their traditional faith and culture against the relentlessly modernizing forces of the western world, spearheaded by the United States.

9. **for•ti•fied** (fôr′tə-fī′) *v.* Made strong.
10. **lurked** (lûrk) *v.* Lay in wait, as in an ambush.
11. **pro•tract•ed** (prō-trăkt′) *tr.v.* Drawn out or lengthened in time.

Confronted with this unconventional, diffuse menace,[12] anti-terrorism experts called for new tactics of "asymmetrical warfare," employing not just traditional military muscle, but innovative intelligence-gathering, economic reprisals, infiltration of suspected organizations, and even assassinations. The new war against terror also compelled the Bush administration to back away from the unilateralist foreign policies it had pursued in its early months and seek anti-terrorist partners around the globe, as evidenced by the surprisingly warm relationship that emerged after September 11 between the United States and its former adversary, Russia.

6   The terrorists' blows diabolically[13] coincided with the onset of a recession. The already gathering economic downdraft worsened as edgy[14] Americans shunned air travel and the tourist industry withered. Then, while the rubble in New York was still smoldering, a handful of Americans died after receiving letters contaminated with the deadly respiratory disease, anthrax. The gnawing fear spread that biological warfare would be the next threat facing the American people.

7   In this anxious atmosphere, Congress rammed through the USA-Patriot Act, permitting extensive telephone and e-mail surveillance, and authorizing the detention and deportation of immigrants suspected of terrorism. The Justice Department meanwhile rounded up hundreds of immigrants and held them without habeas corpus (formal charges in an open court). The Bush administration further called for trying suspected terrorists before military tribunals,[15] where the usual rules of evidence and procedure did not apply. Public opinion polls showed Americans sharply divided on whether the terrorist threat fully warranted such drastic encroachments on America's ancient traditions of civil liberties.

12. **men•ace** (mĕn´ĭs) *n.* A possible danger; a threat.
13. **di•a•bol•i•cal•ly** (dī´ə-bŏl´ĭ-kəl) *adv.* Wickedly or cruelly; of the devil.
14. **edg•y** (ĕj´ē) *adj.* Nervous or irritable; worried about a bad situation becoming worse.
15. **tri•bu•nals** (trī-byōō´nəl) *n.* A military term for trials.

8   Catastrophic terrorism posed an unprecedented[16] challenge to the United States, but the world's oldest republic remained resilient and resourceful. Born as a revolutionary force in a world of conservatism, the United States had emerged in the twentieth century as a conservative force in a world of revolution. It held aloft the banner of liberal democracy in a world wracked by revolutions of the right and left, including fascism, Nazism, and communism. Yet through it all, much that was truly revolutionary also remained a part of America's liberal democratic heritage, as its people pioneered in revolutions against colonialism, racism, sexism, ignorance, and poverty.

9   The terrorist threat reminded Americans of the urgency of resolving the ethnic and cultural conflicts that continued to plague[17] the planet after the Cold War's end—and of the urgency of making America's own character better understood around the world. Americans still aspired to live up to Lincoln's prediction that they and their heritage represented "the last best hope of earth"— but in the twenty-first century they would have to work harder than ever to prove it, to themselves as well as to others.

Source: Kennedy, D. M. (2002). *The American Pageant* (12th ed.). Boston: Houghton Mifflin, pp. 1033–1034.

○ Assessing Your Learning

Demonstrating Comprehension

Earlier in this chapter, you explored how authors use facts, explanations, and commentary. To review, explanations usually give more information or an objective definition to make a subject clear, whereas a commentary is an interpretation or personal view of a subject. In Reading Selection 3, the author mixes these elements together as he concludes the chapter and the textbook.

16. **un·prec·e·dent·ed** (ŭn-prĕsʹĭ-dən-tĭd) *adj.* Having no previous example.
17. **plague** (plāg) *tr.v.* To afflict with or as if with a disease.

◯ Assessing Your Learning at the End of a Chapter

Revisiting Objectives

Return to the first page of this chapter. Think about the chapter objectives. Put a check mark next to the ones you feel secure about. Review material in the chapter you still need to work on. When you are ready, answer the chapter review questions in Exercise 18.

◯ Practicing for a Chapter Test

EXERCISE 17   Reviewing comprehension

Check your comprehension of main concepts, or ideas, in this chapter by answering the following review questions. First, write notes to answer the questions <u>without</u> looking back at the readings. Then, use the readings to check your answers and revise them, if necessary. Write your final answers in <u>complete sentences</u> on separate paper as short-answer responses of three to five sentences each. Choose one question to develop more deeply, and prepare an essay response.

1. How is America both an old and new nation?
2. How has America's global significance increased over the last hundred years?
3. Describe the economic revolutions that occurred in the twentieth century.
4. How has the disparity between the rich and the not-so-rich widened in the last twenty-five years?
5. How has the ethnic makeup of America changed over the twentieth century?
6. How have racial and ethnic tensions worsened in America's cities?
7. What positive gains have been achieved for African Americans in recent history?
8. Why did America overthrow the government of Afghanistan in 2001–2002?
9. What were some legislative responses to the events of September 11, 2001?
10. The author begins and ends this chapter with a quote from President Abraham Lincoln. Reread those quotes. How do they reflect this chapter's theme?

EXERCISE **18** **Participating in small-group discussion**

Deepen your understanding of the author's perspectives on American history by responding to the following questions about specific statements he made. First, write brief personal notes on separate paper to answer the questions. Then, meet with a group of three or four classmates to discuss your ideas and opinions together. Finally, check back with the reading selections for extra supporting material or clarification if needed.

1. The author calls September 11 "catastrophic terrorism." How was that day of terrorism catastrophic? How was it different from other events involving terrorists? How did you personally react to this catastrophe?

2. The author states that America "remained resilient and resourceful" after September 11. Use examples from the text and from your own knowledge to support or refute this opinion. (*Note:* To refute means to argue against a point of view.)

3. In describing America in the twentieth century, the author indicates that the United States "held aloft the banner of liberal democracy in a world wracked by revolutions of the right and left, including fascism, Nazism, and communism." Can you give an example from recent history that supports or refutes this commentary?

4. America is described as having "a liberal democratic history." What does the author mean by this expression? Do you agree with the author? Why? Why not?

5. The author sees America as "leading revolutions against colonialism, racism, sexism, ignorance, and poverty." Do you agree or disagree with that assessment of America's history and its role in the world? How do people from other countries view America?

6. What do you believe Abraham Lincoln meant when he called America "the last best hope of earth?" From your understanding of history, do you believe that is a true statement? Do you think most Americans believe this statement? What do you think people from other countries think of this statement?

7. In referring to Lincoln's statement, the author states, "in the twenty-first century they [Americans] would have to work harder than ever to prove it, to themselves as well as to others." Do you think Americans are "working harder than ever" to show they are "the last best hope of earth?"

◯ **Linking Concepts**

EXERCISE 19 **Writing in your reading journal**

Write in your journal your reflections on the following questions.

Reflections on Learning

1. What is a theme?
2. What is the purpose of a chapter title? How can a chapter title help you understand a chapter?
3. What is the purpose of an introductory quote? How can an introductory quote help you understand a chapter?
4. How can noticing a repeating pattern in a passage help you understand?
5. How can graphics help you understand the text?

Reflections on History

1. Write a definition of history that includes its different elements. Give examples from this chapter.
2. How is history greater than the listing of events that happened? What value is there in studying history?
3. Is the writer of the history textbook used for this chapter's readings objective or subjective? Support your answer with examples from this chapter.

My Reading Journal
Reflections on learning

1. A theme is _____

2. The purpose of a Chapter title is to _____
_____

3. _____

4. _____

EXERCISE 20 Reviewing academic words

Assess your knowledge of the academic words from the crossword puzzle used in Exercise 21. Prepare a word list in a chart with headings like the example below. Check how well you know each word, and study them until you know all the words well.

Academic vocabulary words	I always know this word.	I usually know this word.	I need to study this word.
benefited			

○ Learning Vocabulary

EXERCISE 21 Reviewing academic vocabulary

Remember that every subject of study uses specialized academic vocabulary. Some of this chapter's vocabulary is used mainly for studying history, whereas AWL words are used in many academic fields. Complete this crossword puzzle. Use the chapter AWL words listed in the box and the clues provided below. If you need additional help, refer to the reading selection and paragraph numbers in parentheses. For example, (RS 1: ¶ 7) means Reading Selection 1, paragraph 7. All definitions were taken directly or adapted from the American Heritage College Dictionary *(2002).*

Use these words to complete the puzzle on the following page:			
benefited	civil (civil rights)	complexity	compounded
constituencies	demonstrated	discrimination	emphasized
environment	ethnic	evident	institutions
isolated	justified	majority	minority
percent	presumably	reaction	revealed
revolution	status	sustain	tensions
whereas			

Crossword Puzzle Clues

Use these clues to complete the puzzle on p. 298. Use the references to find the words in the chapter. RS = Reading Selection. ¶ = paragraph number.

Across

2. A sudden and/or major change in a situation (RS 3:¶ 7)

6. Demonstrated or proved to be just, right, or valid (RS 2:¶ 6)

10. Shown clearly and deliberately (RS 2:¶ 8)

13. The circumstances or conditions that surround a person (RS 2:¶ 9)

18. Mental, emotional, or nervous strains (RS 2:¶ 5)

19. To have received some good from (RS 2:¶ 7)

23. Set apart or cut off from others (RS 2:¶ 8)

24. To keep in existence; maintain (RS 2:¶ 7)

25. One part in a hundred (RS 2:¶ 8)

Down

1. Groups of supporters (RS 2:¶ 8)

3. Established organizations, especially dedicated to education, public service, or culture (RS 2:¶ 7)

4. While at the same time (RS 1:¶ 11)

5. By reasonable assumption (RS 2:¶ 6)

7. Stressed or gave emphasis to (RS 2:¶ 9)

8. A reverse or opposing activity (RS 2:¶ 6)

9. The quality or condition of having interconnected parts (RS 1:¶ 7)

11. To be made known (RS 2:¶ 6)

12. Added to; increased (RS 2:¶ 9)

14. The greater number or part; a number more than half the total (RS 2:¶ 2)

15. An ethnic, racial, religious, or other group having a distinctive, but not dominant, presence within a society (RS 2:¶ 1)

16. The legal character or condition of a person or thing (RS 2:¶ 4)

17. Of, relating to, or befitting a citizen or citizens (RS 3:¶ 7)

20. Being a member of a particular group, by heritage or culture, but residing outside its national boundaries (RS 2:¶ 5)

21. Easily seen or understood (RS 2:¶ 5)

22. Negative treatment or consideration based on class or category rather than individual merit (RS 2:¶ 4)

Academic Crossword

Text Credits